THE FIFTEEN
BIGGEST LIES
IN POLITICS

THE FIFTEEN

BIGGEST LIES

IN POLITICS

MAJOR GARRETT
AND
TIMOTHY J. PENNY

ST. MARTIN'S GRIFFIN ▨ NEW YORK

PRODUCTION EDITOR: DAVID STANFORD BURR
DESIGN BY ELLEN R. SASAHARA AND MIA IHARA

Library of Congress Cataloging-in-Publication Data

Garrett, Major.
    The fifteen biggest lies in politics / Major Garrett and
Timothy J. Penny.
        p.   cm.
    ISBN 0-312-18294-5 (hc)
    ISBN 0-312-25459-8 (pbk)
    1. Political ethics—United States. 2. Deception—
Political aspects—United States. 3. Rhetoric—Political
aspects—United States. 4. Journalism—Political aspects—
United States. 5. United States—Politics and govern-
ment—1993–   6. United States—Economic policy—
1993– 7. United States—Social policy—1993–   I. Penny,
Timothy J.   II. Title.
JK468.E6G37   1998
172'.0973—dc21   98-20636
                                                             CIP

First St. Martin's Griffin Edition: January 2000

10   9   8   7   6   5   4   3   2   1

To our fathers

MAJOR EDWARD GARRETT

AND

JAY CLAIRE PENNY

CONTENTS

———————◆———————

ACKNOWLEDGMENTS

◆

In our first book, *Common Cents*, we were derelict in neglecting to thank so many. To right this wrong we want first to thank Tim's congressional staff: chiefs of staff Steve Kingsley and Steve Bosacker; press secretary Teresa McFarland and her predecessors; policy advisers Jim Haggerty, Joe Thiessen, Jane Shey, Glenda Kendrick, Mark Mullenbach, and Chris Hoven; and numerous other who helped Tim serve his constituents and his country.

As for this book, we wish first to thank our researcher, Brian Eleam, an indefatigable gatherer of facts and able adviser on the cogent use thereof. We also thank Kristin Wilson for so ably proofreading large sections of the manuscript, Mark Bentele for providing crucial advice and counsel in the book's earliest stages of development, Pat McCartan for reviewing and measurably improving the abortion, religion, and corruption chapters, and Westwood One's Jim Bohannon for his advice, counsel, and support.

A few lines of type falls well short of the gratitude we extend to our mentors, but it is the best this limited medium allows:

Major wishes to thank the teachers who made a difference: Judy Fogel, John Lester, Maria Theodore Benedict, Joan Zeno (San Diego Unified School District), Hal Lister (deceased), George Pica, and George Kennedy (University of Missouri); bosses who made a difference: Garet Von Netzer, Charles Zobel, Margaret Downing, Francis B. Coombs Jr., Josette Shiner, and Wesley Pruden; and friends who made a difference: Steve Albrecht, Randy Repaci, Chet Burchett, John St. Clair, Chris Tlapek, Jon Ralston, Warren Strobel, Mark Russell, Don Lambro, Jim Saris, Nancy Roman, Anne Veigle, and Susan Feeney.

Tim wishes thank Don Zwach and his wife Fran. Don served for eighteen years as treasurer for all of Tim's campaigns and remains his closest political confidant and adviser. Also thanks to Jim Eddy, a college professor of Tim's at Winona State University and always the No. 1 volunteer in Tim's campaigns, and his wife, Mary; Marvel Prafke, the campaign chairman for Tim's first run for public office in 1976; and Mankato State professor Dan Burton (deceased), who worked in Tim's Washington office every winter and inspired and edified all whom he met, and his surviving wife, Ronnie, a dear friend and inspiration in her own right.

We wish to again thank our mothers, Kay Garrett and Donna Penny. We dedicated *Common Cents* to them but forgot to share their names with the world. Both of us have traveled much further in life than our roots would have suggested possible. Our success is a reflection of their love, support, and guidance.

Lastly, we thank our families: Major's wife, Julie, his daughter, Mary Ellen, and his son, Luke; Tim's wife, Barbara, his sons Jamie, Joey, and Marcus, and his daughter, Molly. All have offered unflagging support and encouragement. For this and so much more we shall remain eternally grateful.

—Major Garrett
Tim Penny

THE FIFTEEN
BIGGEST LIES
IN POLITICS

◆

POLITICAL LIES:
A SELF-DEFENSE MANUAL

"A harmful truth is better than a harmless lie."

—THOMAS MANN

POLITICIANS LIE ALL the time. Yet the word *lie* is rarely invoked to describe how they turn blatant untruths to their advantage. Politicians who lie are said to be "disingenuous," "misinformed," "less than candid," "unfamiliar with the truth," or "at odds with reality." Rare is the politician who will publicly call another a liar.

This book is not a polemic against political lies, though we certainly wish there were fewer of them. It is an attempt to identify the most-prevalent and damaging lies in our political culture—and to reveal the truths behind them.

There is a hierarchy in the art of political lying. The most-damaging lies are those politicians tell about their ethical conduct, hoping the ugly truth never emerges. President Nixon spun such lies, lost his presidency, and undermined public confidence in all public servants. Then there are lies meant to conceal political cowardice: politicians regularly describe their positions as matters of principle when they are actually concessions to special-interest pressures. There are demagogic lies, in which politicians intentionally distort statistics or hurl sensational charges at political enemies to incite popular support for their causes. And then there are lies of decorum, in which politicians overdo the rhetoric of kindness when referring in public to political enemies they would just as soon spit on.

With the exception of the first, all of these lies play a semiuseful role in American political life. Politics would surely be better off without them, but it would be naïve to discount the value many of these tactical lies have in the long and sometimes torturous pursuit of political consensus. Absolute truth is elusive in any arena—and, from a politician's point of view, not always a worthy quarry. Successful politicians know the hazards of clinging to truth in the face of popular hostility. After all, our democratic process is not about pursuit of absolute truths, but about the peaceful assembling of a consensus measured regularly at the ballot box.

The art of persuasion involves the use of both truth and lies. Most smart politicians—even basically ethical ones—use both as conditions require. If speaking the truth means losing the battle, political calculations often call for a lie. Which raises a thorny question: if the people are willing to believe a lie, is only the liar to blame?

In his 1980 presidential campaign Ronald Reagan promised to cut taxes, increase defense spending, protect Social Security and Medicare, and balance the budget in four years. He said he could do all of this by eliminating wasteful government spending. Reagan may have believed this was possible, but his top economic advisers clearly did not. President Carter said it was impossible, and many independent economists agreed. Political scientists familiar with voting patterns were certain that Congress wouldn't have the political will to cut spending enough to offset the tax cuts and defense-spending increases Reagan was sure to seek.

But the people were willing to believe Reagan. After suffering through high inflation (11.3 percent in 1979, 13.5 percent by 1980) and high interest rates (the annual prime rate averaged 15.3 percent in 1980), voters were willing to gamble on Reagan because they had grown so resentful of Carter's domestic economic record. Americans were willing to believe Reagan's political lie because they felt it offered a better prospect for the future than another term with Jimmy Carter. Reagan's lie was abstract, Carter's record concrete—and wildly unpopular.

As we know, Reagan could not cut taxes, increase defense spending, and balance the budget in four years. He did not do it in eight years. As Lou Cannon recalled in *The Role of a Lifetime,* his biography of Reagan, the president's advisers knew from the start that Republicans in Congress would refuse out of hand to support the administration's domestic spending cuts, dooming hopes for a balanced budget and guaranteeing an era of unprecedented budget *deficits*. The advisers knew this long before Reagan actually signed his historic 1981 budget into law.

And yet Reagan repeatedly told the public that his plans would balance the budget *if only Congress would implement them*. And a majority of the public believed him. Politically, Reagan did the right thing—admitting what he and his advisers knew would have cost him the confidence of the American public and brought into question all the other promises he made during the 1980 campaign. In other words, telling the truth would have hurt more than it helped.

The 1984 presidential campaign dramatized the flip side of this phenomenon, when Democratic presidential nominee Walter Mondale showed how dangerous it can be to speak truth to a public interested only in comfortable fictions. In his acceptance speech at the Democratic National Convention in San Francisco, Mondale spoke these memorable words: "Let's tell the truth. Mr. Reagan will raise your taxes, and so will I. He won't tell you. I just did." Mondale spoke what Ralph Waldo Emerson, in his essay "Self-Reliance," called the "rude truth." Emerson said the rude truth set the courageous apart from the timid, mealy-mouthed mob. Mondale set himself apart all right. Voters treated him rudely in return. They saw neither candor nor courage in his vow, only an unqualified promise of higher taxes. Reagan, predictably, denied he would raise taxes. Even though such a promise sounded improbable by 1984, many voters decided it was better to stick with a president who held out a hope of no new taxes than to support a challenger who guaranteed them.

Presidents Bush and Clinton have also lied about taxes.

Trailing in the polls, Vice President Bush arrived in New Orleans in August of 1988 hoping to rebound at the Republican National Convention. With no momentum to speak of, and Dan Quayle already dragging down the ticket, by the night of his acceptance speech, Bush knew he had to stir the blood of the many GOP delegates still devoted to Reagan. In one of the most-cynical speeches in American political history, Bush, who had no intention of governing as Reagan had, hit every note in the Reagan songbook. The delegates' euphoria was peaking when Bush told the most-memorable lie since Nixon swore he was "not a crook."

"Congress will push me to raise taxes, and I'll say no, and they'll push and I'll say no, and they'll push again," Bush said, preparing for his memorable windup. "And I'll say to them: 'Read my lips. No new taxes.'"

The delegates read those lips, and so did a majority of voters in that year's presidential election: Bush overcame a seventeen-point handicap to defeat Democratic nominee Michael Dukakis handily. The no-new-taxes speech was the turning point. After Bush turned the promise into a lie by signing on to a 1990 budget deal that included tax increases, he never recovered.

Unlike Bush, Clinton survived his tax lie—but many Democrats in Congress didn't. During the 1992 campaign Clinton promised a middle-class tax cut. For this he was attacked by liberals, which made his New Democrat costume appear authentic. At his first town-hall meeting as president, Clinton took a question from Katie Rabkin, who said she voted for Clinton because he promised during the campaign not to raise taxes on the middle class (in fact, he had promised to *cut* taxes for the middle class), but who had noticed that since assuming office Clinton seemed to be backing away from that pledge.

"I'm concerned about your campaign promise to not raise taxes for the middle class and how you intend to keep that promise," Rabkin asked the president.

Clinton responded as follows: "Now, what's happened since the election? We have been told since the election that the federal debt, every year, is going to be $50 billion bigger than we were told it was before the election. . . . I'm doing my best. . . . But we've got to change what we're doing."

It wasn't true. In the summer of 1992—months before the election—the Congressional Budget Office had published revised deficit and debt projections showing that both would be far higher than it had projected in January. Clinton used those very Budget Office projections in his campaign manifesto *Putting People First,* and his aides and Democratic allies in Congress understood well before the election that the deficit and debt would be up to $50 billion higher per year than they were projected to be when Clinton's campaign began. Like Reagan a decade earlier Clinton was promising a tax cut when even his own advisers knew it was impossible. The sudden $50 billion increase in the deficit that Clinton cited in his response to Rabkin was, in fact, a complete fabrication. The numbers were available for all to see in August of 1992.

One week after that town meeting, Clinton unveiled a budget plan that sought $250 billion in higher taxes, including an increase in federal taxes on gasoline and on middle-class Social Security recipients. Lies about taxes cost Bush his presidency; Clinton hung on to his—but in 1994 lost the Democratic control of Congress. Sometimes lies have consequences.

The Reagan, Bush, and Clinton lies are not the biggest or most outlandish our country has seen, but they are examples of premeditated political deception. Tactical lies such as these are meant to deceive voters until the last possible moment—until, that is, the politician has devised a countervailing strategy to protect him- or herself from the consequences of his or her dishonesty. Tactical lies are exactly what we want to expose, because they always work best on an inattentive or uneasy populace—even one that is pretty well informed, as Ronald Reagan learned.

This book is designed to serve as a self-defense manual in this upcoming political season, and for the presidential campaign in 2000. It's a subjective manual: these are the fifteen lies *we* think are the most damaging to America. We realize the lies found in this book may not be on your list of the worst lies in American politics. But we are confident that you will encounter nearly all of these lies this fall, as Republicans and Democrats vie for control of the Senate and the House, and next year (1999) as Republicans and Democrats begin tuning up for the presidential campaign.

It should be clear by now that we are not interested in exposing lies about the ethical or personal conduct of politicians. Lies about individual behavior tend to catch up with the politicians who spin them. President Nixon's Watergate lies caught up with him. If President Clinton is lying about Whitewater or Monica Lewinsky or the solicitation of campaign donations, we are confident that his lies too will catch up with him.

This book is about exploding systemic lies in American political debate. We have chosen fifteen topics that haven't had a fresh word said about them in years. The speeches, editorials, press releases, and news accounts of these fifteen issues resemble so much dead skin, dust mites, and mold spores. We're developing a bit of an allergic reaction to this rhetorical detritus, and we imagine you are too. Consider this book a tool you can use to cleanse the air of political hyperbole, deception, and fluff, a filter of facts designed to trap the noxious lies of contemporary politics. So armed, you can better evaluate these important issues for yourself and, more important, judge the truthfulness of your candidates as the upcoming debate gathers steam.

This book is about lies dealing with abortion, gun control, religion, immigration, public corruption, campaign spending, the federal budget, Social Security, Medicare, taxes, education, pollution, and Republicans and Democrats. Politicians are responsible for spinning most of these lies. But we would be derelict if we only blamed politicians.

The American news media are also to blame. They spin lies of their own that disserve the public. Moreover, the media help politicians to peddle their lies by cynically judging said lies on the basis of their political utility, rather than helping the public cut through the deception to see something a bit closer to the truth. Reporters have grown so accustomed to thinking like politicians that they too measure the success of a lie not against the needs of the nation but against the yardstick of political expediency. If the lie works, it's a good lie, and the politician has succeeded. If the lie doesn't work, then it's a bad lie. *That it was a lie in the first place appears not to matter.*

We write this book from two very different perspectives. One of us is a journalist who has observed politicians. The other has been a politician who has observed journalists. Together we have concluded that an informal conspiracy between the American political class and the news media consistently deprives American voters of the essential information they need to adopt new solutions to some very old problems.

Consider the most-stubborn of these problems. If it's taxes, Republicans want to cut them, and Democrats want to raise them (at least for the rich). If it's abortion, pro-life politicians want a constitutional ban on the procedure, while pro-choice politicians want no limitations on the right of a woman to abort a fetus at almost any time in her pregnancy. If it's gun control, progun politicians find treachery lurking behind any attempt to limit the distribution of cop-killer bullets and assault rifles. On the other hand, gun-control advocates cling to the fantasy that gun-control laws have appreciably reduced crime.

For reasons we will dissect more carefully later, the dominant political parties and the special-interest groups that influence them talk about certain issues the same way year after year after year. If the dominant media outlets policed the partisan propaganda more aggressively, voters might develop a clearer view of their options. But media passivity deprives most voters of a coherent understanding of these issues.

Others have done the honors more than adequately, so we refuse to beat the dead horse of "sound-bite" news coverage. Our gripe is not so much with politicians' use of sound bites as with the media's passive acceptance of them as sufficient vehicles for the truth, when in fact they are no more than cleverly honed phrases meant to incite passion among an otherwise distracted public.

Politicians and special interests give ideas brand names and market them as aggressively as Colgate-Palmolive markets Tide. They hope the brand name catches on with the media and the public. If it does, chances are their objective will be realized.

Here are a few examples. When Bill Clinton wanted to require insurance companies to provide two-day hospital stays for new mothers, he took to calling any shorter hospital stays "drive-by deliveries," which could only have reminded voters of drive-by shootings. When Republicans called for reduced estate taxes, they started using the phrase *death taxes*. Who wants a tax on death?

When issues get hot enough, the public must endure a barrage of such brand names from both sides—names that grotesquely oversimplify the truth and leave us understandably confused about the real alternatives we face. Often the rhetoric can grow so inflated that the two sides seem to be talking about entirely different universes. When Republicans wanted to reduce future Medicare spending in 1995, they said their goal was to "preserve, protect and strengthen" the health-insurance program. Looking at the same proposal, Clinton said Republicans wanted to "devastate Medicare."

Senator Daniel Patrick Moynihan has observed that politicians gain control of political debate when they define the terms on which an issue is debated. If Republicans had succeeded in making the Medicare debate about ways to "preserve, protect and strengthen" it, then their proposals would have succeeded. Clinton prevailed because he turned debate into a choice between the status quo and "devastation." Politicians and special-interest groups know they're trying to limit the range of options with their brand names. It's an inevitable temptation, though politicians should rise above it more often. What is more surprising is that the dominant media outlets refuse to scrutinize political brand names and slogans with the same vigor they show in exposing fraudulent advertisements for soap, automobiles, or over-the-counter medicines.

So far, the dominant media outlets have been willing accomplices in the practice of political deception, though not witting conspirators in the mold of the politicians themselves. Politicians and special interests make it easy for the media to tell complicated stories in a simple, melodramatic fashion. Almost every political issue that rises to national consciousness ends up being summarized as a matter of white hats fighting black hats. Political brand names make this a very easy story to tell, and the media find the script irresistible.

Instead of complaining about this problem in general terms, we have decided to write this book to help at a nuts-and-bolts level—to give voters information that most politicians and special interests would just as soon keep to themselves. Voters who have the facts—and who can sniff out the truth behind the double-talk—are much harder to delude.

The real reason for so much of this political deception is simple: absolutism sells. Absolutism is behind the good and evil caricatures that dominate American political debate. Special-interest groups spawn the absolute images that define our political debate. The politicians they influence parrot their absolutism, often leaving mainstream voters with a set of two equally unattractive options. Absolutism serves one useful purpose, however: it inflames. In the absence of nationwide support, most special interests are happy to stoke the fires of a core of fanatics—the surest way for them to bring pressure down on their political allies. Politicians who bow to such pressure merely prolong the hollow political dialogue that permeates American discourse—all in the name of allegiance to their special-interest patrons.

Ah, but where did that allegiance begin? Usually, it begins when a politician is looking for help in his or her long journey to Congress or the White House. And while it's true that in life you can pick your friends, but you can't pick your parents, in politics you can't always pick your friends. Sometimes your friends are predetermined as surely as your parents.

The alliances, and oppositions, are time-honored. Conservative Republicans get the cold shoulder from industrial unions, teachers' unions, trial lawyers, environmentalists, homosexuals, and pro-choice activists. Liberal Democrats don't get much help from big business, small-business owners, social conservatives, or gun owners. There are 435 congressional districts in America and about 35 percent are prime territory for conservative Republicans and about 35 percent for liberal Democrats. The rest are swing districts, where Democrats and Republicans cobble together key parts of the liberal and conservative agendas to capture a small majority they hope someday to enlarge.

In those hardcore conservative and liberal districts, the die is cast long before politicians start trying to recruit their friends or begin discussing the issues. Ideological sensibilities limit the politicians' options, and, in the process, ensure that the wishes of the constituents will by and large be served.

That's not the problem. The problem is that those special-interest groups that are so influential in hardcore liberal and conservative districts have begun to transfer their clout to swing districts.

The ability to mobilize volunteers and grassroots campaign support in swing districts throughout the country, once held by strong political parties, has increasingly become the province of the special interests. Political parties traditionally mediated the influence of special interests by controlling the nominating process, holding back huge blocks of votes, and siphoning money away from wayward party members—punishment that was rarely meted out for any but the most-extreme violations of party orthodoxy. Strong parties kept alliances strong by giving politicians far more leeway than special interests typically allow.

Today, special-interest groups exert inordinate influence over political parties. Since they have overtaken the parties as the principal source of campaign volunteers and political contributions, the parties are forced to do their bidding—while all along maintaining an independent public image. Brian Lunde, a Democratic consultant in Washington and former executive director of the Democratic National Committee, now describes both political parties as little more than mail-drops for huge campaign contributions and advertising agencies for special-interest dogma. Members of each party show up to pocket their campaign cash and memorize their lines. Generally speaking, the two must go hand in hand: politicians who collect the money but fail to recite the dogma often find the mail drop empty during the next campaign. This now applies to virtually all lawmakers in both parties—no longer just those who rise from the hardcore liberal or conservative districts.

We personally know dozens of lawmakers who are terrified of crossing their special-interest benefactors. We know of lawmakers with sterling pro-choice voting records who have lost contributions and endorsements because they cast *one* vote the pro-choice lobby disliked. We know of pro-life politicians who've suffered the same fate.

This paralysis afflicts debate on issues from tort reform to the environment, labor law to affirmative action, along with every other persistent American issue: Social Security, Medicare and Medicaid, welfare, taxes, veterans' benefits, education, defense spending.

It would be unnecessarily alarmist to suggest that special interests control all of American political speech; clearly they do not. But their influence cannot be underestimated. And it's not a matter of money, either. The most effective special interest groups in America mobilize people, not money. Campaign contributions are far less important to politicians than the number of votes a special-interest group can "deliver" or "withhold" in the next election. The elite special-interest groups—the American Association of Retired Persons, the National Rifle Association, the National Education Association, and the Christian Coalition—all wield tremendous power because of the millions and millions of votes they can influence on Election Day. Plenty of special-interest groups throw money around Washington, trying to get their positions heard. Money is easy to collect and contribute. Bringing votes to the table is a much-tougher business.

There's nothing wrong with special interests pursuing their agendas vigorously. Nor is there anything wrong with their raising lots of money and recruiting thousands of volunteers to help them in the trenches. That's a natural form of political expression.

Here's the problem: the very way they recruit volunteers and raise money requires them to exaggerate, mislead, and downright lie about their goals. This process tends to attract zealots to their cause, who then line up one side of the issue against comparable zealots on the other side. And they argue the issues from their entrenched positions, often drowning out any suggestion of alternatives or compromise. Again, this is only natural. But it tends to stifle the debate, not advance it.

Uncomfortable with such black-and-white choices, most American voters give up any hope of contributing to the debate on individual issues and leave the decision to their elected representatives—which makes perfect sense. But since their representatives are often captives of the special interests themselves, the outcome is inevitably predictable. Politicians tend to side with whichever special-interest groups helped them get elected.

The cycle continues. And it rarely produces results that fundamentally alter government policy. The trench warfare between special interests typically ends in hard-fought political standoffs in which both sides pound each other and advance slowly, if at all, toward a solution that addresses the underlying needs of the public at large.

Until now, the special-interest absolutists have thwarted any movement toward a third way in American politics. The polarization of political dialogue is at the heart of voter disgust with our electoral system. It's one of the main reasons that registered voters don't participate in elections as often as they used to. And it is also the reason most voters are inclined to believe the worst about the politicians who represent them. They see the debate replaying itself over and over—*and they know full well that other alternatives exist.* The fact that so few politicians ever bring up such alternatives only reinforces the sense that our representatives are little more than marionettes, willing to dance precisely as their special-interest masters direct.

This book is designed to reveal the most-insidious lies spun by special-interest groups, parrotted by politicians, and accepted by the media. This book will not catalogue every lie in American politics, just the ones we believe are presently the biggest and most prevalent. The facts that follow should make it easier for any voter to judge the candidates who will come asking for your vote this year and in 2000.

THE ABORTION DEBATE MATTERS

T HE TITLE OF this chapter is intentionally inflammatory.
We apologize to anyone on either side of the abortion debate
whom we've offended, or who believes we've been flippant or cruel.

We're not suggesting that Americans who are pro-choice or pro-
life are irrelevant to the ultimate decision the nation reaches on the
question of abortion rights. Clearly they are important voices, and
their interest and dedication to their beliefs are commendable. Would
that other issues in America attracted similar passion.

Nevertheless, we believe that America must reassess the way it dis-
cusses abortion—believe it so strongly that we are compelled to attack, in the strongest terms possible, the tenor, direction, and content
of America's raging debate over abortion.

But let's establish how we, the authors of this book, personally approach this issue.

In a professional context, Tim dealt with abortion issues repeatedly during his twelve years as a member of Congress. He had a generally pro-life voting record and consistently voted against Medicaid
funding of abortion. Contrary to the wishes of the pro-life lobby, he
voted for international family-planning programs that provide access
to birth-control services, but Tim generally enjoyed support from pro-
life groups. He never received contributions from pro-choice forces.

In his fourteen years as a professional journalist, Major has covered many facets of the abortion debate, from clinic protests in Las
Vegas and Houston to the struggle over abortion language in the Republican Party platform at the 1992 National Convention. Major also
observed dozens of abortion debates while covering Congress from
1990 to the present.

Since 1982 we have been participants in, or witnesses to, a good deal of America's abortion debate.

And we're sick of it.

No.

We're *sick at heart* about it.

We're sick at heart because it all seems beside the point.

It's now been twenty-five years since the Supreme Court ruled that access to abortion was constitutionally protected throughout America (it was legal in fourteen states before the Court handed down its ruling in *Roe v. Wade*).

And what has America gained from its inflamed debate over abortion?

What have we to show for all the protests, the court filings, the clinic blockades, the bombings and shootings, the rallies on the Mall, the press conferences, the television and radio commercials, the congressional floor speeches, the presidential speeches and vetoes, the sermons (for and against) from the pulpit? What has all the yelling wrought? Nothing.

After twenty-five years, the abortion debate in America has done *nothing* to reduce appreciably the number of abortions performed every year in this great nation.

Federal law gives every woman in America the right to terminate her pregnancy up until the twenty-sixth week of gestation. In 1973 the Supreme Court ruled this to be the point at which a fetus becomes "viable" outside the mother's womb. The Court did not endorse the feminist concept that a fetus is the property of the woman, only that the fetus is the property of the woman until the fetus is healthy enough to survive outside her womb by means of medical intervention. At that point the fetus, according to the Court, can be subject to state protections if the state decides to impose them. By and large, however, the Court has rejected most attempts by the state to impose restrictions on adult women seeking abortions at any time in their pregnancy. At the same time the Court has upheld various laws meant to discourage and in some cases outlaw abortions obtained by a minor without the consent of at least one parent.

Following the Court's *Roe v. Wade* ruling, the number of abortions doubled—from 744,600 in 1973 to 1,409,600 in 1978. Since then the number of abortions nationally has averaged about 1.5 million per year. In 1992, the last year for which hard statistics are available, the number of abortions was 1,528,900. Estimates from the Alan

Guttmacher Institute, a special-research affiliate of Planned Parenthood, suggest that the number of abortions from 1994 through 1996 fell slightly, to 1.4 million per year. But this decrease is largely attributed to the decline in women of child-rearing age—particularly women in their twenties, who have a disproportionately large number of abortions compared to women in their thirties.

This follows a statistical trend established after the number of abortions reached 1.4 million in 1978. Since then, according to Census Bureau statistics, the aggregate number of abortions has fluctuated primarily in relation to the number of women of child-rearing age. As the number of women of child-rearing age has increased, so too has the number of abortions. As it has declined, so too has the number of abortions, if ever so slightly. The incidence of abortion has remained relatively constant across all demographic and regional groups and subgroups. According to estimates from the Guttmacher Institute, more than 34 million abortions were performed from 1973 to 1996. After twenty-five years of debate, the cultural predisposition toward abortion has neither increased nor decreased.

To our way of thinking, reducing the aggregate number of abortions each year is the *only* rational goal and the *only* worthwhile measurement of the quality, importance, and relevance of America's debate on abortion.

Why?

Because that's the one thing both sides say they want.

Pro-life forces want to make abortion a crime, or at least return the decision on whether to make it a crime back to the states, where the issue could be debated and a majority decision reached. Clearly their intention is to have fewer abortions, since they consider the procedure an act of "killing the unborn."

Pro-choice forces do not, of course, see abortion as murder, but rather as a woman's way of dealing with an unwanted pregnancy *on her own terms*. Pro-choice mores hold that the woman herself is the only one who possesses the moral and legal right to decide the fate of the fertilized ovum in her uterus. The state has no right to force a woman to bring that fertilized ovum to term *if she does not want to*.

But pro-choice mores also hold that abortion is only one of myriad "reproductive health-care" choices a woman can make. Pro-choice forces rarely argue that abortion is the morally superior method of dealing with an unwanted pregnancy. In fact, leaders of the movement take pains to emphasize that they are not "pro-abortion," and are quick to point out that adoption is an equally valid means of dealing with an unwanted pregnancy.

If we take both sides at their word, it would seem they have a common goal: to reduce the number of abortions in America. Pro-life forces would like to see individual states enact laws against abortion, thus using government coercion to reduce abortions. Pro-choice forces, though they support the right to abortion as it now exists, also want women to understand and to make use of available alternatives.

At least theoretically, both sides want to reduce the number of abortions.

Has that message come across to you?

When you think of the abortion debate in this country, do you think of it as a means of building a cultural consensus on sexuality? Does the debate explore the responsibility women *and men* have to themselves and society when they decide to have sexual intercourse? Do you think the abortion debate has in any way helped women *and men* unite in common purpose against the immense psychological and physical angst an unwanted pregnancy unleashes on a relationship? Do you think of the debate as revolving around the individual consequences of abortion—the physical and psychological trauma that accompanies each procedure—*and* about whether society should act to reduce abortion in order to protect as many *women* as possible from such pain and anguish?

Probably not.

The abortion debate in America is really about power, and the combatants are special-interest zealots as politically obtuse as they are morally righteous.

Before going any further, let us briefly summarize the arguments on both sides of the issue—the moral and legal justifications both sides have used to defend their positions in court and in the political arena.

The abortion question turns on decisions societies must make about life, death, the rights of men and women, the rights of the unborn, and the value placed on individual liberties when the exercise of such liberty deprives a potential human being of life itself.

When debating an issue such as this, neither side will cede the moral or legal high ground.

To activists on the pro-choice side, any diminution of abortion rights is, by definition, a blow to the rights of women and a return to a patriarchal society awash in subjugation and oppression. To activists on the pro-life side, the very existence of abortion rights is an affront to God and all civil society, because it's a license to kill a fetus that is unwanted or inconvenient. Those who are pro-choice are no less fervent in believing that morality and law are on their side than those who are pro-life. In short, both sides are sure they are absolutely right. In a battle in which moral and legal certitude is absolute, compromise is impossible. And so it has been.

Pro-choice forces, particularly those with ardent feminist beliefs, see the abortion question as a defining battle in the millennial war women have waged against moral patriarchy and oppression. Take away a woman's rights to abortion and soon enough the right to contraception might also fall away. Take away a woman's right to control her reproductive organs, and you deprive her, and by extension all women, of the precious autonomy they have established in a world previously dominated by men.

It's important to remember that the federally protected right to abortion in America grew out of the federally protected right to contraceptives. The key legal antecedent to *Roe v. Wade* was the 1965 Supreme Court ruling in *Griswold v. Connecticut.* That case arose from the arrest of the executive director of the Planned Parenthood League of Connecticut and its medical director, a licensed physician, for giving married couples information about contraception and providing women with a medical contraceptive device. Connecticut law at the time forbade the use of any drug or device to prevent conception. The plaintiffs sued on the grounds that the law violated the Fourteenth Amendment's due-process clause, which guarantees that the state shall not "deprive any person of life, liberty or property without due process of law."

The United States Supreme Court had over time expanded its definition of "liberty" to include an individual's right to privacy, ruling in previous cases that parents had the liberty to make certain decisions about their children's education without state interference. It also used the connection between liberty and privacy to strike down a law forbidding interracial marriage.

In a seven-to-two vote, the high court ruled that Connecticut had no compelling interest in violating a married couple's right to privacy (and thus their right to liberty as defined by their reading of the Fourteenth Amendment) by dictating what they did about contraception in their own home. Seven years later, the Court ruled in *Eisenstadt v. Baird* that unmarried women had the same right to privacy, and it struck down a law forbidding the use of contraceptives by unmarried women.

The privacy right outlined in *Griswold v. Connecticut* and reaffirmed in *Eisenstadt v. Baird* set the legal precedent for the Court to rule in favor of abortion rights in the landmark *Roe v. Wade* case in 1973. A woman named Norma McCorvey, given the pseudonym Jane Roe in the Court filing, sought to overturn a Texas law forbidding abortions except those performed to save the life of the mother. (Interestingly, McCorvey never aborted the child she was carrying at the time the suit was filed. The child was the third unwanted pregnancy of her life and, as with the previous two, she carried it to term and gave the child, a girl, up for adoption. McCorvey has also backed away from her abortion-on-demand position and now advocates abortion only in the first trimester. This change of heart arose, according to her 1994 autobiography *I Am Roe,* out of her work in an abortion clinic, where she witnessed far too many second-trimester abortions.)

The right to privacy, the Court ruled, was no less valid when it came to ending an unwanted pregnancy than when the issue was attempting to prevent one in the first place. The Fourteenth Amendment right to privacy that the Court construed as protecting the rights of parents to send their children to private schools, of mixed-race couples to marry, and of married couples and unmarried women to use contraceptives was, the Court said, "broad enough to encompass a woman's decision whether or not to terminate her pregnancy."

So, on the one hand, the Court validated the feminists' point that women had a fundamental constitutional (even human) right to control decisions about their own sexuality and motherhood. On the other hand, the Court also validated the pro-life community's contention that a woman's womb is home to more than a mixture of cells, tissue, and genetic codes. The Court came up with a scientifically informed judgment of twenty-six weeks as the point at which a fetus becomes capable of living outside of the womb—and therefore as deserving of state protection from harm as any other human being.

So the Court itself, ironically, provided foundations for the moral certitude both sides have brought to this debate since 1973. Moral certitude is the best weapon any voice in a political debate can have. It establishes rigid principles and sets a high standard for those who wish to join the cause. It calls upon political leaders to reach beyond easy compromise and measure their own moral precepts against prevailing political attitudes.

It was just this kind of moral certitude, of course, that forced America's political and legal system to confront the question of abortion rights.

Those opposed to anti-abortion laws considered it immoral to require a woman to have a child against her will. This they considered the ultimate violation of her rights as a woman. The intricacies of human sexuality and the nuances of each and every sexual encounter were such that mistakes would inevitably occur. Whereas men had the legal right and, usually, the financial power to flee such mistakes (unless they agreed to marry the woman, which many were not prepared to do), women had no legal right to flee the consequences of a pregnancy. Pregnant women were sentenced to become mothers of children they did not want, regardless of whether they had the financial means or emotional and spiritual inclination to raise those children. In the event of a "mistake" between consenting adults, men had options that women simply did not. The conviction that this situation was morally and legally unfair gave rise to the push among feminists first for legal access to contraceptives and then for legal access to abortion in all fifty states. At first, the call for abortion rights was intended to give a woman recourse when, in the most-difficult of personal circumstances, abortion appeared to be the best course of action. The crusade for abortion rights was not motivated by a desire to make abortion available as a method for casual birth control, but by the need to give women a legal method of coping with the extremely difficult circumstance of an unwanted pregnancy. The moral thrust behind the movement was to give women the right to control their destinies in cases—assumed to be rare and acutely painful—when adults who consented to sex could not agree on how to cope with their unwanted pregnancy.

This moral and legal construct remains central to the pro-choice argument in defense of legal abortion. It is a legitimate and entirely defensible argument, honorably conceived and consistent with legal precedents and moral codes that seek to equalize rights and responsibilities in our pluralistic society.

There was also a practical side to the abortion-rights crusade: legalizing abortion, it was hoped, would reduce maternal mortality. The medical community lobbied to legalize abortion because more than five thousand women—predominantly black and Hispanic—were dying annually as the result of botched abortions performed in illegal clinics. Pro-choice advocates were fighting to end the days of such pro-cedures; surprisingly, though, the era of the "back-alley" or "back-room" abortion was not as long as many might guess. From colonial days until the last third of the nineteenth century, abortion was legal before (in the language of the time) "quickening" had occurred—until roughly the fourth month of pregnancy. After the Civil War, the American Medical Association, seeking to bolster the authority of physicians over that of midwives and homeopaths, pushed for legislation to prohibit abortions in state legislatures across the land. Legal prohibition of abortion led many women to seek back-alley abortions—and to accept the considerable risks that went with such measures.

★

NOW let's take a moment to examine the pro-life argument. Pro-life forces contend that life is just as sacred inside the womb as outside. They argue, with more than a slight degree of scientific justification, that most of the genetic coding of a child is laid down in the earliest days of conception. What a child will become at birth—the color of his or her hair, his or her height, his or her weight, the length of his or her fingers and toes, and millions of other genetic characteristics—is determined at, or very soon after, conception. Many also argue that only God has the right to abort a child spontaneously—that is, to cause a miscarriage. Each human being is a divine creation, in their view, and God, as the creator of all mankind, determines whether a fetus will survive in a mother's womb. To abort a fetus, which God gave us the power to create, is to interpose oneself between God and the act of creation. The power to create is a gift from God and must be honored as a sacred blessing, and its defiance through an act such as abortion constitutes a sin of a particularly heinous kind. Aborting a fetus is a greater moral violation than killing an innocent human being because adults and even children would theoretically have some potential of defending themselves—something a fetus surely does not have.

In response to the feminist argument that abolishing abortion puts women at a legal disadvantage to men, pro-life forces argue that women who submit to unprotected sex outside of wedlock are taking an *informed risk*. They know such sexual encounters can result in pregnancy. By agreeing to have unprotected sexual intercourse outside of marriage, they are assuming the biological responsibility to care for any child that union might create. Pro-life forces argue that abortion allows a woman to shirk her responsibilities to herself and society by giving her the right to kill a fetus she agreed to create by having sex in the first place.

How is feminism advanced, pro-life women often ask, by creating a moral and legal climate in which it is accepted that women are powerless to control the outcome of sexual interaction with men? The assumption that women need abortion rights *presumes* that they are incapable of protecting themselves from unwanted pregnancies. If women are so concerned about unwanted pregnancies, pro-life forces can fairly ask, why don't they abstain or make absolutely sure they've taken all the necessary precautions available to avoid a pregnancy— instead of resorting to abortion?

Lastly, pro-life advocates contend that no society should condone, on the grounds of expanding personal liberty, an act that deprives another human being of that same liberty. The transient liberty a woman enjoys once freed from an unwanted pregnancy deprives the fetus she was carrying of all the liberties he or she would have enjoyed if allowed to live.

These arguments are as morally and legally valid as those on the pro-choice side. Those who hold them do so as sincerely and with the same honorable intentions and goals as those on the pro-choice side.

And guess what? Most Americans agree with both sides.

Or, to be precise, they agree with *most* of what both sides have to say about the morality and legality of abortion.

The vast majority of Americans see abortion rights as an important component of women's rights, a reflection of the progress women have made in asserting their right to control decisions involving their own bodies. Most Americans see abortion as a practice that should be exercised with extreme caution, and only under the most trying circumstances. In sum, most Americans want abortions to be safe, legal—and *extremely rare.*

That's why the vast majority of Americans oppose abortion as a means of birth control or sex selection. Most of us also oppose unlimited access to abortions for teenagers, recognizing that teens are unlikely to be mature enough to make such a life decision on their own. Importantly, most Americans do not oppose giving teens access to abortion; they merely want the state to ensure that teenage girls consult with their parents and obtain counseling to help them cope with the trauma. Most Americans are opposed to partial-birth abortions, in which a near-term fetus is partially delivered before the abortion takes place.

Survey data collected in 1987 by the Guttmacher Institute suggest that a high percentage of abortions are performed for "social" rather than medical reasons. The Institute found that among a group of nineteen hundred women who had had abortions, only 6 percent cited potential health problems of themselves or the baby as determining factors in their decisions. Only 1 percent cited rape or incest as the reason. In the vast majority of cases, according to the survey, women had abortions because they had relationship problems with the father or couldn't afford the baby at the time or weren't ready for the responsibility of raising a child. The Institute estimated that 1,559,100 abortions were performed in 1987. According to the survey data, fewer than 150,000 of these abortions were performed on women who reported what most Americans would consider "hard cases," such as rape, incest, or potential health complications for the woman or child. (This is the only year so far in which the Institute has conducted such a survey.)

Overall, most Americans have a strong commitment to maintaining access to abortion but are opposed to the use of abortion in many of its particulars. When it comes to the right to abortion as an abstraction, the vast majority of Americans support it. When most Americans evaluate abortion on a case-by-case basis, ambivalence grows. Many Americans tell pollsters they are *personally opposed* to abortion but nevertheless support the right of others to obtain the procedure. We suspect that most Americans secretly harbor *"there but for the grace of God go I"* sentiments about abortion. We also suspect that a sizable majority of Americans have, at one time or another, placed themselves in a situation in which the need for an abortion *might* have arisen. That's a powerful psychological subtext in this issue, one that sets abortion apart from all other public policy issues. It's one of the many unique characteristics of the abortion debate, and one that makes its resolution particularly difficult.

We believe that the public's ambivalence about abortion should compel pro-choice and pro-life forces to craft a public policy that reflects this ambivalence, and to build *a consensus in the nation on the role abortion plays in a civil society*. There is a crying need for pro-choice and pro-life forces to send a unified message to women and men across the country that we all have a responsibility, to ourselves and society, to avoid unwanted pregnancies and the abortions they needlessly precipitate.

Sadly, they are doing nothing of the kind.

Instead, pro-life and pro-choice forces have done all they can to demonize one another—to question each other's motives, morality, and humanity. In a nation where ambivalence about abortion runs deep, debate has grown increasingly shrill, violent, and meaningless. While most Americans stew in their own mixed feelings, pro-life and pro-choice forces shove down our throats a monochromatic and distorted picture of the choice facing America: a choice between abortion on demand or prohibition except in cases of rape and incest. Intolerant of nuance, indifferent to abortion's inherent moral complexities, the warring voices debase their respective causes and do immeasurable harm to the nation by refusing to devote their energies to any cause but the *absolute political and legal destruction of their opponents.*

We have a message for pro-life and pro-choice forces: no one is listening anymore.

Pro-life America isn't going anywhere and neither is pro-choice America. While the abortion debate is clearly meaningful to activists on both sides, it is utterly meaningless to the vast majority of Americans, who want a halt to abortion hostilities, and a new tone and direction for the discussion.

Why can't pro-life and pro-choice forces see this?

Why can't both sides see the damage this debate has inflicted on innocent people? Why can't both sides see that their moral absolutism and inflexibility have contributed to a sense of helplessness and confusion among many Americans—especially teenage girls—about how to cope with their own sexuality?

The debate has also grown needlessly irrational and even violent.

Let us cite one example from each side of the debate.

Pro-choice forces will not retreat from their defense of abortion on demand, from the protection of abortion access under any circumstances at all times. This rigidity has led them to defend the medically and morally indefensible practice of partial-birth abortion. In their efforts to protect abortion on demand, pro-choice leaders have craftily sanitized the language of abortion—frequently referring to abortion as a "reproductive-health service"—and in recent years they have rejected the use of the very term *partial-birth abortion,* preferring the medical description *dilatation and extraction* (making the process sound beneficent and impersonal, as if it were an abessed tooth and not a fetus under discussion). Pro-choice activists steadfastly refuse to acknowledge that a fetus is a potential human being, preferring to focus their rhetorical firepower on a woman's need to exercise choice over her body—implying that the fetus is an alien force undeserving of protection or humane consideration. This rhetoric intentionally diminishes the value of the fetus and demands that women and society as a whole ignore their moral sensitivity to the potential human life growing by the minute inside a woman's womb.

On top of that, pro-choice activists routinely and intentionally lie about the true state of abortion practices in America. During the 1995 congressional debate over partial-birth abortion, Ron Fitzsimmons, the executive director of the National Coalition of Abortion Providers, said in an interview on ABC-TV's "Nightline" that partial-birth abortions were performed rarely and only on women whose lives were in danger or whose fetuses were unhealthy. This contention was meant to reinforce the argument that it was unnecessary to create a specific legal prohibition against partial-birth abortion.

In an article published two years later, in the March 3, 1997, edition of *American Medical News,* Fitzsimmons confessed he "lied through his teeth" about the number of partial-birth abortions performed nationally every year. After retracting his "Nightline" assertions, which he attributed in later interviews to "spouting the party line," Fitzsimmons estimated that at least five thousand partial-birth abortions are performed each year. Interviews and statistics gathered by journalist Ruth Padawer and published in the September 15, 1996, Bergen, New Jersey *Record* revealed that more than fifteen hundred partial-birth abortions were performed annually at a single clinic in Englewood, New Jersey. The pro-choice lobby knew of these figures, yet its members continued to lie to the public (asserting that only five hundred partial-birth abortions were performed across the country each year) in order to protect the procedure from regulation.

The pro-choice lobby began lying about the frequency of partial-birth abortions after the medical community rejected its claim that the procedure was medically therapeutic. On January 12, 1997, the executive board of the American College of Obstetricians and Gynecologists announced it could identify no circumstances in which a partial-birth abortion would be the only option to save the life of the mother or to preserve her health. And an American Medical Association task force convened to study the issue concluded that "there does not appear to be any identified situation in which intact dilatation and extraction is the only appropriate procedure to induce abortion." Most Americans who support abortion rights would not likely support the pro-choice lobby's practice of misleading the public about the nature or number of abortion procedures performed in America. The philosopher George Santayana once defined a zealot as one who has redoubled his efforts while forgetting his aims. There is no better example of the reckless zealotry of the pro-choice movement than the partial-birth abortion debate.

What pro-choice forces should be made to see is that such tactics and rhetoric have indirectly contributed to a state of moral disintegration in which young women dispose of their newborn children in trash cans and dumpsters. Such was the case with Amy Grossman and Brian J. Peterson, two New Jersey teens indicted for murder in the death of their infant son. The teens, high-school sweethearts, delivered the six-pound-two-ounce boy in a Comfort Inn and proceeded, according to court documents, to shake the boy to death, wrap him in a gray plastic bag, and dispose of him in a trash bin. Equally disturbing is the case of Melissa Drexler, a seventeen-year-old New Jersey teen indicted for murder in the June 6, 1997, suffocation death of her six-pound-six ounce newborn son, whom she delivered and then dumped in a trash can at the banquet hall where she was attending her high-school prom.

In an interview on the NBC-TV program "Dateline," a friend of Drexler's named Amanda Jacobsen said the following about the baby boy's death: "She didn't know it was alive. It came out blue. She assumed it was dead. Melissa told me it wasn't living." Four sentences. Twenty-one words. Four occasions to refer to the baby as a boy, but every time Jacobsen said "it." Jacobsen's words confirm the hollow and terrifying belief among some American teens that newborn children are not, in fact, human. Would anyone deny that the moral ambiguity of the pro-choice camp helped create a climate in which teenagers could act as these did without recognizing that they had committed murder?

These cases are ghastly exceptions, but they are nevertheless relevant as an outgrowth of the pro-choice lobby's refusal to question the validity of abortion as a morally justifiable alternative to abstinence, contraception, or adoption. Because pro-choice activists refuse to acknowledge that some abortions can be both morally and legally wrong, they reinforce the notion that an unborn child (at any stage of development) can be considered no more than an inconvenience and a nuisance unless its mother decides otherwise.

. . .

NOW, for the other side.

The pro-life lobby must assume responsibility for the zealots in their movement who kill and maim abortion doctors and others who work at abortion clinics. Since 1992, pro-life assassins have killed two doctors, two abortion clinic employees, and a clinic escort. Seven others have been shot and wounded. Since 1977 there have been nineteen hundred acts of violence against abortion clinics, including bombings, arson, death threats, kidnappings, and assaults.

While it's true that mainstream pro-life forces have never explicitly advocated the death of abortion doctors or those who work in abortion clinics, their rhetoric is a contributing factor in such violence. They may try to deny it, but that doesn't make it any less true.

Consider the pro-life argument, which, reduced to its core principles, goes as follows: Abortion is the murder of an unborn child, a creation of God. Those who perform abortions are murderers. Those who assist doctors who perform abortions are accessories to murder. Laws must be changed to outlaw such murders.

But some in the pro-life movement, frustrated by their inability to change the law or reverse society's acceptance of abortion as murder, have taken God's law into their own hands—have decided to carry the argument against abortion one deadly step further. If doctors who perform abortions are murderers, then they deserve to die. If society at large will not avenge God by punishing those who kill babies, then individuals must. Those who have shot and killed abortion doctors have found Biblical justification in the New Testament, quoting Jesus' admonition not to live by the rules of man but by the rules of God. Terrorists who have bombed abortion clinics have offered similar defenses for their actions, claiming they had an obligation to God *and society* to stop murders from occurring. Their argument is repugnant not only in its content, but in its consistency.

Bill Price, president of Texans United for Life, once acknowledged that "there has been a philosophical or even moral groundwork laid for assassinating abortionists by certain people in the pro-life movement, and I think they bear some of the blame." But that doesn't make it tolerable or defensible. It's neither. The pro-life community has, through benign neglect, allowed this mentality to take root in some quarters of its movement. It has done far too little to denounce it and drive it out. Until it does, the pro-life movement must accept some responsibility for the slaughter of abortion doctors and civilians who work at abortion clinics.

After twenty-five years, the abortion debate has done absolutely nothing to satisfy the yearning of millions of Americans for a moral and legal consensus about the morally troubling practice of abortion. But it has contributed to behavior that makes one gasp in silent horror. Killing doctors and bombing clinics in the name of pro-life vengeance? Disposing of infant children in dumpsters as a defensible exercise of reproductive choice? At the ragged and immature fringes of American society, the abortion debate has done real and measurable damage.

What has it done for the law? Not much.

What has it done for the rest of America? About the same.

The basic construct in *Roe v. Wade* remains the law of the land, only marginally circumscribed in some states that regulate access to abortion for teens, and in others that require doctors to test a fetus's viability before an abortion is performed after the fifth month.

In Congress politicians fight endlessly over the most miniscule contours of abortion law. There are annual floor fights over whether the federal government should subsidize abortions through Medicaid: the Supreme Court has held there is no such right to funding guaranteed in the Constitution, and Congress, through the Hyde Amendment, has banned such subsidies since 1976. Congress also fights annually over whether the District of Columbia should use its own taxes to pay for abortions for poor women. Other regular legislative scrums include debates over the legality of providing abortion counseling at federally funded family planning clinics, and over the availability of abortion services on United States military bases overseas, and over foreign assistance for family planning clinics overseas. Pro-life lawmakers even used this issue as a bargaining chip with President Clinton in 1997 over issues as diverse and considerable as trade legislation, funding for the International Monetary Fund, and debt payments to the United Nations.

All of these repetitive fights in Congress are perfect illustrations of the special-interest mania that has infected the abortion debate. Members of Congress elected with the support of pro-life or pro-choice forces are on the spot in each and every one of these debates. And they deviate from the party line only at their own peril. We know of pro-choice lawmakers who have lost all of their support from the pro-choice lobby because on one occasion they voted against the lobby's stated position. We know of similar penalties meted out to pro-life lawmakers. For lobbyists on both sides of the abortion issue, support is contingent on 100-percent loyalty. Anything less is treason. And since there are plenty of lawmakers in each camp, legislative stalemate is often the end result.

Presidents can change abortion policy, but only at the margin. When Clinton was elected, for example, he immediately rescinded a Bush executive order forbidding workers at federally funded family-planning clinics from *discussing* (not performing) abortions. As a practical matter the ban had little effect, since it was never enforced in a meaningful way. The clinics that wanted to provide advice and counsel found ways around it. Bush's original executive order, of course, was the result of pressure from the pro-life community to make good on campaign promises to toe the pro-life line; Clinton's action, which disabled the ineffective measure, was just as bold a symbol of fealty to his side of the debate.

Indeed, the entire abortion debate in Congress is about symbolism, not reality. While we recognize why some lawmakers do not want to subsidize abortions directly through Medicaid, this petty skirmish ignores the fact that other kinds of federal assistance, such as the earned-income tax credit, housing subsidies, and Aid to Families With Dependent Children (AFDC), all indirectly subsidize abortions for poor women. Forms of direct cash assistance such as the earned-income tax credit and AFDC are probably a routine source of abortion funds for women across the country. Other subdebates are comparably meaningless: no attempt to regulate where United States service personnel have abortions will significantly effect *whether* they have abortions, merely on whether they have them in a military hospital or at a private facility at their own expense.

This symbolic debate reaches the zenith of banality when it comes to the Republicans' quadrennial battle over the language of their party platform on abortion. Since 1980 the party has called for an amendment to the Constitution abolishing the legal right to an abortion except to protect the life of the mother and in cases of rape and incest.

This is entirely about symbolism. Congress has voted once on such an amendment to the Constitution. (It fell eighteen votes short of passage in the Senate in 1983. The vote was forty-nine to fifty.) It has never again come to a vote in the Senate. The Republican-led Congress of the 1990s did not hold a vote on this proposed amendment in the first four years it held control of the House and Senate. It is not in the

Republican's legislative agenda now or in the immediate future. And yet pro-life forces require that any candidate seeking the GOP's presidential nomination nod to their demand that this amendment be added to the Constitution.

The simple truth, of course, is that such an amendment could, by definition, come only after the abortion debate was already settled.

Think about it: To pass a constitutional amendment, two-thirds majorities must be obtained in both the House and the Senate. Then, normally, three-fourths of the nation's state legislatures must vote to approve the amendment.

For Congress to pass a pro-life amendment and three-fourths of the state legislatures to approve it, the consensus in America would have to be so deep and so profound that virtually no one would be having abortions in the first place. In fact, passage of such an amendment would require an American electorate more hostile to legal abortion than it was *before* the Supreme Court handed down its deeply controversial *Roe v. Wade* decision. In the six years before the Court ruled, fourteen states had already legalized abortion with some restrictions. Four of those states—New York, Washington, Hawaii, and Alaska—had legalized abortion on demand. In the twenty-five years since *Roe v. Wade,* cultural acceptance of legalized abortion has only increased.

Attempting to dismantle *Roe v. Wade* by means of a constitutional amendment is a fool's errand. It won't happen—not in our lifetime, and not in our children's.

That does not mean, of course, that a fetus is of no moral or intrinsic value to our society or to the state until he or she leaves the birth canal. What our society—or *any* civil society—must do is build a consensus that acknowledges and celebrates the potential of every life, a consensus that encourages men and women to do all they can to avoid unwanted pregnancies. Even in the case of unwanted pregnancies, this society should strive to build a consensus that abortion is an option less worthy than adoption. With literally thousands of childless couples eager to adopt, society should use the tax code and other inducements to support women who carry children to term. Congress and President Clinton took modest steps in this direction in 1997, passing laws easing the adoption of foster children. But Congress and Clinton must do more to ease access to adoption in order to make it a viable and practicable option for women with unwanted pregnancies.

Most important of all, pro-choice and pro-life forces must stop arguing with each other over marginal issues and focus together on the central question of abortion in America: *how many fewer abortions were there this year than last?*

Can we not all agree that each and every abortion is a tragedy? Can we not agree that, as a society, we are not doing enough or saying enough to discourage abortion as an option to unwanted pregnancies? Don't we all believe that this fruitless and polarizing discussion over the legality of abortion sidesteps the *real* discussion men and women should be having every day about the responsibility they have to themselves and society to avoid unwanted pregnancies.

Can we not also agree that men have needlessly been excluded from this debate? With feminism at its core, the pro-choice lobby would have you believe this debate is purely about *a woman's right to choose*. What about a couple's obligation to discuss and decide how to handle their consensual sexual relationship? Has it ever dawned on pro-choice activists that among the nation's most-ardent abortion supporters are sexist men who see it as a way to avoid their responsibilities. The right to an abortion has given men a free pass to deal cavalierly with the most-important moral dimensions of sexual activity. It's allowed men to ignore their responsibilities to women they have intercourse with and to a society that, in an earlier day, could realistically expect that men would stand by women they impregnated. To be sure, men were abandoning their pregnant lovers long before abortion was legalized; but that tendency has only been accelerated by full access to abortion services.

It's time for the abortion debate to change course—and we have a modest suggestion.

Here is a press conference we would like to see take place in the next year. Allow us to set the scene.

Phyllis Schlafly, one of America's most vocal pro-life advocates, standing side-by-side with Kate Michelman, one of America's staunchest proponents of abortion rights, enter stage left. Together they speak from a podium to what would surely be a stunned body of reporters. As silence hangs in the air, Mrs. Schafly and Ms. Michelman eye each other nervously, pause a moment, then turn to the podium and read a statement that would forever change the tenor and direction of the abortion debate in America.

"Good morning. You know who we are. You know what we believe about the issue of abortion. But you don't know why we are here. We'll tell you, but first let's make one thing clear: we still disagree on the laws governing abortion in this country. We've argued about them for nearly twenty-five years. Our debate has been helpful in keeping the abortion issue high in public consciousness, but in the process, we have missed an opportunity to say something about abortion—something that, until recently, we never knew how much we agreed upon. What we both believe, and what has brought us here today, is that we must begin together a crusade to reduce the number of abortions in this country. Whether abortions are legal or illegal, American women will have them. History tells us that. But whether they are legal or illegal, the fact is that an abortion is a tragedy for a woman, for her partner, and for their aborted child. There are alternatives to abortion, and we want to announce the formation of a joint effort to expand awareness and availability of adoption services among women considering abortion. We also call for increased public and private funding for contraception services, for the teaching of abstinence as the preferred alternative to sexual activity and promiscuity among teens. We will jointly ask Congress and the president to double funding for family-planning and abstinence initiatives. In addition, we will devote 25 percent of our organizations' budgets to similar activities. We believe the message of abstinence is especially important to send to the children of America, children who are bombarded day in and day out with pop-culture inducements to have sex. Sexuality is about freedom, but it is also about responsibility. We want to encourage all women and all men to join together in a crusade against *the need to have an abortion.* We have never found ourselves in agreement on any aspect of this subject before. But we have seen that our political efforts are missing the most-important point: they are doing nothing to reduce the abortion rate in this country. One and a half million abortions a year is simply too many. We hope that our historic alliance will raise America's consciousness about the tragic personal and societal costs of abortion. Thank you."

Unrealistic? Perhaps. But to the vast majority of Americans such an event would be a revelation—and a welcome one.

THE SECOND LIE

$\blacklozenge$

GUN CONTROL REDUCES CRIME

NEITHER OF US owns a gun, and neither of us anticipates buying one in the near future. We are not interested in arguing a
pro- or antigun philosophy in this book. What we want to do is de-
mystify and debunk much of the false rhetoric that accompanies
America's debate about gun ownership, crime, and the law.

The debate over gun control remains warped by the uninformed
idea that more guns in America leads to more crime. Anxiety among
suburban voters about the proliferation of guns has reached a fever
pitch, and politicians, ever sensitive to voter fears, have grown increasingly supportive of federal efforts to restrict access to firearms.
Federal law now requires a five-day waiting period for the purchase of
handguns and bans the sale of so-called assault rifles. Other laws have
made ownership of any gun illegal for those convicted of misdemeanor
domestic-violence offenses. In 1997 the Pentagon ordered all soldiers
convicted of misdemeanor domestic-violence charges to turn over all
firearms and ammunition immediately—even soldiers stationed in potential combat zones such as Bosnia.

In other words, the political discussion in America is moving toward increased regulation of firearms at just the moment when credible and unbiased research has proven that gun control *simply does not
reduce crime*.

The great irony of the gun debate is that when the evidence was
murkier, the nation was less willing to impose nationwide regulations
on the access to handguns and other firearms. Now, despite far-clearer
evidence about how little gun-control laws actually accomplish, the
nation is moving more aggressively to impose federal regulations on
the ownership of handguns and other firearms.

What's more, the tenor of the gun-control debate, with its irrational focus on access to firearms, ignores far more effective means of reducing crime, such as improved police tactics and stronger community-based anticrime efforts.

And yet the parameters of the crime debate remain frozen between two choices: society regulates access to firearms to reduce crime, or it doesn't.

Consider two representative excerpts from House debate in 1996 on the proposal to lift the ban on nineteen specific assault-style weapons. First, Representative Luis Gutierrez, Democrat of Illinois:

> What is absolutely right is for this Congress to take every step possible to protect our families, our children, and our neighborhoods from senseless gun violence. What is absolutely wrong is to care more about a few thousand bucks from the National Rifle Association than keeping our kids and communities safe. Today let's vote for our kids instead of for the cash. Vote to protect our families and save the assault weapons ban.

Second, Representative Gary Ackerman, Democrat of New York:

> I beg my colleagues, do not defile the memory of those who died in the massacre on the Long Island Railroad. Do not sell your vote for the blood money of the National Rifle Association. Listen to the painful and courageous cries of the victims, your constituents and our police officers, law enforcement officials, and not to the special interest blood money of the National Rifle Association.

Think about the implication of these remarks. Both congressmen contend that those who question the effectiveness of the assault-weapons ban in reducing crime are actively disregarding the "cries of the victims." What's more, Ackerman maintained those who are skeptical of gun control as a crime-fighting strategy are thoroughly corrupted by "blood money."

Of course, harsh and divisive rhetoric about guns is not limited to those on the gun-control side of the debate.

In a memorable gesture, former-president George Bush resigned his membership in the National Rifle Association (NRA) after a group defended a fund-raising letter that referred to federal law-enforcement officers as "jack-booted thugs." The letter was sent to NRA members in March of 1995, a month and a half before Timothy McVeigh blew up the Alfred P. Murrah Building in Oklahoma City, killing 169 civilians, including 19 children. Among other things, the fund-raising letter said that federal law-enforcement officers "have the government's go-ahead to harass, intimidate, even murder law-abiding citizens. Not too long ago, it was unthinkable for federal agents wearing Nazi bucket helmets and black storm-trooper uniforms to attack law-abiding citizens."

Such rhetoric was seen by many as an incitement of the kind of intense antigovernment hatred that fueled McVeigh's murderous assault on the Murrah Building. Even after the bombing, the worst act of domestic terrorism in American history, the NRA defended its rhetoric and the substance of its charges. This pushed Bush over the edge.

"I was outraged when, even in the wake of the Oklahoma City tragedy, Mr. Wayne LaPierre, executive vice president of the NRA, defended his attack on federal agents as 'jack-booted thugs,'" Mr. Bush said in a May 3, 1995 letter to NRA president Thomas Washington.

LaPierre, under whose signature the fund-raising letter was distributed, said the NRA's sweeping denunciation of federal law enforcement was really meant only as a criticism of specific cases in which it believed excessive force was used.

Bush resigned in part to protest the NRA's "unwarranted attack" on all federal law-enforcement officers. Bush was particularly incensed because one of the Secret Service agents who protected him while he was president, Al Whicher, died in the Murrah Building bombing.

"He was no Nazi," Mr. Bush said in his letter. "He was a kind man, a loving parent, a man dedicated to serve his country—and serve it well he did."

So on one side of the gun-control debate you have advocates accusing anyone who disagrees with them of taking "blood money" from the NRA so it can knowingly endanger the lives of innocent Americans. On the other, you have opponents comparing government agents to Nazis when they enforce gun laws passed by Congress and signed by the president. The portrait of America and guns painted by both sides could not be more false or nauseating.

For more than two decades, the debate over gun control and crime has been based on the intuition that there was more than a coincidental relationship between the steady rise in gun ownership and street crime. Intuition can lead to insight. But intuition is no substitute for sound social science. Social scientists and an increasing number of beat cops understand more clearly than ever that gun ownership does not lead to high rates of crime. Indeed, they recognize that regions where gun ownership is highest are also regions where crime is lowest.

But don't take our word for it.

Study the statements of some of the nation's leading *gun-control* advocates about what the scientific evidence dealing with guns and crime tells us.

Consider the words of Professor Hans Toch of the School of Criminology at the State University of New York at Albany:

> When used for protection, firearms can seriously inhibit aggression and can provide a psychological buffer against the fear of crime. Furthermore, the fact that national patterns show little violent crime where guns are most dense implies that guns do not elicit aggression in any meaningful way. Quite the contrary, these findings suggest that high saturations of guns in places, or something correlated with that condition, inhibit illegal aggression.

Professor Toch originally believed that gun-control laws would lead to a reduction in street crime. But after reviewing an increasing volume of data that challenged his pro–gun-control theories, Toch had to concede that the statistical evidence suggested otherwise.

Another authoritative voice provides an even more emphatic rejection of the gun-control-equals-crime-control notion. It comes from Marvin Wolfgang, one of the nation's leading criminologists and a professor of criminology at the University of Pennsylvania. Wolfgang's eyes were opened when he assessed important research concerning guns and violence that was undertaken by Gary Kleck (who originally believed gun-control laws reduced crime and was seeking to prove it by amassing crime data) and Marc Gertz. What Kleck and Gertz discovered was that guns are used far more often by victims to thwart crimes than they are by criminals to commit them. Similarly, Kleck and Gertz revealed that individuals who had a gun were able to escape serious injury far more often than unarmed individuals who surrendered to their assailants.

> I am as strong a gun control advocate as can be found among the criminologists of this country. If I [could] . . . I would elim-

inate ALL guns from the civilian population and maybe even from the police. I hate guns—ugly, nasty instruments designed to kill people. . . .

Nonetheless, the methodological soundness of the current Kleck and Gertz study is clear. I cannot further debate it. . . .

The Kleck and Gertz study impresses me for the caution the authors exercise and the elaborate nuances they examine methodologically. I do not like their conclusion that having a gun can be useful, but I cannot fault their methodology. They have tried earnestly to meet all objections in advance and have done exceedingly well.

A quiet revolution has been taking place in American academia on the question of gun control's efficacy in reducing crime. As the nation learns more about crime, the habits of criminals, the deterrent effect of punishment, and the role guns play in violence, it should come to see that gun-control laws do not reduce crime. In many instances, they create a false sense of security among the population on whom gun-control regulations fall.

As statistics about crime and criminals become more reliable, the science of criminology is beginning to flourish. It was not until the mid-1960s that the nation made a serious attempt to measure the number of crimes and track patterns in the action of criminals. Until then, crime statistics were entirely a local matter, and the uniformity of collection methods was spotty at best.

In 1967, in response to a startling increase in crime, President Lyndon Johnson convened a blue-ribbon commission that produced the first nationwide survey of crime in America since 1931. The report set in motion the first strong federal crime-control program and led to a massive increase in federal funding for anticrime efforts and local and state gun-control laws. The presidential commission found that the nation kept very crude statistics on crime and violence, making it extremely difficult to gauge the scope of crime in America. Soon thereafter, substantial efforts were undertaken to improve the collection of statistics on crime and the use of firearms in the commission of crimes.

For years, the academic community scrutinized gun-control laws in search of evidence to measure their effect on crime. For years, most of the data were inconclusive; as a result academic opinion remained divided. There was anecdotal and statistical evidence throughout the 1970s that crime was rising rapidly, despite the presence of new gun-control laws. But researchers could not be sure that the rise was due to factors beyond the reach of gun-control laws, from ineffective law enforcement, poverty, and drug abuse to gang activity, police-force cutbacks, or the patchwork nature of gun-control laws.

As a consequence, the academic community could not adequately assess the real-world consequences of gun control in ways that taught policymakers or citizens much about their value.

Meanwhile, the crime issue became a favorite of Washington lawmakers eager to exploit voter fear in return for political support. Congress routinely churns out crime bills, even though the federal crimes they address only account for 5 percent of all crime in America. Such measures are taken by and large to "prove" to voters that Washington is doing something about crime; but the laws typically dance around the periphery, providing federal dollars for state and local crime-fighting efforts and increasing criminal penalties on federal crimes that have nothing to do with the mayhem on our streets. But the laws do make for swell press releases, and Washington lawmakers are too willing to deceive voters into believing that each year's new and improved anti-crime laws are helpful.

While Washington has provided more money, states and localities have spent their time beefing up gun-control legislation. Gun-control laws proliferated at the state and local levels in the 1960s and 1970s, particularly in America's largest cities. The District of Columbia banned handgun possession in 1977. Chicago began requiring registration of all newly purchased handguns in 1968 and in 1982 banned them altogether.

Like their federal counterparts, local and state politicians assumed their streets were filled with too many guns—and that limiting access to them would reduce crime. Since gun-control laws were in their infancy, criminologists could not say for sure whether they would or would not reduce crime. Politicians and the public at large reasoned, with some justification, that gun control couldn't hurt and might actually make things better.

That was and remains the fervent hope and belief of gun-control advocates. We do not doubt the sincerity of their beliefs, or the good intentions that underlie them. But the time has come to judge gun control by its results, not by its intentions. Good intentions don't always lead to sound and effective public policy. And clinging to good intentions in the face of a track record of failure is illogical and, in the case of gun control, perilous.

Thanks to vastly improved methods of counting and investigating crimes in America, criminologists have more data than ever before to help them evaluate the role gun ownership plays in crime. The passage of time has allowed criminologists to measure criminal behavior in relation to gun-control laws. After years of study they've proven one thing most of us could have guessed: the criminal class has managed nicely to elude every new law.

The amount of research on crime in America has never been more plentiful—and its conclusions never more significant—in the nation's quest to improve public safety. And yet much of this important new information has been either suppressed or ignored by the national media.

Here, in simple terms, are the facts about guns and crime in America—not the assumptions of the 1960s, but the facts as we have learned them today.

GUN OWNERSHIP DOES NOT INCREASE CRIME. Criminologists Gary Kleck and E. Britt Patterson reported in 1993 that a 45-percent increase in gun ownership from 1973 to 1992 did not increase the rate of murder, rape, robbery, or assault.

GUN-CONTROL LAWS DO NOT KEEP GUNS OUT OF CRIMINALS' HANDS. Criminologists James D. Wright and Peter H. Rossi reported in 1986 that only 7 percent of convicted felons reported obtaining handguns through legitimate retail sources. Three quarters of the felons told interviewers they would have no trouble obtaining a firearm after their release, despite laws forbidding felons from obtaining firearms.

FIREARMS PROTECT POTENTIAL VICTIMS OF CRIME. Gary Kleck reported in his widely acclaimed 1991 book *Point Blank: Guns and Violence in America* that Americans successfully use firearms to thwart a crime between 2.5 and 3 million times per year. Kleck estimated that as many as sixty-five lives are saved each year for every person killed by a firearm. Each year, potential crime victims kill between 2,000 and 3,000 criminals and wound between 9,000 and 17,000.

ACCIDENTAL DEATHS DUE TO FIREARMS ARE DECLINING. Researcher David Kopel, in his 1993 article "Gun Play," revealed that accidental gun deaths in America have fallen dramatically since 1970. That year saw 2,406 Americans die in firearms accidents; by 1991 that number had fallen to 1,441, even as the stock of privately owned firearms rose by more than 40 percent. The rate of death due to accidental discharge of firearms fell from 1.2 per 100,000 Americans in

1970 to 0.6 percent in 1991. Compare the 1991 statistic for accidental firearm deaths to the rates of death for drowning (1.6 per 100,000), inhalation or ingestion of foreign objects (1.3 per 100,000), and complications from medical procedures (1.0 per 100,000).

THE VAST MAJORITY OF MURDER VICTIMS AND MURDERERS IN AMERICA ARE CRIMINALS. According to researchers Daniel D. Polsby, professor of law at Northwestern University, and Dennis Brennen, chairman of the Economics Department at Harper College, there is a widespread myth in America that victims of homicide know their assailants. This myth has led to the assumption, unfortunately enshrined in some gun-control legislation, that limiting access to firearms will discourage or prevent an individual from killing or wounding a member of his family, a friend, or an acquaintance. While it is technically true that most homicide victims know their assailants, it is a lie to suggest they know them as you know your neighbor or your child's homeroom teacher. Polsby and Brennen reviewed the records of the Chicago Police Department for ten years to see what relationship homicide victims had to their assailants.

In the homicide data Polsby and Brennen analyzed, a familiar pattern emerged. On average, 72 percent of murderers had known criminal histories. Of those killed, on average, 57 percent had known criminal histories. Polsby and Brennen also found that in the last year of their survey data (1993) fewer than 3 percent of Chicago homicides involved victims who were married to their assailants and only 3 percent involved relatives. Nearly 50 percent of the cases fell into two categories: half involved victims and assailants police described as "acquaintances" but not "friends," while the other half involved homicides in which no relationship whatsoever could be established between victim and assailant.

To quote from their article, "Taking Aim at Gun Control," published October 30, 1995, by the Heartland Institute:

> The evidence usually given in support of [this] hypothesis is that homicide offenders often know or are related to their victims. That is true, but it hardly proves that these offenders are successful people ordinarily in control of their emotions. Much more plausibly, it shows that members of the criminal underworld often know one another, and that people with predatory, impulsive patterns of behavior attack relatives and associates as

well as strangers. The often-repeated proposition that murder usually occurs between friends and family members is bogus.

Those data surely understate the criminal histories of both offenders and victims. Only about two-thirds of homicides are ever "cleared." Homicides resulting from domestic quarrels are cleared at a much higher rate than killings between gang members or strangers. Furthermore, an unknown proportion of both offenders and victims who are shown as having no police record do in fact have such a record; they only appear not to because of statutes that expunge the records of juvenile offenders.

Most homicides are perpetrated by and upon socially marginal individuals, many of whom, because of prior run-ins with the law, are *already forbidden by law to possess firearms*. Controlling the behavior of this cohort through additional gun control legislation is nearly hopeless.

BELIEVE IT OR NOT, MORE GUNS MEANS LESS CRIME. The authors offer the following observation even though they are personally opposed to concealed weapons legislation. According to a 1996 study authored by University of Chicago law professor John Lott and David Mustard of the university's department of economics, allowing law-abiding citizens to carry concealed weapons is a more effective means of fighting crime than any gun-control law yet passed.

Lott and Mustard analyzed crime data from every county in America from 1977 to 1992 to see what effect, if any, laws requiring right-to-carry permits had on reducing crime. Such permits allow law-abiding citizens to carry a handgun with them whenever they choose.

We find that allowing citizens to carry concealed weapons deters violent crimes, and it appears to produce no increase in accidental deaths. If those states which did not have right-to-carry concealed gun provisions had adopted them in 1992, approximately 1,570 murders, 4,177 rapes and over 60,000 aggravated assaults would have been avoided yearly.

On the other hand, consistent with the notion of criminals responding to incentives, we find criminals substituting into property crimes involving stealth and where the probabilities of contact between the criminal and the victim are minimal.

Concealed handguns have their greatest deterrent effect in the high crime counties.

Thirty-one states now have right-to-carry permit laws that allow citizens to carry concealed firearms. Twenty-two of these states have adopted such laws in the last decade. Eleven states have passed them in the past three years (1995–98). Half of the country's population lives in states with right-to-carry laws. States with such laws have lower overall crime rates than states without them: Total violent crime is 18 percent lower. Homicide is 21 percent lower. Robbery is 32 percent lower. Aggravated assault is 11 percent lower.

Florida passed a right-to-carry law in 1987, and media speculation predicted a surge in crime and accidental deaths and injuries due to improper use of firearms. Here are some interesting facts gathered by the FBI. The rates of homicide, firearm homicide, and handgun homicide in Florida have fallen 36, 37, and 41 percent, respectively, since 1987. Nationally, the homicide rate fell 0.4 percent over that same period. The national rate of firearm homicide and handgun homicide rose 15 and 24 percent, respectively.

There is even fascinating anecdotal evidence that suggests that widespread publicity about increased gun ownership itself helps suppress crime.

From October 1966 to March 1967, the Orlando (Florida) Police Department trained more than twenty-five hundred women to use guns. The training was organized in response to a sharp increase in rapes and was specifically designed to send the message that women of Orlando were armed and trained to defend themselves. The *Orlando Sentinel* cosponsored the program and gave it extensive coverage. The number of rapes in Orlando dropped by 88 percent from 1966 to 1967, even though the rate of rape remained constant in the rest of Florida and nationwide. The rate of burglary also dropped precipitously.

All of this is not meant to suggest that gun-control laws serve no purpose. They can act as a psychological balm to voters who simply dislike guns and wish them to be as scarce as possible. They can also act as a cultural statement that reflects a city's, state's, or nation's attitude toward certain types of firearms. The nation has decided that nineteen specific types of long-rifle firearms that fire bullets rapidly should be banned. As a device to reduce crime, the Assault Weapons Ban, as the law is popularly known, is meaningless. With tiny modifications that can be successfully performed in a garage or by any gun shop, these "assault weapons" can be rendered legal. The Assault Weapons Ban, in other words, is almost purely symbolic—but it is a valid cultural statement. America has decided that law-abiding citizens have no reasonable and legally justifiable need for such weapons. Fair enough. As a member of Congress, coauthor Penny voted for the ban. As long as voters understand this law is a cultural statement and believe that such statements are helpful in defining the standards of civilized behavior, that's fine. But no one should be deluded into thinking the Assault Weapons Ban will significantly reduce crime. The same can be said about the Brady Law, which requires citizens to wait five days before obtaining a purchased handgun. The Brady Law has done very little to reduce crime. Government reports show that the law has resulted in only a handful of arrests and even fewer prosecutions. Criminologists have already documented that criminals avoid precisely the kinds of roadblocks the law erects. What's more, most of the rejections generated by the policy are the result of technical glitches and are eventually revised.

As a symbolic gesture and a legislative opiate, gun control might prove useful to a fearful electorate. As a cultural statement, it might be defensible at the local level. A city, town, or county might reasonably reach the conclusion that there are certain kinds of guns it simply must outlaw. A discrete group of voters may decide that it's worth narrowing Second Amendment rights in order to make explicit its attitude toward guns.

In fact, some local governments have done precisely that. Their stories tell us much about the constitutionality of such cultural statements and their effect on crime.

The town of Morton Grove, Illinois, banned the private possession of handguns in 1981. The Illinois Supreme Court upheld the ban because it was within the "police powers" of the town to enforce the ban. The Seventh United States Circuit Court also upheld the ban, ruling that the Second Amendment prevents Congress, but not a local jurisdiction, from restricting or infringing a citizen's right to bear arms. The Supreme Court declined to hear the case, leaving the judicial precedent for local regulation of firearms intact. That's the legal side of the story.

Most residents ignored the law. Local officials estimated there were three thousand handguns privately owned when the ban took effect. They did very little to collect the handguns, and only twenty were turned in or confiscated. Professor Paul Lavrakas of Northwestern University concluded that 80 percent or more of Morton Grove's residents still had their handguns two years after the law took effect.

Crime had never been much of a problem in Morton Grove, and it didn't rise or fall appreciably after the ban. There was a short-lived increase in burglary, but neither the police nor criminologists have determined its cause.

The move to ban guns in Morton Grove inspired a strong anti–gun-control reaction in Kennesaw, Georgia. In 1982 the city passed an ordinance requiring "every head of household residing in the City Limits of the City of Kennesaw to maintain a firearm, together with ammunition therefor." The ordinance exempted criminals, residents with moral objections, and those mentally or physically incapable of handling a firearm.

Local officials were not trying to increase gun ownership, since most Kennesaw residents already owned guns. The city wanted to make an emphatic cultural statement about its regard for guns and its willingness to use them to defend person and property. They had a hunch that the ensuing publicity would discourage criminals from preying on Kennesaw residents.

Between 1981 and 1985, violent crimes in Kennesaw dropped by 71 percent, burglaries by 65 percent. Between 1981 and 1993, burglaries dropped by 16 percent—even though the city's population doubled.

Oak Park banned handgun sales in 1977. From 1977 to 1984 the rates of homicide, robbery, aggravated assault, and burglary rose dramatically even as they declined or rose much more slowly in other suburbs across the nation.

Here are the numbers:

	Homicide	Robbery	Aggravated Assault	Burglary
Oak Park	+58%	+83%	+113%	+109%
U.S. Suburbs	-13%	-5%	+5%	-19%

Evanston, Illinois, the home of Northwestern University, banned handguns in 1982; researchers who analyzed crime statistics from 1981 to 1983 found the city's robbery rate rose by 8 percent while at the same time the robbery rate in other suburbs in the nation declined by 20 percent and the national robbery rate had fallen 16 percent.

From 1982 to 1994 the robbery rate in Evanston had risen 17 percent, while the national rate has fallen 5 percent.

The tales of these three cities do not prove that gun bans *automatically* lead to increased crime rates. Nor does the story of Kennesaw, Georgia, prove that cultural statements embracing gun ownership *automatically* reduce crime. But such anecdotal evidence does suggest that gun bans have done little or nothing to reduce criminal activity. Similarly, evidence from Kennesaw, Georgia, Orlando, Florida, and Kansas City, Missouri, indicate that well-publicized efforts to arm and train law-abiding citizens in the use of firearms have frequently led to a reduction in violent crime.

By their very nature gun-control laws put law-abiding citizens at a comparative disadvantage to criminals when it comes to accessing guns. Gun-control laws make it harder for those who follow the law to obtain a firearm than it is for criminals. For individuals who dislike guns and would never own one in the first place (and the authors are in this category), this is a relatively academic point. But for those who do feel the need to own a gun, and particularly for those who, for whatever reason, feel menaced, this disadvantage is very important.

The inequity inherent in gun-control laws is central to the gun-control debate, especially when you consider that individuals legally in possession of a gun thwart between 2.5 million and 3 million attempted crimes *each year*. Evidence is also clear that armed individuals are killed, raped, and injured at far-lower rates than unarmed individuals who passively submit.

These are solid facts. As we've already shown, leading gun-control criminologists cannot refute these statistics, though they expressly would like to.

With this information as a guide, the gun-control debate in America must move in a different direction and take on a much more nuanced tone.

We are not suggesting that all regulations on the sale of so-called cop-killer bullets, assault weapons, or handguns should be abolished. But these regulations must be viewed for what they are—cultural statements that reflect society's anxiety about unlimited access to firearms and ammunition. While in Congress, Tim voted for the ban on so-called cop-killer bullets and the assault-weapons ban because he felt that society had no overriding need for either weapon. He was not acting on the argument that such steps would appreciably reduce crime. We evaluate the purpose of these regulations from exactly the opposite perspective: is there a real need for any citizen to own cop-killer bullets or an assault weapon? We don't see one. These laws fall into an area of social policy where the gains are nebulous but worthwhile. The upside of these regulations is not to noticeably reduce crime, but to forge a cultural consensus against unlimited access to all firearms and all types of ammunition. This seems to us a worthy achievement, one gained with only a slight encroachment on Second Amendment rights.

Evidence refuting the value of gun-control laws in reducing crime can also be found outside the walls of academia. Criminologists may reach their conclusions while facing no peril greater than a paper cut, but police officers in one of the nation's most crime-ridden cities, New York, have discovered new tactics that can reduce crime faster and more effectively than gun control. New York City's gun-control laws, among the toughest in the nation, had no effect on crime rates in the 1980s and the early part of this decade. But new crime-fighting tactics introduced by former police commissioner William Bratten, and codified since his departure by Mayor Rudolph Giuliani, have drastically reduced rates of murder, rape, robbery, and burglary in the city. Far more than any gun-control laws, innovative police tactics have driven down crime rates and returned previously uninhabitable neighborhoods into the hands of peaceable, productive citizens. It's worth noting that police officials from across the country (many from communities with tough gun-control laws) have come to New York to study the city's new police techniques.

The last important revelation about crime in America comes from a recent Harvard study on crime in America's poorest neighborhoods. The idea that crime always takes root in areas of urban decay and economic stagnation is deeply ingrained in the American psyche. Most public policy toward urban America operates on the assumption that crime cannot be fought successfully without a dramatic reversal in the economic fortunes of an impoverished neighborhood or city.

New research from Harvard University, however, shows conclusively that crime does not always grow where poverty is high. Dr. Felton Earls, a professor of psychiatry at Harvard, and Robert Sampson, a professor of sociology at the University of Chicago, studied 343 neighborhoods in Chicago and conducted lengthy interviews with 8,872 residents drawn from all of the neighborhoods. The study began in 1990 as part of a research project known as the Project on Human Development in Chicago Neighborhoods. The researchers chose

Chicago because it most closely matches the whole United States in terms of ethnic and racial diversity and offers a wide mixture of rich, middle-class, and poor neighborhoods.

The Earls-Sampson study found that the lowest crime rates came in poor neighborhoods where adults intervened to help children improve themselves and to resist the quick-profit temptations of a life of crime. The researchers described these efforts as "collective efficacy," a term they defined as a "willingness by residents to intervene in the lives of children." The study showed that neighborhoods where adults adopted a zero-tolerance attitude toward truancy, graffiti, and loitering were those with the lowest crime rates.

The determining factor in whether crime took root was not the level of unemployment or the number of business start-ups; it was the level of coordination among the residents in fighting crime in their neighborhoods. In abjectly poor neighborhoods with a strong commitment to fighting crime, crime rates were low. In neighborhoods where the attitude was indifferent or less aggressive, crime rates were higher. The researchers concluded that the citizens' own attitude toward crime was the determining factor. In neighborhoods where citizens took the time to clean up their playgrounds, alleys, and sidewalks, crime declined. In neighborhoods where residents watched out for each other, criminals found less opportunity to prey. In neighborhoods whose citizens were actively involved with their local police precinct, criminals felt the heat. The researchers came to the startling conclusion that even in areas of pervasive poverty, citizens could and did deter crime by simply joining together to clean up the neighborhood, look out for one another, and visibly cooperate with police.

Surprisingly, it did not seem to matter whether there were strong familial ties within the neighborhoods. In an interview with the *New York Times,* Sampson said the most important factor in controlling crime in tough neighborhoods was "a shared vision, if you will, a fusion of a shared willingness of residents to intervene and social trust, a sense of engagement and ownership of public space."

The gun-control debate in America must be replaced by a debate about crime control. It cannot and should not be about whether gun control reduces crime, or whether attempts at greater control would succeed where previous efforts have failed. The days of uncertainty on this question are over.

THE THIRD LIE

◆

RELIGION AND POLITICS DON'T MIX

E VERY ELECTION SEASON brings new expressions of alarm to our newscasts and front pages about the role of religious zealotry in American politics. With furrowed brow, America's political pundits fret over the way evangelical Christians have "taken over" control of local and state chapters of the Republican Party. Many voters are anguished about the notion of politics that seeks to impose a fixed Christian morality on our pluralistic society. Constitutional scholars worry that such incursions into grassroots politics will threaten the integrity of the secular political state and weaken the legal barriers separating church from state.

Is the blending of religion and politics really cause for concern?

Let us answer by examining the role religious activists played in one very important race for the House of Representatives. This race had it all: back-room scheming intended to cut short a promising political career; intense pressure applied by religious "zealots"; and one candidate's about-face on a major policy question, which carried a whiff of political desperation.

Please allow us to set the scene.

An up-and-coming young politician was seeking his first election to Congress in Virginia. His enemies had used their power in the state legislature to draw hostile boundaries in his congressional district, sticking him with four counties that had opposed this young politician's first effort at drafting comprehensive political reform for the nation. The young politician knew the swing vote in this district would rest with the fundamentalist Christians, who were inveterate proselytizers. The cultural elite in the district saw the fundamentalists as wild-eyed fanatics and dangerous political allies. But the young politician knew the Christian right would decide the outcome of his race, so he met with them to discuss his reform document. They pressed for one change he had previously opposed. In fact, the young politician was so proud of his original reform manifesto that for a time he would entertain no changes whatsoever. But eventually he realized that he could not win the support of the evangelicals without acceding to their desires. He vowed to make the change in his manifesto, captured the evangelical vote, and won a seat in Congress.

Sounds like a story right from today's headlines, doesn't it?

Think again.

The race just described occurred in 1788. The young politician was James Madison. The reform manifesto he helped write was the Constitution.

The concession he made was the addition of an amendment guaranteeing religious freedom to all citizens of the new nation. It became part of the First Amendment.

The evangelical zealots Madison faced were Baptists, who refused to endorse any candidate for Congress who would not support an amendment providing for religious freedom. Baptists were unpopular in America and Virginia; only years before this election they had been forced to obtain a special license to preach their brand of doctrine. Those who refused had been horsewhipped. When they made their demands clear, Madison changed his position. In a letter to a Baptist preacher named George Eve, Madison reported that "circumstances are now changed" and that, if elected to Congress, he would press for amendments to the Constitution that would safeguard "all essential rights, particularly the rights of conscience in their fullest latitude, the freedom to the press, trials by jury, security against general warrants, etc."

We happened upon this story in a column on religion and American politics written by Michael W. McConnell (*Newsday*, 22 September 1996), a law professor at the University of Chicago. His take on the current debate over religion and politics is instructive: "It is ironic," McConnell writes, "that the very form of religiously engaged activism that gave us the First Amendment is now said to violate it."

We couldn't have said it better ourselves.

Before we make the case that religion is an essential ingredient of American politics, consider the opposite question: what would America look like without religion? It would not exist.

It was the quest for free religious expression that brought many colonists to the American shores in the first place. Free of theocratic oppression and persecution, the colonists embraced the freedom to assemble and worship as one of the sacred rights and blessings of the new land. They saw religion flourish as it never had in England or the European continent, where the church-state axis made God a handmaiden of government and vice versa, depriving both of legitimacy and vitality.

Which was just the point of the radical new American experiment. The Founding Fathers wanted government and religion to draw strength from the individual's free allegiance to both. In ways citizens of no other nation at the time could imagine, free men in America had the right to question the authority of God and government on the same day.

The Founding Fathers sought to create a new space in the world where religious practices and observances flourished but were not monitored, enforced, or in any way validated by the state. But this does not mean they wanted a country free of religion or a rule of law detached from the Judeo-Christian ethic. As their own words demonstrate, they considered religious faith central to survival of the new nation:

> Before any man can be considered as a member of civil society, he must be considered as a subject of the governor of the universe . . . religion is the basis and foundation of government. . . . We have staked the whole future of American civilization, not upon the power of government, far from it. We have staked the future of all our political institutions upon the capacity of each and all of us to control ourselves, to sustain ourselves according to the Ten Commandments.

> —JAMES MADISON
> Author of the Constitution

Of all the dispositions and habits, which lead to political prosperity, religion and morality are indispensable supports. . . . Let it simply be asked, where is the security for property, for reputation, for life, if the sense of religious obligation desert the oaths, which are the instruments of investigation in courts of justice? And let us with caution indulge the supposition that morality can be maintained without religion. Whatever may be conceded to the influence of refined education on minds of particular structure, reason and experience both forbid us to expect that national morality can prevail in exclusion of religious principles. It is substantially true, that virtue or morality is a necessary spring of popular government. The rule, indeed, extends with more or less force to every species of free government. Who, that is a sincere friend to it, can look with indifference upon attempts to shake the foundation of the fabric?

—GEORGE WASHINGTON
Farewell Address to Congress
September 19, 1796

That religion, or the duty which we owe to our Creator, and the manner of discharging it, can be directed only by reason and conviction, not by force or violence; and therefore all men are equally entitled to the free exercise of religion, according to the dictates of conscience; and that it is the mutual duty of all to practice Christian forbearance, love, and charity towards each other.

—PATRICK HENRY, in the
Virginia Bill of Rights
June 12, 1776

The highest glory of the American Revolution was this: It connected, in one indissoluble bond, the principles of civil government with the principles of Christianity.

—JOHN ADAMS

The First Amendment to the Bill of Rights was designed to provide refuge to those fleeing religious persecution. The wording of the First Amendment is very clear on this point: "Congress shall make no law respecting an establishment of religion, or prohibiting the free exercise thereof." This means that the government is forbidden from establishing a state religion, or the kinds of compulsory observances that would flow from such an institution. The Founding Fathers understood that state-sponsored religion trampled the rights of nonconformists and—worse yet—spawned the kind of empty, ritual religiosity that only undermined the power of sincere morality.

One constant runs throughout the Founding Fathers' understanding of the role of religion in American political life: humility. The founders were enormously suspicious of political platitudes and wary of the ease with which the political process could subvert morality. The founders did not want Americans to look to their politicians or the laws they wrote as moral bellwethers. Instead, they looked to their common understanding of morality to guide their own conduct—used it to help them reach a consensus on how this new nation's laws should create a more-just society.

It has become common in this cynical period of American political life to diminish the founders' deeds by stating the obvious—that the society they created was riddled with cruelty and inequality. And so it was. The hideous institution of slavery remained for nearly a century. A century more of legalized segregation and bigotry followed. Women's suffrage came only after a century and a half of waiting and struggle. Looking back on the nation's origins now, it would seem that slavery and the denial of universal voting rights were premeditated perversions of the Constitution's "We, the people" preamble. How seriously can we today take the founders' passionate entreaties about the centrality of religion in America when the nation they left behind was so despoiled by cruelty and injustice?

This is a fair question—and yet the answer only underscores the role religious and moral values have played in America's quest for justice, equality, and "a more perfect union."

Every important social movement that improved the lives of the disenfranchised or the poor in America found its roots in religious principles: abolition, black suffrage, women's suffrage, the labor movement, and civil rights.

Those who fought for these causes acted out of their understanding of justice. Drawing on the same definition of Judeo-Christian justice that inspired the Founding Fathers, abolitionists, suffragettes, and civil-rights activists waged holy war on a political establishment unwilling to fulfill the high ideals and lofty moral aspirations enshrined in the Constitution. That the nation hadn't yet fulfilled those ideals and aspirations wasn't as important to those activists as the definition of justice the Founding Fathers laid before the world. The nation's dedication to religious freedom, and to virtues enshrined in religious observance, gave the activists the power of moral suasion.

Of course, moral suasion was not enough to carry the day; on its own, it rarely is. But a moral inspiration lifts a movement above simple grubbing for political spoils. It acts as a sextant to guide its followers through the confusing constellation of compromises with which any more-conservative government always hopes to divert them from their ultimate goal—uprooting an immoral or unjust system. Movements without a moral code can replace one system of cruelty and injustice with another even worse. To those who doubt us, we recommend a brief review of the French Revolution's Reign of Terror. After serving for many years as United States ambassador to France, John Adams correctly predicted the French Revolution would fail—because the nation was "a republic of 30 million atheists."

Madison saw the multiplicity of religions in America as a kind of insurance policy on behalf of minority rights. Defending the Constitution in Federalist Paper Number Fifty-Two, he argued that a great variety of political interests and religious sects would, through their own activities, protect the nation from tyrannical impulses.

> It is of great importance in a republic not only to guard the society against the oppression of its rulers, but to guard one part of the society against the injustice of the other part. Different interests necessarily exist in different classes of citizens. If a majority be united by a common interest, the rights of the minority will be insecure. There are but two methods of providing against this evil: the one by creating a will in the community independent of the majority—that is, of the society itself; the other by comprehending in the society so many separate descriptions of citizens as will render an unjust combination of a majority of the whole very improbable, if not impracticable. . . .
>
> The second method will be exemplified in the federal republic of the United States. Whilst all authority in it will be derived from and dependent on the society, the society itself will be broken into so many parts, interests and classes of citizens, that the rights of the individuals, or of the minority, will be in little danger from interested combinations of the majority. In a free government the security for civil rights must be the same as that for religious rights. It consists in the one case in the multiplicity of interests, and the other in the multiplicity of sects. The degree of security in both cases will depend on the number of interests and sects. . . .
>
> Justice is the end of government. It is the end of civil society. It has ever been and ever will be pursued until it be obtained, or

until liberty be lost in the pursuit. In a society under the forms of which the stronger faction can readily unite and oppress the weaker, anarchy may as truly be said to reign as in a state of nature, where the weaker individual is not secured against the violence of the stronger.

Some legal scholars have argued that the Constitution is a "Godless document" and that its lack of reference to a divinely inspired government proves the Founding Fathers wished to keep religion and politics separate and distinct. For these scholars, the fact that the Constitution was criticized at some state ratifying conventions is proof that many Americans feared religion would die without some recognition of God in the Constitution. That the preamble made reference to "We the people" did provoke hostility among some religious activists, as did Article Six, which ordered that "no religious test shall ever be required as a qualification to any office or public trust under the United States." But the preamble and Article Six only speak to a broader point: that the founders labored to craft a constitution that validated *no particular* type of religious faith or practice. The language they chose does not suggest hostility toward religion or imply that they were ambivalent about the role religion would play in a civil society.

Madison makes that point unmistakable clear in the Federalist paper cited above. A multiplicity of political interests and religious sects is the best protection against the tyranny of the majority. Although he could not have foreseen it, Madison was explaining the power of America today—a society of more than 250 million people, most of whom consider themselves people of faith. A sizable majority of Americans regularly practice their religious faith, and a majority of those who do not regularly attend church tell pollsters they pray frequently. America, which offers a home to members of all the dominant world religions and most religious sects, is the most-religious nation of the industrialized world. The foresight of the founders is clear all around us: never has religion so flourished as in the nation where the government has done nothing to institutionalize it.

Religion and politics have always been with us. But the character of religious activity is different now than it has been for previous generations. This seems to be the problem for some. When religious beliefs motivated citizens to press for civil rights or seek nuclear disarmament, this nation's cultural and intellectual elite nodded approvingly. We would ask those discomfited by the role of religion in contemporary politics whether they are similarly uneasy about the role religious interests played in these movements. Similarly, the elite celebrate the presence of religious activists in Washington who lobby for more-generous welfare policies, the maintenance of affirmative action, and the rights of legal and illegal immigrants.

But when evangelical Christian beliefs gave rise to political movements that sought to limit access to abortion, to return prayer to public schools, to prohibit doctor-assisted suicide, or to deny spousal benefits to homosexuals, the nation's cultural and intellectual elite suddenly found cause for alarm.

Clearly, it is the agenda of evangelical Christians, not the political activity of people of faith, that drives this new debate about the role of religion in politics. So the debate about religion and politics is not *really* about religion at all. It's about issues. What could possibly be wrong with that?

Nothing.

Let's dispatch the canard that religion has no role in American political life. Instead, we should ask what has stirred evangelical Christians from decades of political silence to organize and agitate in ways they never have before.

The answer is really quite simple. Evangelical Christians feel that the dominant American culture has, for the first time in history, declared war on their sacred values and beliefs. Though secular America views the last forty years as a period of enlightened liberation, evangelical Christians see it quite differently. From their perspective, popular culture has waged war on American morality, dismantling or weakening cultural institutions and customs they believe gave America its strength, character, and stability.

Here's a short list of defeats most evangelical Christians believe the nation has suffered over the past forty years: Court decisions removed the Bible, the Ten Commandments, and prayer from the public schools. Later decisions drove the Christmas crêche from the public square, and still later ones muzzled prayer at graduation ceremonies. Then came laws legalizing abortion and no-fault divorce. With them came federal welfare rules that discouraged men from living with their wives and removed any political stigma from illegitimacy. Then the homosexual-rights movement sought myriad rights previously available only to heterosexuals: spousal benefits, the right to marry, the right to adopt, the right to sue for discrimination under civil-rights laws that equated discrimination based on sexual orientation with discrimination based on race.

All of these changes flowed directly or indirectly through the political system. Federal judges appointed by elected presidents were shrinking the role of Christianity in the public square. Lawmakers were doling out billions on a welfare system that seemed ambivalent about illegitimacy and family disintegration. Local school boards began moving books on homosexuality into classrooms as city and county governments were debating new rights for homosexuals.

There is a stark us-versus-them dimension to the way evangelical Christians view each of these policy disputes. In every case, biblical teachings and traditional American mores were swept aside by secular celebration of personal liberation.

To the average American evangelical Christian, secular America started the culture war. Halting and ultimately reversing these secular gains are the central political goals of evangelical Christians. That's why they got into politics in the first place.

Starting slowly, these political newcomers began registering to vote and participating in politics at the local level. Evangelical Christians gravitated to the Republican Party because of its opposition to abortion. Arriving in greater and greater numbers, they began to win seats on local Republican Party organizing committees. Before long, they were winning seats on city and county executive committees. Eventually they became county chairmen and delegates to state and national conventions. Only recently have evangelical Christians won election as state-party chairmen. Occasionally these intraparty battles drew national media attention because, it was often said, they were contests between the "moderate" Republican gentry and a new breed of Republican, the "religious hard-liner" or "religious extremist."

There is a word for the increased influence evangelical Christians have gained in Republican Party politics over the past twenty years.

Democracy.

Whether you agree with their agenda or not, you must as an American appreciate the steady effort and patience evangelical Christians have brought to their political activism. They staged no coups. They worked within the system in each and every state and gradually saw their influence grow to such a point that they could control, through their numerical superiority, the agenda and direction of their chosen political party. Woody Allen once observed that 90 percent of life is showing up. The percentage might be even greater in politics. Evangelical Christians have been showing up in increasing numbers for nearly two decades and have earned the right to be the major players they are in national politics.

We hasten to remind those Americans so concerned that the "religious right" is gaining power and using it to influence the direction of a national party that growing influence is not the same thing as a winning coalition or a national consensus. The very problems evangelical Christians have had within the Republican Party and with voters who do not share their religious ardor or partisan inclinations starkly illustrate the limitations of special-interest politics. While the influence of evangelical Christian votes has been decisive in many House and Senate races, the face of cultural conservatism has so frightened key segments of the voting public that Republicans have been unable to run credible national campaigns for two successive elections.

In ways few political observers have been willing to admit, cultural conservatives have been both the greatest strength and the greatest weakness of the Republican Party at the national level. Their role in the GOP is almost exactly like the role of liberal activists in the Democratic Party from late 1968 to 1988. No Democratic presidential aspirant in those twenty years won without the support of the party's liberal core of grassroots activists. Similarly, no Republican presidential aspirant can hope to capture his or her party's nomination without first gaining the allegiance of the party's cultural conservatives. The grassroots power of liberal Democrats from 1968 to 1988 also helped solidify the party's hold on Congress. Liberal activists provided the money and grassroots organizing skill to carry many congressional Democrats to victory in competitive House and Senate races. Today similar power is in the hands of cultural conservatives in the Republican Party. They were most responsible for providing the money and organizational strength that carried Republicans to their first congressional majority in 1994. In House and Senate races across the country, evangelical Christians and other cultural conservatives provided the decisive margins for victory, just as liberal activists had throughout the 1960s, 1970s, and 1980s.

Which leads us to this observation about the direction of American politics: the two major parties are changing places. The Democrats are becoming the party of the presidency, and the Republicans the party of Congress. Republicans have much-stronger grassroots support than the Democrats, thanks in large part to their cultural-conservative foot soldiers. This gives them an advantage in competitive House and Senate races, in which voter turnout is crucial and parties with highly motivated grassroots support invariably prevail. Democrats have lost this grassroots advantage—but have gained national credibility on issues of spending and taxes that their party has not enjoyed since the days of Harry Truman. The Clinton administration will go down in history as the one that killed the deficit dragon, energized a sluggish economy, and led a reluctant party into the rough-and-tumble (but profitable) world of free trade. Nominees who echo this agenda can no longer be credibly labeled "tax-and-spend" Democrats, and those who try to label them as such will be dismissed as the foolish partisans they are.

What does all this have to do with religion in politics?

The role of religion in contemporary politics is changing the nature of the political parties and, by extension, changing the power dynamic between them. Liberal activists a generation ago were motivated by religious principles to fight for civil rights, economic justice, equality for women, an end to the arms race, and federal support for the poor. Their influence gave Democrats sizable political power at the local level, but their message proved too liberal to sustain the party's nominees in presidential elections. The election of Bill Clinton spelled the end of liberal dominance in the party's nominating process and foreshadowed the shrinkage of that grassroots support so important in competitive House and Senate elections.

Voters motivated by religious principles are now predominantly Republican, and they seek to regain control of a culture they contend has been warped and weakened by a creeping secular humanism. Their convictions are no less sincere and their clout is no less significant within the Party than the convictions and clout that liberal activists wielded within the Democratic Party from 1968 to 1988. And just as the face of liberalism was an albatross for all Democratic presidential nominees in these years (Jimmy Carter was an anti-Nixon aberration, as Reagan's 1980 landslide revealed), so too is the face of cultural conservatism an albatross for Republican presidential nominees. As always in American life, religion and politics can and do mix comfortably, but when questions of morality or religious conviction appear to distort or tip a party's governing message toward a liberal or conservative extreme, the American public rebels.

Voters motivated by religious principles led the movements to abolish slavery, establish black suffrage and women's suffrage, mandate fair wage and labor practices, and ensure civil rights for all Americans and most Americans ultimately agreed with these movements. Now voters with strong religious beliefs are pressing for a return to moral values they believe are consistent with this nation's heritage, and most Americans believe the resulting debate is necessary and long overdue. While Americans disagree strongly over the nuances of this debate, survey after survey reveals a profound uneasiness about America's moral and ethical values. This uneasiness has given rise to a new political movement, just as concern over slavery, suffrage, wages, and civil rights gave rise to political movements.

We're not arguing that religious conservatives are right or wrong, and we are not asserting that their agenda is as important or morally powerful as the agendas of the abolition, suffrage, or civil-rights battles. We merely contend that these movements rose from the same intellectual and spiritual wellsprings. They grew in opposition to a political system that was perceived as injurious to, and inconsistent with, America's noblest principles and highest ideals.

There is nothing to fear about that.

Lastly, we wonder how America will cope with some of the issues that lie ahead if voters of deep religious conviction are not involved in the political process.

Forget for a moment the current issues in which religious principles play a prominent role (abortion and homosexual rights), and consider that America will, in the very near future, have to decide how it will regulate the following procedures: doctor-assisted suicide, genetic engineering, and cloning. Consider: the Supreme Court has already ruled that there is no constitutional right to commit suicide with the assistance of a physician. The high court has turned over to the states the power to regulate physician-assisted suicide. Oregon voters approved an initiative in 1997 allowing doctors to assist in suicides under certain conditions. Other states will consider similar initiatives this year. While Oregon is the only state to legalize doctor-assisted suicide, 36 states have outlawed the procedure and 9 others consider the practice illegal under common law. Four states (North Carolina, Utah, Ohio, and Wyoming) have no statutes on doctor-assisted suicide. Many religious faiths believe that assisted suicide is immoral and sets society on a dangerous path to state-supervised euthanasia, in which the "right" to die becomes a "duty" to die.

This is a legitimate issue.

While we do not know how physician-assisted suicide will be administered in the future, we do know that America's baby-boom population is aging and will live longer than any previous generation of Americans. It is clear that America will not, under the current system of Medicare and Social Security taxation, be able to support the entire baby-boom generation when it reaches retirement age. With life expectancy for this generation approaching an average of nearly eighty years, there will be immense financial pressure to reduce the costs of providing Medicare and Social Security benefits. This much we know.

Does our society really want to place the state in the position of sanctioning suicide when the political and economic pressures to reduce the costs of America's aged population will be more pronounced than ever before? This is a question that simply cannot be properly debated outside the moral construct of religion. All of America's major religions—Christianity, Judaism, Islam—consider euthanasia morally abhorrent. These religions do not want to invest in the state a power they believe lies exclusively in the hands of God. Voters cannot adequately debate this issue without weighing these ancient teachings and asking hard questions about the power of the state and the rights of the individual.

The question of genetic mapping is even more difficult to ponder and simply cannot be debated without reference to religious doctrine. The Human Genome Project, a federally funded mission to create a comprehensible genetic map of man, has already made startling discoveries that will force America to make excruciating decisions about medical ethics and individual rights. The project, which is to run fifteen years at a cost of $3 billion, has already uncovered a number of genes that may lead to particular disease or personality traits. Once the science becomes more precise, individuals will be able to learn whether they have a genetic predisposition to certain diseases. Society will have to decide the following question: who is entitled to receive such information? Should an employer or insurance company know whether an individual's genes make him or her a likely cancer patient, a likely diabetic, a likely manic-depressive? If not, why not? Insurers now have the right to demand information about "preexisting" medical conditions. Why not information about genetic maps that suggest serious diseases lie ahead? What about genetic mapping that discloses the presence of diseases in elderly people long before they have become manifest? Would society want to do something to shield itself from future health-care costs? If so, what might the options be? (And so the debate will overlap with that over doctor-assisted suicide.) Or, at the other end of the age spectrum, what about the ability to detect potential defects in an unborn fetus? These are only a handful of questions that techniques such as genetic mapping will force society to consider. The ultimate decisions will be made by politicians, but the debate that leads them to whatever decision they reach *must* be grounded in some understanding of the moral implications of the vast new powers science will soon place in the hands of individuals and the state.

The same is true of the prospect of cloning—perhaps even more so. The awesome and terrifying power of human cloning—which, thankfully, is much farther away than euthanasia and genetic mapping—will put all societies to a severe moral and ethical test. The implications of this science are so overwhelming that it is difficult to imagine how society can confront the subject in a systematic way. Society's first impulse, of course, would be to make cloning illegal. But history is replete with cases in which laws abolishing new technology were powerless to stop it from spreading. The same might be true of cloning. How, then, to regulate an individual's ability to genetically copy himself or herself? This question, like the questions of euthanasia and genetic mapping, simply cannot be pondered, debated, or resolved without a thorough consideration of what religion teaches us about the value of life. Religion will not and cannot give us all the answers to moral questions arising out of science (and cynics would say that religion has been on the wrong side of most debates over science), but it must be a part of the process of finding them.

All of which means the role of religion in American politics will remain with us and will likely take on greater visibility and importance as society tries to cope with new and intimidating scientific breakthroughs the likes of which man has never seen before.

Our conclusion?

We need religion in politics!

Some of this nation's greatest advances in individual rights and freedoms were grounded in religious tenets. Just as in the past, today's religious activists will help enliven the public debate and ultimately help us in establishing a public morality that reflects societal consensus.

Thanks to James Madison and his compatriots, we have *both* religious freedom and the freedom as a society to decide when and how we will base our public policies on the moral and ethical tenets of faith.

THE FOURTH LIE

◆

IMMIGRATION HURTS AMERICA

IRST LET US discuss immigration for what it is and what it is
not. Immigration is not a simple blessing. It is not now and never
has been, in itself, the secret to America's success. America's success
derives from the ideas that form the basis of our society. The mere
presence of immigrants did not ensure America's prosperity. It was the
ideals of America—individual responsibility, republican democracy,
religious tolerance, free markets, and public education—that allowed
free people, native born and immigrant alike, to pursue and achieve
the American Dream.

Keeping faith with the ideals that make America unique is the key
to maintaining a successful immigration policy. Immigrants alone are
not responsible for the existence and continued success of the American Dream. The dream itself is the key. Those who chase it make it
real, but their presence alone does not guarantee its existence. Immigrants shape America, and America shapes them. By necessity, immigrants assimilate. Rarely does this process destroy an immigrant's
culture. Instead, America grows more diverse with each and every new
culture it accommodates; at the same time, though, immigrants themselves become a part of our country when they gain an appreciation
for what makes America unique. Diversity is not what makes America
tick. Diversity may add to our strength, but ultimately our cultural differences are secondary in importance to the unifying values that form
the basis of our national identity.

Freedom is our strength. Lots of countries have ethnic diversity—
and for many it's a huge problem. What unifies so many different people here is our common commitment to a shared set of values. Without
these values, the diversity so many multiculturalists extol would be
meaningless. America would be just another nation filled with com-

peting ethnic groups fighting for economic survival and obliged to turn to their cultural roots for consolation. Freedom is what gives people the courage to look beyond their clan and see the worth of another free man or free woman. Freedom allows men and women to judge one another on individual merit, not on the basis of assumptions about their clan or group. In the end it's America that makes immigrants strong, not the other way around.

And yet the idea that immigration hurts America is another lie that persists in our political discourse—a lie less pervasive than others but perhaps more insidious. As a journalist and a member of Congress, the coauthors have studied the issue of immigration for many years. We sympathize with those Americans concerned about the potentially harmful effects of a huge influx of immigrants competing for jobs at both ends of the skills spectrum.

Clearly, lower-skilled immigrants exert downward pressure on wages by enlarging the number of available job seekers in relation to the number of available jobs. Similarly, higher-skilled immigrants can and sometimes do take jobs from American workers slightly less skilled than they are. Americans caught in the downsizing mania of the early 1990s probably resent the fact that jobs they were retraining themselves to take were filled by better-skilled immigrants. These are real concerns, and we, unlike some immigration enthusiasts, do not diminish their importance.

Nor do we share the anxiety expressed by, among others, conservative commentator and Republican presidential candidate Pat Buchanan. Recently commentators such as Buchanan have worried about how the presence of "new" immigrants from Asia, Mexico, Africa, and Central and South America is weakening America's predominantly "European" stock. It's worth remembering that similar concerns about American "purity" were behind efforts to prevent immigration of Jews and Italians two generations ago. What Buchanan and other critics of immigration fail to appreciate is that the unique quality of American life has led to the assimilation of every ethnic group that has ventured to our shores in large numbers. For the most part, it's courage and desire that brings immigrants the world over to our shores. This is true whether the immigrant is from England, Ireland, Italy, Albania, Ethiopia, Nigeria, El Salvador, Peru, or Brazil.

We respectfully ask Mr. Buchanan or any other critic of generous immigration policies the following questions: Would you prefer that only Europeans found our way of life inviting enough to move here? Is the definition of American exceptionalism meant to stir only the hearts of Europeans? Did we build this nation only to inspire Europeans? Or did we build it to inspire all men and women desiring to be free? Is the desire to be free not universal? And if it is, shouldn't America make itself the repository of this basic and noble human desire?

This is the straightforward argument in favor of immigration. It's the one we believe and intend to defend. Like many Americans, we tend to think of immigration in romanticized terms. Understandably, in contemplating the subject we, like most Americans, conjure images of our own immigrant parents, grandparents, or great-grandparents making the perilous trek to the United States in pursuit of the American Dream. Everyone who is a first-generation immigrant and those of us who are great-grandsons of immigrants can all take justifiable pride in the grit, ingenuity, and courage it has always taken to make it in America as an immigrant. We all celebrate the power of the immigrant's dream and fervently hope the power of this dream will always attract those who yearn to be free and industrious to our shores.

But we must all be honest with ourselves. As romantic as the story of each immigrant can be, the way our government has established its limits on legally admissible immigrants is not now and has never been about romance. Immigration is about hard political and economic decisions. The sooner most Americans realize that, the better.

To give you a glimpse of just how ruthless immigration laws can be, let's take a quick survey of the major changes in the history of United States immigration law.

The first attempt to limit immigration came in 1882, when Congress passed and President Chester A. Arthur signed the Chinese Exclusion Act, which suspended Chinese immigration and naturalization for ten years. It also forbade U.S. courts from granting citizenship to Chinese immigrants already in the country. The exclusion act violated the spirit and the letter of the Treaty of 1880, a pact President Rutherford B. Hayes negotiated with China to limit Chinese immigration.

The Burlingame Treaty of 1868 had opened the door to a massive flow of Chinese labor into the country, welcomed by railroad barons eager to exploit immigrant workers. When the railroad boom began to die in the early 1880s, Chinese immigrants began to compete for other jobs. This competition irked voters throughout the western states, where Chinese immigration was highest. As a result, Congress passed a bill in 1879 to reverse the Burlingame Treaty. President Hayes vetoed the bill but, sensing the mounting political opposition to Chinese immigration, ordered his secretary of state to negotiate a new immigration treaty with China. The Treaty of 1880 restricted but did not ban Chinese immigration. Congress forced President Arthur to do so in 1882.

While Chinese labor was blocked, immigration continued from Europe. From 1881 to 1924 this nation admitted 25.8 million immigrants. Of this total, 8.7 million immigrants arrived between 1901 and 1910.

The next effort to halt legal immigration came in 1924, when President Calvin Coolidge signed the Immigration Act, cutting the quota of legal immigrants by one-third and placing strict limits on the number of immigrants from southern and eastern Europe. Under the new law, 60 percent of the visas were awarded to immigrants from Germany and England.

Our nation, in essence, was trying to keep Jews, Italians, and others of Mediterranean stock out of the country.

The next big change in immigration policy came in 1965, when President Johnson signed legislation that radically altered qualifications for immigration to this country. While laudably lifting the quota restrictions imposed on eastern and southern European nations (and nations the world over, for that matter), the legislation wrongly dismantled a historic bias that favored skilled and well-educated immigrants over unskilled and poorly educated ones. This policy shift was driven by a desire to unify families separated by immigration in the first place. The new law gave preference to immigrants who already had family in this country. This new policy dramatically increased the number of semiskilled and unskilled immigrants coming into the country and reduced the number of skilled immigrants. This change in the law has altered the composition of the immigrant class in America.

From 1931 to 1940 more than 65 percent of all new immigrants hailed from Europe, and more than 20 percent from Canada. Between 1981 and 1990 the percentage of European immigrants fell to 10.4, and the percentage of Canadian immigrants fell to 2.1 The percentage of Asian immigrants rose from 3.1 in the 1930s to 37.3 in the 1980s. The percentage of immigrants from Mexico rose from 4.2 in the 1930s to 22.6 in the 1980s.

We believe current immigration policy could be improved by placing a higher emphasis on importing workers with specific skills instead of providing blanket preference to immigrants who simply wish to be reunited with their families. We sympathize with the desires of immigrants who want to join their families as soon as they can, but we also believe that reuniting families should take a backseat to filling immediate needs in the work force. Immigrants who arrive in pursuit of jobs should understand that coming to America and gaining the immense benefits of working here can come with a price, including a temporary separation from one's family. By placing a higher priority on plugging holes in the work force, United States immigration policy would do more to bring the most-productive and disciplined workers here. Unifying families may be a noble aim, but in our opinion it should be secondary to filling the needs of the economy.

Here are the numbers: Today's immigrants are less skilled than those who arrived in 1970, and the skill differential between natives and newly arrived immigrants is growing larger. In 1970 the mean educational attainment was 11.5 years of schooling for natives and 11.1 years for immigrants who had arrived in the previous five years. In 1990 the mean educational attainment was 13.2 years for natives and 11.9 years for immigrants who had arrived in the previous five years. The gap between native and immigrant education levels is growing. Fully 40 percent of recent immigrants are high-school dropouts, and a Harvard University study in 1997 showed that immigrants have increased the number of Americans without high-school diplomas by 20 percent from 1980 to 1995.

Immigration experts believe the educational-attainment differential is primarily responsible for a widening gap in wages for native workers and new immigrants. The wage differential between these groups was 16.6 percent in 1970; by 1990 that differential had risen to 31.7 percent, meaning that native workers now earn nearly one-third more than new immigrants, largely because the new arrivals lack the proper skills to land jobs in a work force that increasingly demands technology-based skills. Even if these new immigrants find jobs, as many do, their earnings will be so far behind that of native Americans that most immigrants will not close this wage gap in their lifetimes.

Immigration surged in the decade from 1981 to 1990, as more than 7.3 million immigrants entered the country. As a result, that decade saw America's highest percentage of population change since the decade from 1911 to 1920, the end of the nation's First Great Migration. The portion of America's population that is foreign born is now 7.9 percent, the highest it has been since 1940 and double what it was in 1970.

The National Academy of Science's 1997 study "The New Americans: Economic, Demographic, and Fiscal Effects of Immigration" reported the following:

- The yearly economic gain derived from current immigrants is between $1 billion and $7.5 billion per year—a pittance in a $7 trillion economy.

- When the cost of government aid to immigrants is calculated as a percentage of each state's budget, the costs appear small. In reality, the 1990 census shows that six states in the union have become home to most of the immigrant population: three quarters of the new arrivals migrated to California, New York, Texas, Florida, New Jersey, and Illinois. And the costs of serving these new residents are high indeed. In California, home to the highest percentage of new immigrants, each household contributes a staggering $1,174 per year to the various government services immigrants use. In New Jersey, the cost is $229 per year. To reduce the costs immigrants inflict on native taxpayers, the Academy recommends shifting immigration laws to favor those applicants with higher skills and better education. "If the only policy goal were the maximization of the positive fiscal impact of immigrants, the way to accomplish it would be to admit only those with the highest education." The Academy cites the fact that European and Canadian immigrants have had a net positive economic impact on New Jersey, contributing far more to the economy than they consume in government services—a point that has nothing to do with ethnic qualities and everything to do with educational standards in their native lands.

- Nearly half of the ten-cent-per-hour wage decline that has hit high-school dropouts can be attributed to competition from low-skilled immigrants. Since blacks drop out of school at a statistically higher rate than whites, the influx of low-skilled immigrants has hit American blacks the hardest. Nearly two-fifth of immigrants who arrived since 1965 are high-school dropouts.

• The 1990 census showed that 21 percent of immigrant households received some type of government assistance, in contrast to 14 percent of native households and 10 percent of households headed by white non-Hispanic natives.

• A recent study by Ohio State University economists Randall Olsen and Patricia Regan shows that immigrants who receive government assistance are much less likely to return to their native country when they fall on hard times than those who don't. Programs that do not allow certain immigrants to "fail" in America disproportionately reward less-skilled, poorly educated immigrants who receive assistance while punishing skilled and educated immigrants, who immediately begin paying taxes to pay for these additional social costs.

• While many immigrants come seeking work, some arrive seeking only income. And it appears that generous welfare benefits in some states have attracted a higher proportion of immigrants, suggesting that welfare itself can be an immigration magnet. Consider the case of California: In 1970 the state offered welfare benefits that were 68 percent of the national median income; by 1990 the value of those benefits was 250 percent (2.5 times) the median national income. From 1980 to 1990 the number of immigrants who did not receive welfare and chose to live in California dropped from 30.1 percent to 28.9 percent. Meanwhile, the fraction of immigrants who received welfare benefits and chose to live in California increased from 36.9 to 45.4 percent. According to George J. Borjas, an economics professor at the University of California at San Diego: "Immigrant use of welfare programs would be greatly reduced if we improved the skill composition of the immigrant flow. It makes a great deal of economic sense to restrict the entry of persons who will probably become public charges. We could set up a point system—à la Canada—where the success of a visa application would depend not only on whether the applicant had relatives in the United States, but also on the applicant's education, age, occupation, and job prospects."

Before we can create the best immigration policy, we must answer the following question: what is our goal?

Should it be simply to maximize America's economic well-being? Is

admitting one more immigrant to the marginal cost of the immigrant.

It is reasonable to suppose that the net fiscal costs of immigration are larger for unskilled immigrant flows. After all, unskilled immigrants are more likely to use many government services *and* pay lower taxes. In addition there are economic reasons, arising mainly from the complementarity [*sic*] between capital and skills, that suggest that the immigration surplus might be larger when the immigration flow is composed exclusively of skilled workers. It seems, therefore, that on purely efficiency grounds there is a strong economic case for an immigration policy that uses skill filters in awarding entry visas.

Borjas emigrated to the United States in 1962, a refugee from Cuba who entered through a special program President Kennedy established to aid Cubans fleeing the communist regime of Fidel Castro. Borjas's family had owned a clothing factory in Cuba, but the government seized it after the revolution. Borjas arrived with his mother, who had only a high-school diploma. They settled in Hoboken, New Jersey. His mother went to work as a seamstress, and Jorge quickly adapted to life in America, changing his name from Jorge to George.

Borjas's experience taught him that many of the first immigrants from Cuba came from families with good education and some experience in business—the elite, in other words. These immigrants tended to adapt well to the rigors of life in America; later waves of immigrants, on the other hand—who had less education and fewer skills— did not. On the basis of these observations, Borjas began to examine the experiences of European immigrants after the First Great Migration, from 1900 to 1930. His research confirmed what he had observed among Cuban immigrants: the earnings of eastern and southern Europeans who arrived before 1924 took four generations to catch up with those of native Americans.

Until Borjas's research uncovered these findings, it was widely assumed that immigrants naturally reached wage parity with native Americans in one or two generations. This trend is even more pervasive among new immigrants, who are even less educated and possess fewer skills than European immigrants of the First Great Migration. What's more, Borjas's research has shown that new immigrants are more sophisticated in adapting to the nation's welfare policies, and the cost of their assimilation into the welfare system has been disturbingly high.

Even though he and his mother arrived under a special immigration exemption that ignored skill levels and education, Borjas still believes that America must shift its immigration priorities and create a system that favors skilled, educated immigrants over less-educated applicants. Under this policy, of course, neither Borjas nor his mother would have been allowed to emigrate to the United States. "Should the fact that I would get hurt under different circumstances be the thing that drives policy?" Borjas asked in a profile published in the August 26, 1996, edition of *Wall Street Journal*. "It would be wrong to set policy on the basis of an egotistical attachment to a particular group. You have to look to the concerns of the nation as a whole."

In the fall of 1997 the United States Commission on Immigration Reform issued its final report, which recommended a gradual reduction in legal immigration, a new emphasis on immigration of skilled workers, and a national effort to accelerate assimilation of those immigrants already here. The commission said that it was essential for current and future immigrants to rapidly develop proficiency in English, and a firm comprehension of America's "core civic values."

"It's absolutely critical that we have a clear message out there that we invite people to come here and we expect them to take on the American Dream and culture and everything else," Harold Ezell, a member of the commission and the former western-states chief for the Immigration and Naturalization Service, told the *Los Angeles Times*. "We're not creating separate little Baltic enclaves. We want [immigrants] to become Americans, not hyphenated Americans."

We could not agree more.

The sensible path for immigration reform is to shift emphasis gradually from family reunification and political asylum toward a system that rewards skilled applicants *from all countries*. We need not return to the northern-European xenophobia of the mid-1920s. The American Dream is as universal today as it ever was, and those immigrants with the skills and education suitable to pursuing it should be welcomed with open arms. But it's foolhardy for our nation to ignore the real costs current immigration policies impose. Doing so will only intensify the political movement to halt or to severely restrict legal immigration, which would be a serious mistake. Better to maintain a relatively open immigration policy that admits roughly 500,000 to 600,000 applicants a year (as recommended by the United States

Commission on Immigration Reform) and place visa restrictions that limit the number of unskilled and poorly educated immigrants to less than 100,000. Skilled immigrants receive only 10 to 15 percent of the annual visas awarded by the Immigration and Naturalization Service. That percentage should be lifted to at least 50.

These changes may happen to reduce the percentage of legal immigrants from Mexico, South America, and, possibly, Asia. But immigration romantics who claim that such changes would be motivated by racism or xenophobia are simply wrong. On the contrary, they would be designed to increase the chances that immigrants who do come can make it here without damaging the country whose qualities attracted them in the first place.

As the statistics noted above clearly show, it is now time for the nation to pause and assimilate immigrants who arrived in the Second Great Migration. Moving to a skill-based policy need not reduce the total number of immigrants. Initially there might not be enough applicants who possess the requisite skills to qualify for a visa, but the skill requirement would, of necessity, be phased in over time. America's economy will continue to be the most innovative and technologically advanced in the world, and the demand for skilled workers will only intensify in the twenty-first century. Considering the difficulty the American education system is having creating a high-skilled work force, it seems safe to assume the demand for high-skilled immigrants will remain high. Immigrants with high skills who land well-paying jobs will help reduce the costs imposed by immigrants who have already arrived, thereby diminishing the burden currently being borne by native taxpayers.

It is important to understand that proposing such changes is entirely consistent with the positive view of immigration we articulated earlier in this chapter. Immigration is valuable. Immigrants do enhance our quality of life and add strength by merging the best of other cultures with the best of ours. Immigration also reminds the world of our optimism and confidence, our ability to share our ideals with any immigrant with the skills and desire to make a new life here.

Nevertheless, it is time to calibrate immigration policies more carefully to match the needs of our economy. Choosing skilled over non-skilled immigrants will accelerate economic growth, increase tax revenue, and protect the low-skilled native workers and low-skilled immigrants who are already here from further declines in wages wrought by the influx of more unskilled immigrants. All of these benefits will also increase domestic political support for increased immigration and undermine any attempts to demagogue this issue.

Now, a few words about illegal immigration.

It remains a problem, but one Congress is dealing with aggressively. Patrols of our border with Mexico have increased dramatically, and Congress appears willing to increase the Border Patrol's budget as long as the situation demands. Importantly, the political will to blunt illegal immigration has finally begun to surface in Mexico, where the political elite previously chose to look the other way, hoping that emigration would help alleviate domestic unemployment and reduce the drain on government services. But recent studies in Mexico have brought home the point that many illegal immigrants who leave for the United States are depriving the country of a potential source of motivated and trainable workers. If not a "brain drain," Mexico certainly has been suffering from a "potential drain," as its most ambitious young laborers have fled for America.

Mexico now sees that it will need more workers to make the most of the intentional free trade opportunities offered by NAFTA and is now laboring to control professional immigrant smugglers, known as coyotes, who have exacerbated the problem. Tougher border-patrol efforts have forced many illegal immigrants to turn to the coyotes to increase their chances of safely entering the United States. Organized efforts within Mexico to combat the coyotes offer substantial hope that illegal immigration from that country can soon be brought under control.

And, surprising as it sounds, there is actually some other important news about illegal immigration from Mexico (the largest source by far) that suggests the problem may be on the way to solving itself.

The 1997 report "Binational Study of Migration Between Mexico and the United States," commissioned by the two governments and written by ten experts from both countries, boldly predicts a decline in legal and illegal immigration from Mexico: "There is reason to believe that the currently high levels of migration may represent a 'hump' or a peak. Within the next decade, changes in Mexican demographics and other structural changes should begin to reduce emigration pressures."

The report provides these interesting statistics:

- Using census data from both countries, it estimates that the number of Mexicans who have settled illegally in America has averaged 105,000 per year since 1990—far lower than estimated in previous reports.

- The number of workers between fifteen and forty-four years of age in Mexico will decline from 1.05 million in 1996 to 430,000 by 2010. If Mexico achieves the rather-modest goal of 3-percent annual economic growth (which appears within range thanks to NAFTA, a stabilized currency, and fewer nationalized industries), more than 800,000 new jobs will be created, thus reducing the need for Mexican workers to seek employment or income in America.

- Labor shortages in America will lift wages for low-skilled native workers, who have already gotten some help through an increase in the minimum wage.

- The number of low-skilled job seekers in America will increase due to new federal welfare laws that curtail benefits to the able-bodied after a fixed period of time set by each state.

After reviewing the report's conclusions, Frank del Olmo, a columnist for the *Los Angeles Times,* reached the following conclusions:

> We got ourselves all worked up over a problem that pretty much is solving itself, which is what usually happens when human nature and the free market are allowed to operate unfettered by government-imposed controls. We may not be over the demographic hump yet, but we can see light at the end of the tunnel. Once Congress looks beyond the Mexican border, it can focus on long-term immigration challenges . . . such as ensuring that the foreigners we will want and need—investors, inventors, artists and the like—can immigrate with a minimum of hassle.

It's also important to remember that half of all illegal immigrants—there are about 300,000 each year—are individuals who entered the country legally but have violated their short-term visas. The only way to address this problem successfully is to increase the Immigration and Naturalization Service budget, and substantial changes appear possible in the near term.

So there is plenty of room for optimism in considering the future of immigration. There will be plenty of room for immigrants, now and in the future, if we adopt new policies that place a higher priority on education and skills. Doing so will benefit natives and immigrants alike and deepen the historic consensus in favor of relatively open immigration policies—while denying the xenophobic fantasies of those who would like to seal America off hermetically from the rest of the non-European world.

Not a bad deal, eh?

THE FIFTH LIE

◆

ALL POLITICIANS ARE CORRUPT

T HIS IS SIMPLY not true.
Yes, most Americans believe it. You can see it in national polling data, hear about it incessantly on talk radio, and read about it in letters to the editor.

But that does not make it so.

If you take nothing else from this book, please consider carefully the argument we're about to make on behalf of today's American politician. You may not believe it, but America is blessed with the most ethical, hardworking, and intelligent breed of politician it has ever had.

Corruption does exist. We don't deny that. Generally speaking, however, the conduct of most politicians is exemplary. What's more, new laws requiring disclosure of campaign contributions and forcing once-private meetings into public view have made government at all levels more visible and accountable. We're not saying today's politicians are genetically predisposed to virtue in ways their predecessors were not; we're only saying that times have changed.

Corruption is not rampant in the way we elect members of Congress, state legislators, city councils, or county school boards. Thousands of campaigns—big and small—are conducted every year in America, and the instances of graft or corruption are rare. Big-city machines have gone the way of the dodo bird. Civil-service protections at the federal, state, and local levels prevent powerful politicians from packing agencies with cronies.

Laws now prevent White House officials from leaving office and immediately cashing in on the access they once enjoyed—the so-called revolving-door effect. While this practice did not constitute actual corruption, trading in on previous work for the public was rightly frowned upon. These laws should reassure the public that work carried out on its behalf will not be immediately exploited for private gain.

One of the most-impressive but underappreciated accomplishments of American politics over the century has been the virtual elimination of systematic political graft and corruption. This nation has by far the highest standards of political conduct of any industrialized democracy and, happily, an abundance of politicians who meet those standards with regularity.

Think of the requirements that local, state, and federal politicians disclose their annual earnings. These requirements have made it virtually impossible for politicians to hide ill-gotten gain. Any attempt at collecting illicit money can and often is spotted by inquiring reporters and political opponents almost immediately. The kind of land speculation that was commonplace among local and state politicians two generations ago has almost vanished, because land records are easily accessible and meetings dealing with public lands are open to the public. Most site-selection procedures take months and years to complete—thus complicating the kind of quick-strike real-estate transactions local and state politicians used to exploit. In short, we have a variety of disclosure laws now in place that have effectively eliminated pure corruption—or at least made it vastly simpler to uncover and prosecute.

American politicians are more visible and more accessible than ever before. The average voter knows or can know more about the inner workings of their local, state, and federal government that any voter anywhere in the world. In person, by mail, phone, fax, or e-mail, voters can communicate with their lawmakers in ways that would have astonished voters a generation ago. At last count, 382 of 435 members of the House of Representatives and all 100 members of the Senate have their own Web sites. At these sites, voters can download information on legislation these lawmakers have introduced, minutes and reports of proceedings for the committees they belong to, and complete texts of all floor speeches they've delivered. Often, members of the House and Senate provide on their Web sites Internet links to other key government agencies.

These are reference tools most newspapers were without *when George Bush was president!* And they are now in the hands of any voter with a computer or access to a public library. We realize that not every American voter is hooked up to the Internet, and we know that many who are don't really care what their members of Congress are up to. But that doesn't matter. One of the few iron rules of politics still applies: disclosure equals accountability. Supreme Court Justice Louis Brandeis said it best: sunshine is the best disinfectant.

Does this torrent of information flowing over the Internet guarantee the end of corruption? Of course not. Nothing can end corruption forever. Lawmakers in Washington or in your state or in your city will still try to tuck a special favor or two into legislation at the last minute. If they can persuade all of their colleagues to go along, the special favor might even make it into law. But this laborious process rarely succeeds. Often such special favors die in the legislative incubator. Those favors that do survive Congress are frequently discovered by an inquisitive press corps. If sufficiently egregious, the favors are usually rescinded in short order.

Such was the case in 1997 when the tobacco industry sought a $50 billion exemption from a fifteen-cent tax increase, phased in over three years, imposed as part of the so-called balanced-budget deal. Tobacco interests, working with the congressional Republican leadership, wrote into the new budget law one simple sentence saying that $50 billion in new tax revenue would count against the $368 billion the industry agreed to pay in its settlement of pending lawsuits brought by several state attorneys general.

The tobacco lobby's intentions were straightforward. The $368 billion settlement was its final offer to the state attorneys general—and to Congress and Clinton. The industry would not pay one penny more, and if required to do so, it was prepared to walk away from the deal and take its chances in court. Since the higher excise taxes were meant to cover the costs of a new health-insurance entitlement program for children, the industry reasoned, those taxes would achieve some of the same goals as the $368 billion settlement package. Why pay for the same public-health services twice? the industry argued.

Congressional leaders *and* President Clinton agreed. The outlines of the $50 billion rebate were hammered out in a closed-door session with congressional leaders and top Clinton administration officials, including the president's chief of staff, Erskine Bowles. President Clinton signed the budget knowing that the tobacco lobby's $50 billion rebate was included. And yet, when the time came, the public outcry was so intense that Congress and Clinton reversed field and repealed the rebate.

The lesson here is that even sweetheart deals do not last long under intense public criticism. And what of the other, less-publicized sweetheart deals? Of course they exist. But their numbers are far smaller than in days gone by, and almost all are eventually exposed—if for no other reason than that no special deal leaves everyone unharmed. With each tax break or regulatory shield comes a set of winners and losers; typically the losers outnumber the winners, and they swiftly alert reporters to the story. (Note: we are not referring here to pork-barrel spending. This time-honored practice is still quite prevalent and remains inimical to the interests of most taxpayers. But pork-barrel spending does not qualify as a corruption.)

Still, the public believes politics is rife with corruption. So how is it that higher standards in public service have led to greater cynicism about public servants?

It's interesting to ponder the following chain of events. Government institutions were generally held in high esteem until the Watergate era. Congress enacted "corrective" measures dealing with the disclosure of campaign contributions, along with other reforms, in the aftermath of Watergate. Governments at the state and local level followed suit. These reforms were followed by efforts at the state and local levels to bring "sunshine" into the governing process by opening previously closed meetings of city councils, state commissions, and county councils. These moves greatly enhanced the public's ability to scrutinize the political process. Voters could see more, and the press had ready access to information that allowed them to police corruption more thoroughly than ever before.

Then came the television cameras. C-SPAN began covering House proceedings in 1979 and Senate proceedings in 1986. This brought the public unprecedented access to the debates within Congress. When C-SPAN expanded coverage to include important committee action, voters around the country suddenly had the same access to important government activities that Washington's most-powerful reporters enjoyed.

C-SPAN took it a step further, bringing its cameras into the hallways of Congress to capture impromptu press conferences with key congressional leaders. Voters so inclined could actually watch lawmakers respond to questions on issues of the day from the nation's best political reporters. What's more, a community's voters could see their own members of Congress in action. They could judge for themselves how these members were handling their legislative duties in Washington. The menu of options on C-SPAN is mind-boggling: White House briefings, State of the Union speeches, on-the-spot presidential campaign coverage, House and Senate floor proceedings, key committee hearings, important policy speeches delivered by lawmakers, annual conferences sponsored by the nation's most-powerful political interest groups, academic seminars on American politics, and call-in programs with lawmakers.

C-SPAN alone provides access of the kind no American voter could imagine a generation ago. Americans can learn more about the federal government in one week of average C-SPAN programming than their parents could have learned in a year of reading the nation's best political journals.

By any rational standard, Americans can see more and learn more about their government—whether in Washington or their own hometown—than at any time in history. Government is more open and accessible and, by definition, more accountable than ever before.

Which brings us to another lie we wish to obliterate. "Politicians are out of touch." Equally phony, this is a cousin to the lie this chapter is dedicated to refuting.

Every step along the path toward greater public access—open meetings, disclosure of campaign accounts, disclosure of personal finances, and televised coverage of Congress—has increased the level of contact between politicians and voters. So have the arrivals of the fax machine and e-mail. Members of Congress and their staffs now wade through piles of letters and faxes, answer hundreds of phone calls, and filter dozens upon dozens of e-mail messages each day. In ways positively unimaginable to federal lawmakers a generation ago, members of Congress are hard-wired to their constituents.

At times, the provoked public's roar paralyzes, as the lawmaker's staff tries to answer ceaselessly chirping phones, processes page upon page of invective-laden faxes, and reviews acidic e-mail messages. For federal lawmakers the phone, the facsimile machine, and the e-mail box act as a three-pronged political seismograph to measure the volatility of certain issues, and most analyze the results with the anxious intensity of geologists checking the San Andreas Fault.

These readings weigh far more heavily on the minds of the typical politician than any individual political contribution. The newfound ease with which voters can contact their members of Congress has increased the importance of their voices relative to that of the special interests. Although, to be sure, organized groups of voters can and do influence members of Congress by peppering them with faxes, phone calls, and e-mails. Nonetheless, today's communication technology offers an average voter an overwhelmingly positive means of contacting elected officials.

But there is a downside to a nation of hard-wired national legislators. At times they can be *too* responsive—too distracted by the rumblings back home or by an orchestrated barrage of "grassroots outrage" generated by special-interest groups—to do what their consciences instruct or what the needs of the nation require. This relationship is growing dangerously one-sided. Public demands for accountability have grown so vociferous that more and more voters are coming to see their elected officials in Washington as little more than trained seals. There's an increasing tendency to believe that any politician who does not act upon his constituent's every wish is corrupt and unfit for office—living proof that voting is a futile gesture. This sentiment, like the notion of rampant political corruption, can be found in letters to the editor, ravings on talk radio, and impromptu political conversations in virtually any coffee shop in America.

The life of a politician should be a life of public service. But public service is not the same as political servitude. Trust is an essential element of the relationship between lawmaker and citizen. Citizens must trust politicians to exercise their judgment as best they see fit, even if that means that citizens and politicians occasionally disagree over particular issues. Yes, politicians have to be responsive to the wishes of their constituents. Yes, they owe their allegiance first and foremost to those citizens who worked hardest to elect them. But federal lawmakers have a higher duty, an obligation that calls them to serve their nation as they do their constituents. Many lawmakers today are terrified to cross the home folks even once on a high-profile issue, for fear that their next election will become a referendum on their political "treason"; the result is a legislature often too timid to take a bold stand on hot-button issues under public discussion.

Voters are right to demand courage, foresight, and wisdom from their elected officials. The nation needs all of these qualities. But voters cannot denounce political cowardice unless they are willing to support politicians who take risks, especially when that risky position *conflicts with their own point of view.* By all means, hold politicians accountable. Avoid, however, the presumption of corruption simply because you disagree with a politician's position or vote.

We know this sounds hopelessly old-fashioned, naïve, and nostalgic.

Too bad.

One of the problems we have with today's unremittingly hip, ironic, and sardonic popular culture is that it discounts or disdains value judgments. It sneers at virtue and leers at vice. In such a cynical world it's easy (and intellectually lazy) to conclude that all politicians are corrupt. If there is by definition no virtue possible in politics, then virtually anything can pass for corruption.

One of the reasons it's so hard to see the goodness in American politics is that the media continue to redefine corruption. Corruption used to be easy to spot: any politician who traded votes or government perks for cash was corrupt. Today, however, the media have an entirely new criterion for corruption. It's a sticky, convoluted web of so-called standards that generate plenty of sensational headlines but do nothing to protect the public from true political corruption.

As we mentioned earlier, much of this started with Watergate. President Nixon's misdeeds were not unique. But they were excessive and constituted a real threat to the Constitution. Nixon tried to cover up crimes. He created a constitutional crisis and brought the nation to the brink of its first attempt to impeach a president since Andrew Johnson.

The Nixon standard for political corruption was clear and indisputable. But the media have led the public down a delusional path toward "cleaner government" by constantly redefining corruption. After Watergate, the press began to scrutinize all manner of political activity in search of similarly brazen acts of corruption. The good news for America was, there wasn't much to be found.

But what was good news for the country was bad news for the bloodthirsty news media. The absence of Nixonian corruption demanded a new definition of corruption. Subject to many subsequent rewrites, the new corruption code began with an attack on conflicts of interest.

If a politician was found to be consorting with those who had interests that appeared to conflict with the loosely defined "public interest," he or she found himself or herself under fire. Conflict of interest was never about actual corruption, never about the straight trading of votes for money. It was about doing things or meeting people who *might* exert undue influence.

Might: that's a pretty slippery word, and an even more slippery concept when you're talking about politicians who have a legitimate need to meet with powerful figures; for example, leaders of big business or of the labor movement. The conflict-of-interest standard was most aggressively applied against members of Congress who received speaking fees from associations that lobbied Congress. The fees received were known as honoraria. The media and so-called good-government groups, "goo-goos," said that the fees, in and of themselves, constituted a conflict-of-interest problem for any politician who accepted them. The logic flowed this way: a member of Congress who accepted a fee for a speech might at some future date change his or her vote to favor the interest group that paid for the speech. Remember, all honoraria income was published for all to see.

But none of that mattered. Jittery politicians, unable to adjust to this new standard, waved the white flag and banned speaking fees, trading the lost honoraria revenue for higher salaries. The ensuing public outcry over the pay increase showed what voters really cared about. (Count coauthor Penny among the jittery politicians, as he voted to ban honoraria *and* reject the pay raise.)

As soon as Congress buried honoraria, the goo-goos and the media changed the ethics standards again. Now politicians were being scrutinized for doing things that *might create the possibility* that a corrupt act might be suggested to them by a contributor and that they might eventually act upon the suggestion. The buzzword for this newly defined corruption was *access*. Politicians were suddenly accused of trading access for political contributions. This standard made it quite easy for the media to tar any politician. All politicians in Congress raise money, and they must, on occasion, meet with their contributors. Therefore the very process of raising money—this fundamental mechanism of American politics—now qualifies as a potentially corrupt activity.

This preposterous standard is routinely applied to campaign contributions; sinister motives are imputed to virtually everyone who contributed money to a politician and, of course, to the politician who accepted the money. If, for example, a corporation or labor union gave a congressman or senator $1,000 and the lawmaker at some point in the future voted for some legislation that assisted that group, even indirectly, then that qualified as corruption under the new *appearance of conflict of interest* standard. The Center for Responsive Politics, one of Washington's leading goo-goos, goes so far as to publish a "scorecard" that shows money received by members of Congress and legislation that may have benefited the donor. On these scorecards, contributions of as little as $250 or $500 (out of campaign accounts where more than $600,000 is routinely raised) are listed as potentially decisive in the politician's vote on a particular piece of legislation.

Rubbish.

The premise of this standard is that all contributions are made to buy votes. If you accept that premise, then you must assume that every politician who accepts a contribution is willing to sell his or her vote, and that every company, union, special-interest group, and individual is giving money *only because it will elicit a favor in return*. In essence, this standard *assumes* that all contributors and all politicians are corrupt, which is intellectually indefensible.

A typical, and to our way of thinking, reckless example of this new standard for "corruption" occurred in the October 13, 1997, edition of the *New York Times* in a story about Senate Majority Leader Trent Lott, jointly reported and written by Allison Mitchell and Eric Schmitt. The headline read: "Lott, Champion Money-Raiser, Still Champions Rules of Game." The piece speaks for itself:

> After ringing the death knell for a campaign finance overhaul on the floor of the Senate last Tuesday evening, the Senate Majority Leader, Trent Lott, had other pressing business. From the Capitol, the Mississippi Republican sped to a cove of luxury homes in Potomac, Md., where, as a guest of the hotel executive J.W. (Bill) Marriott Jr., he attended a fund-raising reception for his political action committee. More than 100 guests paid $1,000 each to rub shoulders with the Republican leader, who, just hours earlier, had blocked a bill to slow Washington's chase for campaign dollars by overhauling the current campaign finance system.
>
> So far this year, Mr. Lott's political action committee, the New Republican Majority Fund, has raked in an impressive $2 million. . . . Since becoming majority leader last year, Mr. Lott has become one of his party's most prodigious fund-raisers. . . . Since 1995, Mr. Lott has used his fund-raising prowess to raise the millions necessary to help cement the Republican majority in the Senate and, he hopes, expand it in 1998.
>
> . . . Indeed, his zealous opposition to campaign finance legislation is tied to the fund-raising advantages his party now enjoys, say a number of Republicans who allied with Mr. Lott in

his so-far successful effort to stave off such a bill. The legislation Mr. Lott blocked, the McCain-Feingold bill, would, among other things, ban corporate "soft money" contributions, the unregulated money that flows in ever bigger waves to the national Republican Party, the Republican senatorial committee and their Democratic counterparts . . .

In the current campaign finance system, the Republicans enjoy big advantages over the Democrats in almost every area of fund-raising. Republicans have a deeper base of small donors, and their committees far outstrip the Democrats in tapping the richest vein of donations: soft money, the unlimited contributions from corporations, unions and wealthy individuals that can be donated to the political parties, as opposed to hard money, the limited contributions that go to candidates.

. . . What distinguishes Senator Lott's fund-raising success, particularly in a city where $1,000-a-plate receptions are a nightly staple when Congress is in session, is that most of the money he raises is not for himself. Although his own campaign coffers contain a healthy $782,000 (he is not up for reelection until 2000), most of the Mississippian's fund-raising is to benefit other Republican senators and Senate candidates.

Senator Lott's PAC, for example, doled out $292,000 to Republican Senate candidates in 1996 and $117,000 to Republican House candidates. Though a good chunk of the contributions from Mr. Lott's PAC went to fellow incumbents, he sent most of it to Republicans running for open seats and to those challenging Democratic incumbents. That helps the majority leader expand his base of Republican allies.

. . . At the expensive Breakers Hotel in Palm Beach, Fla., Mr. Lott defended the current system of raising campaign money as "the American way." Advocates of a campaign finance overhaul immediately denounced Mr. Lott for using such patriotic terms to describe what they view as a cash-for-access system that encourages influence peddling.

It all sounds so sinister, doesn't it?

Raking in money while rubbing shoulders with contributors, in a home nestled in an enclave of luxury and privilege. Raising money and giving it to challengers just to expand his Senate majority. Killing a "reform" that would eliminate a fund-raising advantage.

Gosh. It sounds worse than sinister. It almost sounds criminal.

But it isn't, not by a long shot.

Let's take the accusations one at a time.

Hours after killing a bill designed to "slow Washington's chase for campaign dollars," the *Times* piece asserts, Lott attended a fund-raiser where those who donated one thousand dollars each were allowed to "rub shoulders" with him.

First of all, Lott and other Republicans successfully filibustered a bill that would have made small changes to campaign-finance laws but would in no way have slowed "Washington's chase for campaign dollars." The tone of the *Times* piece also leaves the impression Lott was raising money the new bill would have outlawed. Not true. The contributions of one thousand dollars raised by Lott, would have remained legal under the McCain-Feingold bill the Senate killed. As the story later pointed out, McCain-Feingold sought to ban only so-called soft money, contributions that national parties receive for party-building activities such as voter education, get-out-the-vote drives, and membership recruitment. Political consultants in both parties agree that such a ban would not slow "Washington's money chase" but simply send it in a different direction.

Lott was acting in a perfectly legal manner, raising money at a private residence from citizens who have a legal right to contribute to him or to anyone else. The money he raised would even have been legal under the campaign-finance bill the Senate had killed earlier that day, proving there was no underlying hypocrisy to Lott's accepting donations.

Let's look at the next charge: *Lott raises a lot of money.*

You don't say.

Every party leader in Congress raises a lot of money. Lott and House Speaker Newt Gingrich are the Republicans' top two fund-raisers. Senate Minority Leader Tom Daschle and House Minority Leader Richard Gephardt are the Democrats' top fund-raisers. It comes with the territory, folks. *Party leaders exert tremendous influence over their party's legislative and political agenda.* As long as contributions from private citizens are legal (and there are those who want to abolish this cherished First Amendment right), party leaders will always receive more contributions than anyone else. If you don't like that, then you have no other choice but to put your tax dollars on the line to finance every congressional campaign in America, providing funds for candidates you fundamentally disagree with.

Next charge.

Lott is a "zealous" fund-raiser.

Hmm. Well, if money naturally flows to party leaders, is it fair to charge Lott with zealotry? Could it be that there are zealous contributors eager to assist him, just as there are zealous contributors eager to assist him, just as there are zealous contributors who help Daschle and Gephardt to raise more money than any of their Democratic colleagues?

Next charge.

The current system favors Republicans, and Lott is wrong to oppose changing it.

And why does it favor Republicans? Because they are corrupt? No, it's because they have "a deeper base of small donors" and their committees "far outstrip the Democrats in tapping the richest vein of donations: soft money."

First, let's separate apples from oranges. Small donors are people who typically give less than one hundred dollars. Their contributions are not regulated by federal law. Their names are not even disclosed on Federal Election Commission reports because the amounts are so small that no one, not even the advocacy groups, can make a credible case that they "buy access" or contribute to an atmosphere of "influence peddling." These donations would not be changed by McCain-Feingold. Republicans have more of these small donors than Democrats. And this is a bad thing? Why does the *New York Times* care which party has more small donors? If the Democrats don't have as many, that's their problem, isn't it? Wouldn't it be the Republicans' problem, not the public's, if it were the other way around?

We thought so.

Next charge.

Republicans also have an advantage in raising soft money.

Well, so did the Democrats when *they* ran Congress. This advantage comes with the majority. In fact, when Democrats ran Congress, they attracted more big-business money than Republicans *because they were in charge of federal regulations affecting business.* When you have a strong hand in writing the laws, those affected by the changes will do what they can to make you hear their voices. Getting one's voice heard is not a crime. It's not a scandal. It's not questionable or inappropriate. It's democracy.

Next charge.

Lott distributes money to Republican candidates running in open-seat races or challenging Democratic incumbents.

What is he supposed to do? Give the money to the Democrats? Lott is raising money legally, following logical tactics to keep his party in power, and looking around the country to find like-minded Republicans he can help in order to enlarge his majority in the Senate. Folks, that's exactly what he's supposed to do. It's what Democrat George Mitchell of Maine did when he was Senate Majority Leader, what Democrat Tom Foley did when he was Speaker of the House. It is what current Democratic leaders Daschle and Gephardt do. It's been the practice of every party leader since the dawn of the republic. The only difference now is that more of this activity happens in full public view than ever before. Virtually all fund-raising events are publicly disclosed (though not all are open to the press), and campaign contributions and disbursements are publicly recorded and available for all to see.

Even though everything Lott did was legal, logical, and fully consistent with past political practices in this country (except that they were far more visible), such behavior still drives the government-watchers crazy. Why? Because it's all part *"of a cash-for-access system that encourages influence peddling."* Everyone who contributes simply wants access, they claim. Everyone who contributes wants to encourage lawmakers to bow to their influence, in other words, break the law. It's just not true.

It would be hard to imagine the criterion for corruption becoming any sillier, but it has. The new standard, three times removed from actual corruption, is "the appearance of a *potential* conflict of interest."

This would be hilarious if it wasn't so serious—and so damaging to our democracy.

What constitutes an appearance of a potential conflict of interest? Well, just about anything. It was applied most recently to casual meetings between politicians or their staff members and lobbyists. Congress in 1994 passed a ban on gifts from lobbyists. Under this legislation, a "gift" could be a lunch, a dinner, a basket of fruit, a ticket to a sporting event, or tickets to charity fund-raisers. Critics argue that the receipt of gifts from lobbyists creates an "appearance" that lawmakers could be influenced to assist lobbyists in the future. This new standard asserts that politicians are so craven that they will change their votes if someone buys them a tuna sandwich for lunch. It also assumes that lobbyists are so gullible that they think buying a congressman a tuna sandwich will get them a vote.

Unable to pacify the critics, the House voted to ban all gifts to lawmakers or their staff in excess of twenty dollars, and the Senate voted to ban all gifts valued at more than fifty dollars. What was the result? Well, Congress now has a mini–police force that inspects every reception on Capitol Hill to make sure the value of the food consumed does not exceed the twenty-dollar limit per person for each lawmaker and congressional staff member present. Government employees now count the number of pastries, melon wedges, and bottles of Coke to make sure your government is "clean."

And there's another little problem with the gift ban. Because lobbyists cannot meet lawmakers for lunch and dinner anymore, they have to meet them at fund-raisers. To attend the fund-raisers, of course, they have to contribute money. (And now we are taking much higher sums than twenty dollars.) In other words, by complying with the gift ban, which is designed to rid government of the appearance of a potential conflict of interest, lawmakers and lobbyists instead engage in conduct that, at minimum, constitutes a potential conflict of interest. It might even be a pure conflict of interest. We can't keep up. Only the media and the goo-goos can explain it.

And while they're trying to untangle this web of contradictions, perhaps the critics can pause to explain what they have accomplished. Is government cleaner? Has public confidence been bolstered?

Let us remember that our goal should be to root out truly corrupt behavior. Over the years, a few spineless weaklings have come to Washington and sold their votes for money, yes. Of course it was dirty. Before Watergate, politicians weren't obliged to disclose from whom they accepted political contributions or in what amounts. Before Watergate, some members of Congress accepted cash contributions in their offices on Capitol Hill. Each member of the House had a safe in his office, often used for just this purpose. According to Barbara Wolanin, curator of the Architect of the Capitol, the safes were in each House office until the 1960s and 1970s, when they were removed one by one as congressional offices were renovated. Wolanin said there were no permanent safes for senators, but those who requested one received a small portable model. Wolanin would not verify whether these safes were used to accept cash contributions, only that they were used for a variety of purposes.

But even in the pre-Watergate era, few who accepted a cash contri-

bution ever traded a vote. Vote selling has always been a rarity, if for
no other reason than that such behavior would instantly brand the offenders as unreliable among their colleagues. Without the confidence
of their peers, lawmakers simply cannot get things done in Washington—or in a state legislature or city council, for that matter. Lawmakers who can't get anything done soon run into difficulty with their
constituents back home. If word spreads that the lawmaker in question is corrupt and untrustworthy, defeat at the polls almost always
follows. The democratic process is remarkably efficient at punishing
actual corruption.

However, the goo-goos are not content to let voters sort this out
for themselves. Authors Peter W. Morgan and Lenn H. Reynolds observed in their fine 1997 book, *The Appearance of Impropriety: How
the Ethics Wars Undermined American Government, Business, and
Society,* that the process of seeking funds leads some good government
groups to use flimsy ethics complaints against politicians to raise
money from donors eager to know they are still out there fighting the
good fight for "clean government."

But the impact of this phenomenon on public interest organizations specializing in promoting government ethics is significant,
too. The reason is the relationship between direct-mail fund-
raising, the public relations efforts needed to sustain it, and the
proliferation of appearance standards in government ethics
realm.

Appearance ethics is ideally suited for such advocacy
groups. First, the promotion of appearance standards allows
such groups to adopt a posture of strictness: "We're not just for
clean government, we're for government that doesn't even look
dirty." Second, appearances provide ready-made grist for public relations and direct-mail mills. Showing impropriety may require real work, but showing the *appearance* of impropriety is
often much easier: a few vaguely worded statements about an
official's "links" to unsavory characters, a raised eyebrow at
some campaign contributions, and *Voilà!* A scandal (or at least
a mini-scandal) likely to last long enough to get mailings out
and money back. A few press releases, a few items on the
evening news and in newspapers, a little footage of the Executive Director standing in front of the Capitol, and the organization has created an image as a real go-getter.

Senator Daniel Patrick Moynihan of New York laments how popular culture has defined deviancy down by accepting aberrant behavior as the norm. This has led society to abandon standards that used to unite us. He's right, and everyone in society has paid a terrible price. But just the opposite has happened with politics. Sadly, we have defined deviancy up in politics—to the point where almost every act of a politician is suspicious and assumed to be either corrupt or criminal.

This pursuit of fictitious corruption puts all politicians in the impossible position of having to prove a negative. How can a politician prove that having dinner with a lobbyist did not change his or her vote? That a five-thousand-dollar contribution from a special-interest group did not affect his or her voting record? That receiving a speaking fee did not compromise his or her ability to judge an issue fairly? No one can prove a negative. All politicians can do is plead with the media and the advocacy groups that it's unfair and undemocratic to *assume* corruption on the basis of appearances alone.

No court of law in this country convicts a defendant on the basis of the appearance of a crime. No one in this country is even indicted for the appearance of a crime. A crime must certainly have been committed, and the accused must be proven guilty, before he or she is convicted. Of course, we want politicians to uphold a higher standard than that of common thieves, but we also want government critics to understand that their maniacal pursuit of "clean government" has led us nowhere.

Instead of increasing public confidence in government, the crusade against fictitious corruption has only increased cynicism and undermined confidence in all politicians. As a consequence, a generation of decent and honorable men and women in politics labor under a cloud of suspicion they are powerless to expunge. It's almost as if every politician is on a blacklist. The goo-goo advocacy groups and the scandal-starved media are responsible for this hideous stain on our political system. By placing the appearance of a conflict of interest on a par with true corruption, they have effectively equated politicians with criminals. The American people—whose ranks, of course, they represent—should be wise enough to reject the equation.

Teddy Roosevelt once observed that when they take roll in the Senate, members "don't know whether to respond 'present' or 'not guilty.'"

It was and is a funny line. In the time of railroad, steel, and sugar trusts that routinely bribed compliant senators, Roosevelt's barb had an undeniable ring of truth to it.

Contemporary comedians are even more savage when they poke fun at members of Congress. Sadly, the jokes have gotten tougher while the behavior of politicians has grown noticeably better. It's time for what the British call a rethink on this whole subject.

THE SIXTH LIE

◆

MONEY BUYS ELECTIONS

MUCH LIKE THE lie we debunked in the previous chapter, this is a delusion most Americans believe. Like the notion that all politicians are corrupt, the idea that all elections are won by the candidate with the most money is now an article of common faith, an understood and accepted principle of political science. Pundits, professors, and political watchdog groups, when accounting for the outcome of an election, all typically cite money as the decisive factor. When they try to explain the outcome of legislative votes, they add up the amounts of money contributed to legislators. When trying to explain complex actions of the president, they attribute them to the presence or absence of political contributions.

In short, money is the easy answer most "experts" give to political questions. It's a convenient answer. It sounds like a credible answer. In some cases, it's even the correct answer. But in most cases, it's neither credible nor correct.

The role money plays in politics is inherently complex. To say that money explains everything in politics is like saying that gasoline explains why stock cars go fast in a NASCAR race. Gasoline explains why cars go. Money explains why politicians go. But gasoline doesn't explain why some cars go faster than others, why some crash and others do not, why some win and others lose. Similarly, money doesn't fully explain why some candidates rise in the polls or why others fall, why some win and others lose.

Let's take the race-car metaphor a little farther: In a car race, all drivers use the same fuel. The race cars also have to meet certain specifications, so all competitors have roughly the same equipment. The track is the same length for all divers, and all rules of the race apply to all drivers. What the race is designed to test is the skills of the driver, the quality of the team he or she works with (the pit crew that maintains the car before and during the race), and the quality of the driver's car. The winners are the best drivers, who drive the best cars and work with the best teams.

Before each race drivers compete against one another for starting position. The fastest cars start at the front, and the slower ones are placed in order behind them. Those who start in front have a better chance of winning, while those at the end of the pack have to work that much harder to prevail. Being a front-runner does not guarantee victory. Many early leaders lose races due to driver error, an error on the part of the pit crew, or a defect in the car itself. Sometimes, near the end of a race, drivers low on fuel decide not to refuel so they can stay on the track and gain on drivers who do stop for fuel. When this gamble works, drivers have just enough fuel to cross the finish line. When it fails, the cars stall as drivers who stopped for fuel whiz by on the way to the checkered flag. Outside forces can also conspire against the leader of a race: debris that flies onto the track can disable his engine, or he can be sucked into the swirling vortex of a crash started by other drivers. There are countless variables that determine the outcome of any car race.

It's the same with politics.

Just as drivers cannot compete without a car or fuel, politicians cannot compete without a party and some money. To compete and win, politicians must have a message and a proven ability to raise money to communicate that message.

Just as not everyone who owns a car is a race-car driver, not everyone with a political message is a credible political candidate. Every type of competition has barriers to entry. Message and money are the barriers to entry in politics. Without them, you cannot compete.

So not everyone can run for office in America. Who would want that anyway? Would you really like a ballot that read like the White Pages? Of course not. The key question is whether the barriers to entry in American politics are too high. Most people interested in seeking elective office have some message they want to spread. It may not be a winning message, but the lack of a winning message isn't a barrier to entry (we'll show later how plenty of candidates who thought they had winning messages lost badly). So how much money is enough?

Well, that depends on where you live and the office being sought. Let's look at the House and Senate. We have to look at House and Senate seats separately because of the fundamental differences in running for them: statewide Senate campaigns cost more to staff, advertising costs are higher, travel expenses are greater, and the time involved to build a campaign is much greater. It's impossible to draw any coherent conclusions about the role of money in politics by comparing House and Senate elections.

As we will soon discover, it's difficult to draw a definite conclusion about money in politics even when you examine *only* House or *only* Senate races.

Let's start with the House.

In 1996 the average amount spent on a victorious House campaign was $673,739. That was substantially higher than the 1994 average of $516,126. These averages don't tell us much, however, because the cost of campaigning varies widely across the nation. House campaigns in big cities cost far more than in rural districts—primarily because television and radio advertising are much more expensive. Also, incumbents who represent safe districts often spend far less than the average. Similarly, incumbents in swing districts who often battle for reelection spend far more than the average. Open-seat races in swing districts also attract more money than this average.

Even accounting for inflation, the costs of the average competitive House seat for an incumbent have grown dramatically since 1976, the first year when campaign-finance reforms were applied to congressional elections. If the costs had merely kept pace with inflation, the average incumbent Democrat or Republican would have spent about $300,000 to keep his or her seat in a competitive race in 1992.

But does this cost represent an insurmountable barrier to entry? Does it prevent competitive challengers from running for Congress? Does the cost of campaigning drastically limit the number of competitive races, thereby limiting voters' ability to effect change? More to the point, is money the decisive factor in whether a challenger wins?

A review of spending habits in House elections dating back to 1976 shows the number of challengers in competitive races remaining relatively constant, rising and falling as *political tides in the nation tended to benefit or hurt the candidates' own party.*

To gain a better understanding of the role of money in House races, it's important to understand the four distinct types of races that occur each two-year election cycle. The role money plays in the ultimate outcome varies from each type to the next. Here they are:

1. Safe races: These are races in which the incumbent (Democrat or Republican) faces no challengers or only token opposition. These typically occur in the "safe" districts we referred to in our introduction, districts where the political alignment overwhelmingly favors one party over the other and the representative in Congress holds a powerful advantage over challengers from the opposing party. In such cases, the incumbent must first and foremost worry about challengers from within his or her own party. If the incumbent avoids a primary challenge, reelection is a virtual certainty.

2. Competitive races: These are races in which the incumbent wins with less than 60 percent of the vote. When an incumbent falls beneath this threshold, it's a sign of potential vulnerability and suggests his or her opponent had at least a fighting chance. Typically, these races occur in swing districts, where political divisions are acute and there are roughly equal numbers of registered Democrats and Republicans.

3. Weak-incumbent races: These races frequently end in a loss for the Democrat or Republican seeking reelection. Typically the incumbent's vulnerabilities are well known before the race, and the opposition party has recruited a strong challenger and given him or her a promise of substantial financial backing. These races often go to the wire—and a heavy financial advantage for the incumbent in such cases can be the decisive factor. As you will soon see, however, these races always have well-funded candidates, and the disparities between amounts spent by the incumbents and challengers are far smaller than the disparities in any of the other three types of House races we describe. Typically no amount of money can save a vulnerable incumbent, especially if his or her problems are related to personal or ethical problems or are his or her own creation.

4. Open-seat races: These are elections in which the incumbent has resigned or retired from Congress, leaving his or her seat available to anyone who can win it. We must stress that not all open-seat races are alike. Powerful Democrats and Republicans from safe districts usually turn their seats over to a handpicked successor—or at least try to. The only race for this seat is the party primary, in which challengers vie for support among the various constituencies that previously supported the powerful incumbent. It's an iron rule of politics that the endorse-

ment of the outgoing incumbent is the most-valuable commodity—worth more to the recipient than any amount of money he or she could raise. Open-seat races in competitive districts, however, usually attract capable candidates from both parties, as well as substantial financial backing from the local, state, and national levels of the party.

Now that we have our definitions straight, let's look at the spending habits for all four types of House races since 1976.

The first general observation we can make is that the cost of all types of House elections has risen steadily since 1974, when new election laws were written with the goal of reducing campaign costs.

But let's start with safe seats.

In 1976 the average Democrat spent $56,937 to win reelection in a safe-seat race, while the average challenger spent $24,865. The average Republican spent $77,855 to win a safe seat, while the average challenger spent $26,606.

In 1992 the average Democrat spent $494,885 to keep a safe seat, while the average challenger spent $93,346. The average Republican spent $485,010 to keep a safe seat, while the average challenger spent $79,808.

The number of Democrats and Republicans who fall into the safe-seat category has remained remarkably constant since 1976. In that year 185 Democrats ran and won in safe-seat races. The average number of Democrats to do the same per election over the next eight election cycles was also 185. Similarly, in 1976 there were 87 Republicans who won safe-seat races. After eight subsequent elections, the average number of Republicans who won safe-seat races per election was 90.

It's reasonable to conclude, therefore, that in roughly 275 House races money is a factor secondary to the incumbent's party affiliation, since the underlying politics of the districts are so hostile to candidates from the opposing party. Under the existing system of laws, money is no barrier to entry in these districts and does not inhibit the political process from offering voters suitable choices.

Let's go now to competitive races.

In 1976, the first election conducted under the new campaign laws, the average incumbent Democrat in a competitive race spent $119,440, while the average Republican challenger spent $109,079. The average incumbent Republican in a competitive race spent $104,465, and the average Democrat challenger spent $77,075.

In 1992 the average Democrat incumbent in a competitive race spent $835,238, while the average Republican challenger spent $284,831. The average Republican incumbent in a competitive race spent $698,912, while the average Democratic challenger spent $275,058.

The number of Democrats and Republicans who fall into the competitive category varies widely from election to election, depending on the relative national popularity of each party. The average over the nine election cycles for incumbent Democrats was 44. For incumbent Republicans it was 30.

But let's look at the three post-Watergate elections, in which Democrats running for reelection in the House encountered some tough times nationally—1976, 1978, and 1980. In 1976 Republicans were trying to regain the forty-three House seats lost to Democrats when many once-safe GOP districts turned Democratic in the 1974 midterm elections, when revulsion over Watergate was at its peak.

In 1976 Republicans fought hard to win back some of those seats and fielded numerous challengers against the new Democratic incumbents. As a result, the number of Democratic incumbents in competitive races in 1976 was 62—the highest number in any of the next nine election cycles. Republicans only gained one seat in the House in 1976, so they came back at the Democrats in 1978. In that election, 51 Democrats seeking reelection to the House were involved in competitive races, and 14 lost bids for reelection. Only 20 Republicans, however, were involved in competitive House races, and only 5 incumbents lost bids for reelection. Republicans gained eleven House seats in this election and vowed to press for more in 1980.

Let's pause a moment to look at the money spent in these two election cycles on races in which incumbents were defeated. As you will see, all these races attracted adequate funding from both sides.

In the seven races in 1976 in which a Democrat incumbent lost, the average spent by the Democrat was $97,874—in sharp contrast to what the average Republican spent to defeat a Democrat, which was $144,883. In the five races that year in which a Republican incumbent was defeated, the Republican spent, on average, $234,435—much more than what the average Democrat spent to defeat a Republican, which was $144,491. As you can see, the incumbents and challengers had plenty of money to spend. What's also clear is that Republicans who spent more money in 1976 were not safe. Five of them lost despite outspending their Democrat challengers by an average of nearly $90,000.

In the fourteen races in 1978 in which a Democratic incumbent lost, the average spent by the Democrat was $189,994—in contrast to the $226,028 an average Republican spent to defeat a Democrat. In the five races in which a Republican incumbent was defeated, the Republican, on average, spent $230,323—more than what the average Democrat spent to defeat a Republican, which was $192,037. Again, the incumbents and challengers had plenty of money to spend—and Republicans who outspent their Democratic rivals still lost.

By the time of the presidential election of 1980, the nation had begun to sour on President Jimmy Carter, and nationwide support for the Democratic Party was plummeting. With Ronald Reagan as their nominee, Republicans ran an aggressive national campaign against Democrats, urging voters to give the new president a congress willing to pass his agenda. Republicans were riding high. Fifty incumbent House Democrats were involved in competitive races, and 28 lost bids for reelection. Only 26 Republicans were involved in competitive House races, and only 3 Republican incumbents lost. Overall, Democrats lost thirty-three House seats in that election, the largest party losses in one election since 1920. In six years Republicans had gained all the seats lost in the 1974 election.

The fate of a candidate's party during any give election can exert far more influence on the outcome than the amount of money raised. For example, let's examine what happened to the number of safe seats in America during the 1978 and 1980 congressional elections.

The momentum Republicans gained can clearly be seen in safe Democratic and safe Republican House seats in those two elections. The number of Democrats who won with more than 60 percent of the vote fell from 184 in 1978 all the way down to 170 in 1980 (the lowest that number would drop for the next twelve years). Meanwhile, Republicans who won with more than 60 percent of the vote rose from 87 in 1976 to 103 in 1978. In 1980 the number of Republicans who won with more than 60 percent rose higher still, topping out at 114.

As swing districts were moving toward Republicans in these two elections, so too were safe districts. National political trends were affecting voting patterns far more strongly than the presence or absence of money.

Democratic incumbents who lost in 1980 were slightly outspent, on average, by their Republican challengers. The average Democratic incumbent who lost that year spent $285,636, while the average that a Republican spent to defeat a Democrat was $341,499. As we've shown, it was a bad year all over for Democrats, and the national mood was far more important in all House races than the amount of money spent by individual candidates in their own races.

This phenomenon reversed itself in 1982, the year one of your coauthors first ran for Congress. The first election after Reagan's election was a debacle for Republicans. The nation's heartland was in deep recession, and the populous East and West Coasts were not much better off. Unemployment was 9.7 percent; inflation, while declining, was still at 6.2 percent; interest rates remained high at 15 percent. Reagan's economic program had become law, but very few of its eventual benefits could be seen, let alone spent. Negative reaction against Republicans in Congress was palpable, and Democrats exploited it in the same way Republicans two years earlier had capitalized on unhappiness with President Carter.

In 1982 the number of safe Democratic House seats jumped from 170 in the previous election to 178. More important, the number of Democrats running in competitive House races fell from 50 in the previous election to 35. Twenty-six Democrats defeated Republican incumbents that year. Among these Democrats was your coauthor, Timothy J. Penny.

Before we get to the dynamics of Tim's race, let's look at what the national uprising against Reagan meant to his party's prospects in Congress. The number of safe Republican incumbents fell from 114 in the previous election to 86. The number of Republican incumbents who found themselves in competitive races rose from 26 the previous election to 55 (the highest total since 1974 and the highest total in any election since 1982). Only one Republican challenger defeated a Democratic incumbent that year. (Two other Democratic incumbents lost in primary fights brought about by redistricting.)

In all of these elections, the amount of money was not nearly as decisive in the final outcome as the underlying mood of the electorate. The mood of the electorate is what drove the number of safe and competitive seats up or down for the two major parties, not the amount of money raised.

A check on incumbents who ran in 1982 further underscores our point. Only three Democratic incumbents lost that year, and two were eliminated in party primaries brought about by redistricting. On average, Democratic incumbents who lost spent $353,201, while the lone Republican who defeated a Democrat spent $373,093. As for Republican incumbents, they knew they were in trouble and spent vast sums to protect their seats, to no avail. The twenty-six Republican incumbents who lost spent, on average, $465,027. Compare this with what the average Democrat spent to defeat a Republican, which was $282,781.

Now, let's look a little more closely at your coauthor's race for Congress to gauge the importance of money in such a contest.

For most of his career in politics, Tim was a goo-goo public-interest advocate and promoted the same approach to campaign reform as such groups as Common Cause and the Center for Responsive Politics. While he continues to admire the stated intentions of these and similar organizations, he has come to doubt the efficacy of the reforms they advocate. Only eventually did his own experience teach him that such bureaucratic schemes, designed to limit and regulate expenditures, are not necessary.

In 1982, when he first ran for Congress, Tim was a decided underdog. He was a Democrat in a district that had only elected one other Democrat—ever. He was battling an incumbent Republican with a substantial financial war chest. His opponent had been in Congress for eight years and had been reelected handily on each occasion (he never won with less than 60 percent of the vote). Only thirty years old, Tim was relatively inexperienced, though he had already served six years in the Minnesota Legislature.

Despite these initial handicaps, there were several factors working in favor of challengers in the 1982 election cycle. The national trend was moving against President Reagan due to the deep recession. Many special-interest groups, including the American Association of Retired Persons (AARP), the National Education Association, and public-employee unions, were upset about some of Reagan's proposed budget cuts. This hostility provided some impetus to Tim's campaign. While Tim's moderate record in the Minnesota Senate did not always line up with the agenda of these traditionally liberal special-interest groups, he was nevertheless perceived as preferable to the incumbent Republican.

By necessity, Tim's campaign was based on volunteer efforts and door-to-door and town-hall style appeals to voters; in short, it was a shoe-leather campaign. By the end of the race, Tim's opponent had spent nearly $400,000 to his $182,000. Yet he benefited from a general sense that Reagan and congressional Republicans were to blame for the weak economy. His campaign was energized by groups of voters who felt victimized by the policies of the Reagan administration. Of equal importance was the growing belief in Minnesota that his opponent had lost touch with his roots. These factors, in combination, more than offset any spending disadvantage, and Tim won 51 to 49 percent.

In his first bid for reelection, Tim and his opponent spent roughly the same amount—about $350,000. Naturally, Tim benefited from the fund-raising advantages of incumbency. Nonetheless, his opponent raised as much money as Tim did because national Republican leaders considered Tim a comparatively easy target and devoted extensive party resources to defeat him (while the national Democratic organization gave Tim almost no financial help). Prominent Republicans such as Vice President Bush and Congressmen Jack Kemp and Newt Gingrich traveled to the district to campaign against Tim. Then, too, Republicans were faring much better everywhere; the national mood had swung back to Reagan, thanks to a booming economy and the lackluster campaign of Democratic presidential nominee Walter Mondale. Trying for a fifty-state sweep over Mondale, Reagan made a last-minute swing into southern Minnesota and campaigned for Tim's opponent.

Despite the many factors working against Tim, the campaign boiled down to the strength of Tim's grassroots network of volunteers, his lifelong roots in the district (his opponent was a recent arrival), and his moderate voting record. In the end, Tim's home ties and strong grassroots network led him to a handy 57-to-43-percent victory.

As we have said time and time again, elections are influenced more by the mood of the electorate, the candidate's message, and the quality of his grassroots campaign than by dollars spent. Naturally money was necessary for Tim to be able to compete when he ran in 1982, but it was not the key element. It was only one of several factors. Many candidates win without a spending advantage. Tim is living proof of that.

Just for fun, let's look at a more-recent election to help confirm our point.

The presidential election year of 1988 was the most incumbent-friendly election since the new campaign laws took effect in 1974. Incumbents now must look back on it with astonishment; no election since has proven as tranquil for candidates who already hold their offices. The battle between Vice President George Bush and Michael

Dukakis did not spark a national mood change, largely because the issues debated had little do with taking the nation in a new ideological direction.

What's more, contentment with the economy was very high. There were signs on the horizon that the Cold War was beginning to ebb, though no one could have predicted how rapidly it was to conclude. The nation was at peace and enjoying a level of prosperity not seen since the late 1950s. Pleased with the overall direction of the nation, voters decided to cast ballots for Bush or Dukakis on the basis of their personal qualities (or lack thereof) and not on the basis of sending a message to Washington. Consequently, the choice between Bush and Dukakis had little or no bearing on votes cast in congressional races.

In that election 218 Democrats and 139 Republican incumbents won with more than 60 percent of the vote. It was the highest total since 1974, and it has not been equaled since. When the dust settled, it looked as if the number of safe districts had jumped suddenly from its average of 275 to 357.

Only 23 Democratic incumbents and only 21 Republicans won with less than 60 percent of the vote. That was the second-lowest total for Democrats since 1974 (the lowest came the year before, when only 22 Democrats finished below 60 percent in an election in which Republicans lost ground). It was the third-lowest total for Republicans since 1974 (the best year was Reagan's 1984 landslide, when only 16 incumbents fell below the 60-percent mark). As for incumbents, only 2 Democrats and 3 Republicans lost. In all five races, the incumbents outspent their victorious rivals. The 2 Democrats outspent the Republicans, on average, $935,494 to $349,438. On average, the 3 Republicans outspent their Democratic challengers $969,806 to $809,908. Clearly money was not decisive in those races.

As difficult as it is to draw reliable conclusions from House races, it's trebly hard with Senate races. The Senate never stands for election all at once, as does the House. Consequently, lucky members of the Senate are far more likely to dodge shifts in the national mood by not having to stand for reelection. There are also far fewer safe Senate seats based entirely on geography or ideology. Some states reliably send Republicans and Democrats to the Senate, but these voting patterns are far less predictable than they are for the 275 safe House districts. Senators also have more time to build up a record of legislative accomplishment and constituent service than do House members. This can also allow them to rise above a negative national trend that might pull a House member under. The power of incumbency, of course, provides advantages, but these can dissipate far more rapidly than for a member of the House. Inevitably, there is at least one electoral surprise, in which an overconfident senator assumes he can count on the same support he received six years before, only to discover (usually too late to do anything about it) that the public has turned against him. Under such circumstances, neither money nor high position in Washington can save him.

With these caveats in mind, it's instructive to look at some of the same elections and see what they tell us about the relationship between money and victory.

Let's examine the two years when turnover was highest in the Senate, because that can help us chart tendencies with a higher degree of confidence. In 1980 nine Democratic incumbents were defeated, and Republicans won three open-seat races, giving them a net gain of twelve seats, the worst defeat for Senate Democrats since they lost twelve seats in 1946. The Democratic majority before the election was 59 Democrats to 41 Republicans. After the election it was 53 Republicans to 47 Democrats.

As we noted earlier, this was the year of the decisive Reagan presidential victory. Not one Republican Senate incumbent lost. In those nine races in which Democratic incumbents lost, the Democrats spent, on average, $1.7 million on the election, while the average Republican spent $1.4 million. In the competitive Senate races that year, there was no shortage of money for either party. Four Democratic incumbents won with less than 60 percent of the vote, and two Republicans won with less than 60 percent. On average, the victorious Democrats spent $796,984, while Republicans on average spent $727,617. The two Republicans who won spent, on average, $1.2 million, while the two Democratic challengers spent $1.2 million. Clearly, money was not the decisive factor in these races.

In 1986 Democrats defeated 6 Republican incumbents and won two open seats for a net gain of eight seats. This year wasn't a memorable one for House races, as only 6 incumbents from either party were defeated. But this year was special because all of the Republicans elected to the Senate for the first time in 1980 ran for reelection. Democrats had been gearing up to defeat these Republicans for six years as part of a long-term strategy to regain control of the Senate. Since many of these seats were based in the deep South, Democrats spent two years registering black voters and building a strong get-out-the-vote effort. This was a tactical decision that united campaigns throughout the South and benefited all the Democratic challengers. Republicans could have used the same tactic by mobilizing more of their voters in the South. But they didn't. Thus, individual Democratic candidates gained due to the work of the national party, while individual Republicans candidates suffered due to their party's lethargy. This tactical difference proved critical.

Let's look at the dollars spent to see if the trends present in other elections held for this one. The 6 Republican incumbents who lost spent, on average, $3.8 million on their campaigns, while the average Democrat spent $2.9 million. On average, the Republican incumbents spent nearly $1 million more than their Democratic challengers but lost nevertheless. Again, message or mood or tactics are often more important than the amount of money raised in deciding the outcome of political races.

We have looked at many campaign years to prove our point that money is not the decisive factor in House and Senate elections. There is a very good reason why we looked most closely at the years immediately following the 1974 campaign-finance reforms. These are the years cited as virtually idyllic by those who perpetuate the lie that money buys elections. They look back on these years with nostalgia because candidates spent less than they do now to win seats in Congress. Yes, that's true. *But it simply does not prove money buys elections.*

As we've shown, there are far more variables that must be weighed to understand what tilts a House race one way or another. We've shown repeatedly how national trends were far better at foreshadowing the number of close races and the number of defeated incumbents than the average amount of money spent. National trends are but one factor. None of these numbers measures the incumbent's relative standing back home, his or her ethical or morale woes, the quality of his or her political message, the skill of the campaign team he or she put into place, or, more important, the dedication the candidate showed to campaigning. All of these variables are as important as the amount of money raised. In some cases, they are intertwined. It's difficult to spread a powerful political message if you don't have the money. But as we have shown, in races involving vulnerable incumbents, there's always been enough money. So, if there are at least six variables affecting each House race—national mood, strength of message, candidate's appeal, skill of campaign team, dedication of candidate to campaign, and *amount of money available*—it's impossible to argue credibly that money alone determines the outcome.

To further underscore our point, let's highlight some examples from the 1996 election to show that money alone does not guarantee a seat in Congress.

In 1996 there were fifteen Senate races in which the winner's margin was 8 percentage points or less. In six of these contests, the candidates who spent less actually won. There were 104 House races in which the winner captured 55 percent of the vote or less. In these competitive races, twenty-six candidates who spent less actually won.

Here is a list of the states where these races took place, who the candidates were, who won, and what each candidate spent in the 1995–96 election cycle.

Colorado: Republican Representative Wayne Allard defeated Democrat Thomas Strickland 51 to 46 percent. Strickland spent $2.8 million, and Allard spent $2.1 million.

Georgia: Democrat Max Cleland, Georgia's secretary of state, defeated Republican Guy Milner 49 to 48 percent. Milner spent $9.2 million, and Cleland spent $2.8 million.

North Carolina: Republican Senator Jesse Helms defeated Democrat Harvey Gantt 53 to 46 percent. Gantt spent $7.9 million, and Helms spent $7.7 million. Helms spent $14.4 million from 1991 to 1996, less than he had spent in his two previous reelection campaigns ($17.7 million in 1990 and $16.9 million in 1984). His election-year spending in 1996 was 43 percent less than 1990—a clear indication that money was not a dominant factor in his rematch with Gantt.

South Dakota: Representative Tim Johnson, a Democrat, defeated Senator Larry Pressler 51 to 49 percent. Pressler spent $5 million, and Johnson spent $2.9 million.

Virginia: Senator John Warner defeated Democrat Mark Warner 53 to 47 percent. Mark Warner spent $11.5 million, and Senator Warner spent $5.7 million.

Wyoming: Republican Mike Enzi defeated Democrat Kathy Karpan 54 to 42 percent. Karpan spent $934,308, and Enzi spent $855,267.

Statistics from 1996 also show that several candidates were able to raise enough money to remain competitive against better-known challengers.

In Illinois, for example, Republican Al Salvi spent $4.6 million in his race against six-term Democratic Representative Dick Durbin, who spent $4.8 million. Both candidates had more than enough money to wage intense statewide campaigns, and yet Durbin won in a landslide, defeating Salvi 56 to 41 percent. The two candidates ran competitively for most of the campaign until Salvi made a huge tactical blunder. Gun control was proving to be an important issue, especially in the heavily populated Chicago suburbs, where neither candidate was particularly well known. Durbin had been endorsed by gun-control advocates Sarah and Jim Brady, which clearly helped cement his credibility on the issue. Then something fascinating happened. According to *National Journal's Almanac of American Politics*, Salvi made an "astonishing mistake." In late October, someone Salvi met at a rally told him Jim Brady used to sell machine guns, an accusation he then repeated, without checking it first, in a radio interview. There was no truth to the story, and Salvi had to apologize. The flub destroyed his credibility on the issue of firearms and made him appear to be the "extremist" Durbin regularly suggested he was. A race that had been neck-and-neck for weeks turned into a rout—Durbin won by fifteen points.

In New Jersey, three-term Republican Representative Dick Zimmer spent $8.2 million against seven-term Representative Robert Torricelli, who spent $9 million. Together the two waged the most-expensive Senate campaign of the cycle, but in the end Torricelli prevailed, 52 to 43 percent over Zimmer, who clearly had enough money to wage a strong statewide campaign against Torricelli. The decisive factor here was Torricelli's relentless attacks on the Republican's "Contract with America." He attacked Zimmer for slavishly following House Speaker Newt Gingrich. According to the *Almanac of American Politics,* "Torricelli was going with the flow: opinion in New Jersey was clearly hostile to the Gingrich Republicans, and Zimmer did not emphasize enough the issues—abortion, environment, campaign finance—on which he disagreed with most House Republicans."

In Oregon, Republican Gordon Smith defeated Democrat Thomas Bruggere 49 to 47 percent in a race in which the two matched each other dollar for dollar. Smith spent $3.4 million to Bruggere's $3.2 million, a small difference that cannot by itself account for the outcome of the election.

Lastly, in Massachusetts the race was well-funded from the start; both candidates had immense name recognition and powers of incumbency to draw upon. In the end, Democratic Senator John Kerry defeated Republican Governor William Weld 52 to 45 percent in a race that drew national media attention. Kerry spent $12.3 million, and

Weld spent $7.8 million. The race seesawed back and forth through-out the fall, proving that Weld had the resources necessary to run a competitive race. Kerry prevailed in part due to the strong turnout among Democrats eager to vote for President Clinton, and to some tactical blunders associated with the Weld campaign in the final stages of the campaign.

What's clear from these four Senate races is that both candidates raised and spent enough money to wage competitive campaigns. The outcome was determined by other factors—namely, message, tactics, and candidate appeal.

Of the 435 House elections conducted in 1996, the winners in 104 prevailed by 55 percent of the vote or less. In 23 of the contests the candidate who spent less won. In eight other races, the candidate who spent less won with more than 55 percent of the vote—evidence that again challenges the lie that money is the key ingredient to victory.

Here is a list of the congressional districts where the victors were outspent, the candidates in the races, the outcome of the elections, and the amounts spent by each candidate.

Alabama District 4: Republican Robert Aderholt defeated Democrat Robert Wilson 50 to 48 percent. Wilson spent $1,004,788, and Aderholt spent $712,199.

Arkansas District 3: Republican Asa Hutchinson defeated Democrat Ann Henry 56 to 42 percent. Henry spent $441,060, and Hutchinson spent $340,689.

California District 22: Democrat Walter Capps defeated freshman Representative Andrea Seastrand 51 to 45 percent. Seastrand spent $1,158,068, and Capps spent $855,878.

California District 27: Republican James Rogan defeated Democrat Douglas Kahn 50 to 43 percent. Kahn spent $1,041,426, and Rogan spent $739,269.

California District 38: Republican Representative Steve Horn defeated Democrat Rick Zbur 53 to 43 percent. Zbur spent $1,007,199, and Horn spent $463,633.

Connecticut District 5: Democrat James Maloney defeated three-term Republican Representative Gary Franks 52 to 46 percent. Franks spent $620,975, and Maloney spent $596,720.

Illinois District 20: Republican John Shimkus defeated Democrat Jay Hoffman 50.3 to 49.7 percent. Hoffman spent $790,530, and Shimkus spent $615,982.

Indiana District 10: Democrat Julia Carson defeated Republican Virginia Blankenbaker 53 to 45 percent. Blankenbaker spent $637,171, and Carson spent $567,533.

Iowa District 1: Republican Representative Jim Leach defeated Democrat Bob Rush 53 to 46 percent. Rush spent $429,600, and Leach spent $366,851.

Kansas District 2: Republican Jim Ryun defeated Democrat John Frieden 52 to 46 percent. Frieden spent $748,108, and Ryun spent $400,216.

Kansas District 3: Republican Vince Snowbarger defeated Democrat Judith Hancock 50 to 45 percent. Hancock spent $816,100, and Snowbarger spent $424,824.

Maryland District 6: Republican Representative Roscoe Bartlett defeated Democrat Stephen Crawford 57 to 43 percent. Crawford spent $387,807, and Bartlett spent $249,540.

Massachusetts District 3: Democrat James McGovern defeated Republican Representative Pete Blute 54 to 46 percent. Blute spent $1,093,507, and McGovern spent $796,828.

Massachusetts District 6: Democrat John Tierney defeated Republican Representative Peter Torkildsen 51 to 49 percent. Torkildsen spent $1,113,951, and Tierney spent $767,827.

Michigan District 8: Democrat Debbie Stabenow defeated freshman Representative Dick Chrysler 54 to 44 percent. Chrysler spent $1,483,348, and Stabenow spent $1,445,057.

Michigan District 13: Democrat Representative Lynn Rivers defeated Republican Joseph Fitzsimmons 56 to 42 percent. Fitzsimmons spent $1,221,652, and Rivers spent $1,115,447.

Mississippi District 5: Four-term Democratic Representative Gene Taylor defeated Republican Dennis Dollar 58 to 40 percent. Dollar spent $458,783, and Taylor spent $435,599.

Missouri District 8: Republican Jo Ann Emerson defeated Democrat Emily Firebaugh 50 to 37 percent. Firebaugh spent $824,711, and Emerson spent $758,541.

New Hampshire District 1: Republican John Sununu defeated Democrat Joseph Keefe 50 to 47 percent. Keefe spent $577,362, and Sununu spent $481,473.

New Hampshire District 2: Representative Charles Bass defeated Democrat Deborah Arnesen 51 to 44 percent. Arnesen spent $691,931, and Bass spent $602,864.

New Jersey District 8: Democrat William Pascrell defeated Republican Representative Bill Martini 51 to 48 percent. Martini spent $1,362,208, and Pascrell spent $937,603.

New Jersey District 9: Democrat Steven Rothman defeated Republican Kathleen Donovan 55 to 43 percent. Donovan spent $787,521, and Rothman spent $779,904.

New York District 3: Republican Representative Peter King defeated Democrat Dal A. LaMagna 56 to 42 percent. LaMagna spent $1,066,717, and King spent $635,490.

North Carolina District 2: Democrat Bobby Etheridge defeated Republican Representative David Funderburk 53 to 46 percent. Funderburk spent $1,031,004, and Etheridge spent $692,578.

Ohio District 3: Democrat Representative Tony Hall defeated Republican David Westbrock 64 to 34 percent. Westbrock spent $402,931, and Hall spent $240,142.

Ohio District 6: Democrat Ted Strickland defeated Republican Representative Frank Cremeans 51 to 49 percent. Cremeans spent $1,705,602, and Strickland spent $706,097.

Ohio District 10: Democrat Dennis Kucinich defeated Republican Representative Martin Hoke 49 to 46 percent. Hoke spent $1,382,187, and Kucinich spent $686,822.

Oklahoma District 6: Republican Representative Frank Lucas defeated Democrat Paul Barby 64 to 36 percent. Barby spent $474,756, and Lucas spent $421,459.

Texas District 20: Democrat Representative Henry Gonzalez defeated Republican James Walter 64 to 34 percent. Walker spent $137,577, and Gonzalez spent $124,055.

Washington District 9: Democrat Adam Smith defeated Republican Representative Randy Tate 51 to 46 percent. Tate spent $1,554,870, and Smith spent $686,890.

Wisconsin District 3: Democrat Ron Kind defeated Republican James Harsdorf 52 to 48 percent. Harsdorf spent $505,655, and Kind spent $466,770.

Wisconsin District 8: Democrat Jay Johnson defeated Republican David Prosser 52 to 48 percent. Prosser spent $517,295, and Johnson spent $271,841.

These statistics do not include funds that paid for party-building activities, issue-advocacy advertisements, or independent expenditures. We do know, though, that such contributions flowed to competitive races in which the combatants were already well funded and running strong campaigns. And since the impact of these contributions is hard to gauge, the best measure of competitiveness can be found in what the candidates themselves raised and spent.

The statistics above do not prove that money is not essential to mounting a successful campaign for the House or the Senate. What they do reveal is that the amount of money spent does not determine the eventual winner, in spite of the widely held notion—propagaged by the media and proponents of campaign spending limits—that the candidate with the most money always wins.

What's even more important about the statistics from the 1996 elections is that most of the candidates seeking House and Senate seats in races deemed to be competitive early on had enough money to compete.

The vast majority of candidates from both parties were able to raise the funds necessary to stay on a roughly equal footing with their rivals. This was true in most every hotly contested open seat in the House and the Senate. It was generally true in races involving a well-known challenger and a potentially vulnerable incumbent in the House and Senate.

What's more, challengers in fifteen House races raised more in contributions than the incumbents they were hoping to unseat. In seven races, the challengers won (five Democrats and two Republicans).

Here are the congressional districts where this phenomenon occurred: the amount of money raised, the candidates involved, the election results, and the amounts spent.

Alabama District 7: Republican Joseph Powell raised $223,208, compared to $213,782 raised by Democratic Representative Earl Hilliard. The two spent almost identical amounts. Powell spent $218,751, and Hilliard spent $218,624. Hilliard won 71 to 27 percent.

California District 10: Democrat Ellen Tauscher raised $2,512,231, compared to $1,430,126 raised by Republican Representative Bill Baker. Tauscher spent $2,491,293, and Baker spent $1,378,068. Tauscher defeated Baker 49 to 47 percent. Tauscher contributed $1,673,346 to her own campaign and raised $822,096 from other sources.

Maine District 1: Democrat Thomas Allen raised $972,946, compared to $901,833 raised by Republican Representative James Longley. Allen spent $933,425, and Longley spent $898,669. Allen defeated Longley 55 to 45 percent.

Michigan District 13: Republican Joseph Fitzsimmons raised $1,228,268, compared to $1,097,857 raised by Democrat Representative Lynn Rivers. Fitzsimmons contributed $566,325 to his own campaign and raised $661,943 from other sources. For election results, see above.

Mississippi District 5: Republican Dennis Dollar raised $466,010, compared to $407,721 raised by Democrat Representative Gene Taylor. For results, see above.

Missouri District 9: Republican Kenny Hulshof raised $622,643, compared to $532,703 raised by ten-term Democratic Representative Harold Volkmer. For results, see above.

New Hampshire District 2: Democrat Deborah Arnesen raised $690,963, compared to $679,845 raised by Republican Representative Charles Bass. For results, see above.

New York District 3: Democrat Dal A. LaMagna raised $1,071,385, compared to $655,785 raised by Republican Representative Peter King. LaMagna contributed $991,000 to his own campaign. For results, see above.

New York District 4: Democrat Carolyn McCarthy raised $1,086,507, compared to $1,025,927 raised by Republican Representative Daniel Frisa. McCarthy spent $943,547 compared to the $850,929 spent by Frisa. McCarthy defeated Frisa 57 to 41 percent.

North Carolina District 4: Democrat David Price raised $1,145,022, compared to $988,943 raised by Republican Representative Fred Heineman. Price spent $1,146,441, and Heineman spent $989,340. Price defeated Heineman 54 to 44 percent.

Ohio District 3: Republican David Westbrock raised $399,786, compared to nine-term Democratic Representative Tony Hall's $311,302. For election results, see above.

Oregon District 5: Democrat Darlene Hooley raised $984,019, compared to $568,794 raised by Republican Representative Jim Bunn. Hooley spent $982,416, and Bunn spent $548,754. Hooley defeated Bunn 52 to 45 percent.

Texas District 20: Republican James Walker raised $138,627, compared to $123,375 raised by eighteen-term Democratic Representative Henry Gonzalez. For results, see above.

Utah District 3: Republican Chris Cannon raised $1,748,626, compared to $695,964 raised by Democratic Representative Bill Orton. Cannon spent $1,747,490, and Orton spent $705,716. Cannon contributed $1,446,133 to his own campaign and raised $302,493 from other sources. Cannon defeated Orton 51 to 47 percent.

What these statistics suggest is that it's far from impossible for challengers to raise enough to compete against incumbents—and that even outspending an incumbent does not ensure victory.

To summarize: money is not now, nor has it ever been, the decisive factor in most election outcomes. There is a long list of variables that weigh as heavily or even more heavily than the amount of money raised and spent on a given campaign. As we said at the outset, money is like fuel. If you don't have enough to run around the track, you have no hope of winning. But as our statistics clearly show, in races that are truly competitive, the candidates almost always have enough fuel. After that, it's a race decided by the quality of the candidate, the quality of the message, tactics, and national mood.

◆

FAT CATS ARE THE PROBLEM

T HE LAMENT CAN be heard all over the land. Monied interests are everywhere. Their monstrous influence warps the people's will, controlling lawmakers as if by marionette strings in a gaudy Machiavellian dance that desecrates democracy.

Or so the popular mythology goes.

The power and influence of monied interests, to be properly understood, must be placed in some historical context. Let us take this chapter to deconstruct the arguments against monied interests, supposedly engaged in single-handedly destroying our democratic republic.

The central argument is that special interests exert undue influence over policy-making, thereby thwarting the will of the people who elect members of Congress. Sounds familiar, right? You can hear this argument parroted all over the mass media anytime the topic is "what's wrong with American politics."

Its expression, sadly, can be found in a Gallup/CNN/*USA Today* poll of 872 adults in October of 1997. Respondents were asked to choose which of the following two statements they believed to be more accurate.

Number One: Elected officials are influenced mostly by what is in the best interests of the country. Answer = 19 percent.

Number Two: Elected officials are influenced mostly by pressure from campaign contributors. Answer = 77 percent.

If that poll is to be believed (and not all polls are), then most Americans believe that money makes the world go round in Washington. It's a very popular notion, and one that conveniently explains just about every phenomenon in American politics. And it's an answer used more and more often to explain political motives. Why does a politician oppose abortion? Answer: his contributors are pro-life. Why does a politician support abortion rights? Answer: his contributors are pro-choice. Why does a politician support existing labor laws? Answer: his contributors are big-labor bosses. Why does a politician oppose new environmental regulations? Answer: his contributors are big-business leaders.

Money is the cause of every complex problem in Washington, or so the goo-goo advocacy groups (and many of their megaphones in the dominant media) would have you believe. And the problems are getting worse all the time. How do we know? Because there is more money in politics than ever before!

More money equals more corruption.

But does it?

Let's travel back to the days when American politics was, the advocacy groups contend, full of innocence and virtue——those halcyon days just after Watergate when the sight of well-dressed White House aides being marched off to jail scared everyone straight.

Back then there was far less money in American politics, and there were far fewer special-interest groups.

Just to get our nomenclature straight, for the purposes of this chapter special interests are synonymous with political-action committees (PACs). They are what most Americans think of when asked to describe what ails politics in this country. It's those dirty special-interest political-action committees that use contributions as leverage to get what they want out of Congress and/or a president.

Since we hear so often that government was so much better after the 1974 reforms, and that changes to our existing campaign-finance system should extend these reforms, let's use 1974 as our baseline for measuring the importance of special interests and their financial contributions on American politics.

Now, imagine it's 1976 all over again and we're just pulling into Washington to survey the fund-raising scene. This is the first election cycle conducted under the new campaign finance laws. What do we find? Well, we find that there are 608 registered political-action committees that, over the course of the two-year election cycle (1975–76) donate $22.6 million to congressional candidates.

How do these numbers compare with our current situation?

In 1997 there were 3,875 political-action committees registered with the Federal Election Commission. In the 1995–96 campaign cycle, these PACs donated $169.5 million.

Some PACs contribute more than others, and taking an average of these two different election cycles is useful only in comparing the average PAC contribution. In 1976 the average was $37,171 per PAC. In 1996 the average was $42,164 per PAC.

So what, you say? Of course the average is only slightly higher. Look at the enormous increase in the number of PACs! No one would have predicted in 1976 that six times as many PACs would exist twenty years later.

True enough.

But where did the PACs come from? They came from us. The PACs organized exactly as the reformers of 1974 intended. The reforms created PACs to *increase* the power of small donors relative to wealthy individual donors. Donors of modest means are allowed to set aside, through their companies or associations, a small amount of their wages, which are then combined with the wages of their co-workers to create a fund that the PACs board can use to make contributions.

The proliferation of PACs simply reflects the desire of more and more Americans to play a small role in the American political dialogue. The contributions are passed on to politicians who support policies consistent with the PACs' legislative goals. Is that surprising? For example, an employee of a large telecommunications firm can, through a PAC, exert more influence with her $50 contribution to her company's PAC than she can by sending a single $50 check to one politician. And she can hardly be blamed for using her company PAC to make her precious disposable income go farther than it would if she sent her contribution by herself to one politician. By necessity, PACs focus their contributions on lawmakers who wield influence over their industries. That's their job. The employees who give to a company PAC want their small contributions leveraged to make sure Washington does not harm their interests. The reformers in 1974 saw this political activity as morally superior to contributions from wealthy individuals. As a result, the reformers allowed PACs to make contributions of up to $5,000 per election. Individuals were limited to contributions of only $1,000 per election.

In other words, we have more PACs today because more Americans *choose* to belong to them, and because that's what the reformers who created PACs intended.

We still have the argument, though, that there's simply too much money floating around Washington—whether the PACs like it that way or not.

Fair enough; let's tackle that issue.

Let's go back to 1976, when there were only 608 PACs that together donated $22.6 million to congressional candidates. In that election cycle, all House and Senate candidates spent $98.2 million (with primary and general elections included). Contributions from PACs accounted for 23 percent of what was spent. In 1996 all House and Senate candidates spent $451.1 million (with primary and general elections included). Contributions from PACs accounted for 38 percent of what was spent. While the number of PACs increased sixfold, the amount of contributions as a share of total expenditures rose by only 15 percent. What that tells us is that there were other sources of contributions that competed with the staggering increase in the number of PACs. The other source was individuals, who became involved in politics in consistently higher numbers with each succeeding election. In other words, after the reforms of 1974, the number of Americans who organized themselves in PACs grew substantially—as did the number of individual Americans who donated directly to politicians. This is as it should be.

Now, let's assess the value of these contributions, those from both PACs and individuals. With all the money flowing into political campaigns, the opportunity for influence peddling must be higher than ever. Right?

Not necessarily. We contend that the value of contributions from PACs and individuals is less now than ever before. How, you ask?

In two very significant but routinely overlooked ways, contributions now are worth less on a case-by-case basis than at any time since 1974. And each and every year that campaigns grow more expensive, the relative value of each contribution decreases.

It's simple mathematics. Let's say you were a member of the House running for reelection in 1996. On average, you were likely to spend about $800,000 on your race. The law prohibits a PAC from giving you more than $10,000 for the entire two-year election cycle. So, the most a PAC can give you is a contribution worth 1.25 percent of your entire reelection budget.

OK. Let's transport you back to 1976 and imagine you ran for reelection. Besides the color of your hair, the size of your waistline and the cut of your suit, what would be different? First of all, you would have spent less on your campaign. Second, the proportional value of a PAC contribution would have been substantially higher than today.

The average incumbent in 1976 spent $79,398 on his campaign. A

PAC contribution of $10,000 in that election cycle would have represented *13 percent* of your campaign budget.

We repeat. A full PAC contribution to the average incumbent's campaign in 1996 amounted to 1.25 percent of his or her reelection budget. A full PAC contribution in 1976 amounted to 13 percent of a reelection budget.

In other words, a full $10,000 PAC contribution in an election cycle (primary and general elections) in 1976 was ten times more valuable, in terms of financing the next campaign, than the same full contribution in 1996. If you assume that politicians simply collect contributions to fund their next election and that they make rational decisions about the value of each contribution on the basis of its ability to help get them elected, *you must conclude that contributions today are worth less than ever before.*

When we approached one of Washington's foremost watchdogs, executive director of the Center for Public Integrity Charles Lewis, he had to concede our point. "You're right," Lewis said. "The value of these contributions is smaller than it used to be."

But that's only part of the story.

The value of contributions to politicians has diminished in proportion to the volume of contributions overall—and *in relation to what the contributions would be worth if indexed for inflation.*

The limits on legal contributions have not been adjusted for inflation since 1974.

Each and every year inflation has diminished the value of these contributions relative to what it was in the 1975–76 election cycle.

If you were to adjust the legal limits for contributions to 1996 values, individuals would be allowed to contribute roughly $3,500 per election (not the current $1,000 limit), and PACs would be allowed to contribute roughly $34,000 per election cycle (primary and general election) and not the current $10,000.

To illustrate the point, let's look at how much of a campaign budget a $34,000 PAC contribution would have "bought" in a typical 1996 House reelection campaign. Remember, our standard of good government is the 1975–76 election cycle, the first one conducted under the new campaign-finance laws. A legal PAC contribution back then financed 13 percent of the cost of the average House reelection campaign. An inflation-adjusted PAC contribution of $34,000 would have financed *4 percent of the average House reelection campaign in 1996.*

Four percent.

As we said earlier in the book, a lawmaker who wants to be bought will be bought. It doesn't matter what the laws are. But the good-government advocates argue tirelessly that today's money chase vastly increases the likelihood that votes will be bought or access sold.

False.

As we've shown, the relative value of legal contributions now is much, much smaller than it was in the days just after the 1974 laws were codified. After all, wouldn't you be more concerned about what influence a PAC could wield in 1976 when its legal contribution covered *13 percent* of a lawmaker's reelection budget, versus the *1.25 percent* it covered in the 1996 election?

Which proves our larger point about money and politics: they are inseparable and always will be. Now, it's clear that politicians have to spend much more time raising money than in 1976. Many politicians complain that they spend more time raising money than they spend discussing legislation or studying the issues. A fair point. But time spent raising money does not equal time spent *being corrupted by money.*

Now, you may be asking yourself, how come these guys are making arguments in defense of money in politics?

In our introduction we pointed out that astute politicians do not speak unpopular truths; they are far more comfortable spouting popular lies. So it is with money and politics. The public believes there's too much money in politics and that its influence is corrupting. Consequently, politicians don't even try to argue the point; most simply shrug their shoulders. But others summon what appears to be righteous indignation about the current system, denouncing the corrupting influence of money with rhetorical flourishes on a par with those of this century's last great reformer, William Jennings Bryan.

Clearly many politicians are annoyed at how much time they have to spend raising money.

"Today, a Senate candidate in California can expect to have to raise up to $10,000 per day, including Saturday and Sunday, 365 days a year, for six full years," Senator Barbara Boxer said on March 18, 1997, as the Senate debated a constitutional amendment to limit campaign spending. "That is too much time away from work, too much time away from doing the kinds of things that we want to do here, making life better for people."

Mrs. Boxer is running for reelection this year. She and other in-

cumbents regularly lament how much time they have to spend protecting their seats in Congress. Yet they obviously believe their candidacies,
their ideas, and their service are important to their states. They would
not run again otherwise; thus they must believe it is important for
PACs and individuals to contribute to their campaigns. So it's not the
fund-raising Boxer and others oppose nearly so much as the *amount* of
fund-raising they have to do.

That is why so many politicians support reducing the cost of campaigns by setting legal limits on how much candidates can spend seeking public office. Tim Penny was among their number while he served
in Congress. Perhaps Boxer and those who share this view in Congress
look back on the post-Watergate era as a wonderful time for incumbents, a time when campaign costs were lower, the value of PAC contributions was higher, and the rigors of fund-raising were less taxing.
She and thirty-seven other senators in 1997 actually voted for a constitutional amendment to place limits on the cost of campaigns. Costly
campaigns force incumbents to raise money and also open up the possibility that a challenger can raise more money than they do, which, as
we've seen, can be a factor in the outcomes of their races.

So incumbents who argue for less-expensive campaigns are asking
society to place a higher value on incumbency than on the free flow of
ideas in an election. There is no other conclusion to draw. Incumbents
are always using the tools of incumbency to prove their worth to voters. In any race for federal office, challengers have a comparative disadvantage raising money. They have less access to PAC contributions,
to begin with. PACs understandably give more to lawmakers than to
challengers. PACs are in business to protect the interest of their members or their industry, and that typically means funneling money to
powerful incumbents. (More on that later.)

But first, it's important to stress that incumbents have the inside
track on PAC contributions—a structural flaw that would be horribly
compounded by limits on the amount a challenger could spend to defeat an incumbent. Incumbents will always reach this fund-raising
threshold faster than challengers, giving them more time to use the
powers of incumbency unavailable to challengers. Spending limits
make it doubly difficult for challengers to defeat incumbents.

We have devoted a lot of space in this chapter to developing the
practical arguments against spending limits, and to breaking down the
widespread myth that monied interests exert undue influence over
American politics. But the debate over money and politics will rage in

this country long after this book is published, and our efforts to articulate a new point of view would not be complete without an examination of what the Constitution says about the value of political speech.

When the Democratically controlled Congress rewrote America's campaign laws after Watergate, it had three goals: to reduce the costs of campaigns, to reduce the influence of monied interests, and to enhance public confidence in government. We would argue that these goals are mutually exclusive. If you reduce the cost of campaigns, you increase the potential influence of special interests, as we have shown. Lowering the cost of campaigns also places the nation decidedly on the side of incumbents—which hardly seems like a way to improve confidence in government.

We've been down this road before; it didn't work then, and it won't work now. The original 1974 law imposed limits on contributions from individuals, including the candidates themselves, and from PACs. It established spending limits for House and Senate races and provided public financing for presidential elections, with the stipulation that candidates forswear use of private contributions to aid their campaigns.

Several groups filed suit against this law, on the grounds that imposing limits on contributions and expenditures violated the First Amendment's protection of free speech and deprived the citizenry of a thorough airing of competing ideas in all federal campaigns. Among those involved in the lawsuit were the American Civil Liberties Union, the American Conservative Union, and Democratic Senator Eugene McCarthy (who knew firsthand the value of unlimited political contributions, as we'll see in a moment).

The Supreme Court ruled in 1976 in *Buckley v. Valeo*. What it had to say about free speech and the role of money in politics is essential to appreciating what's at stake when the nation debates the financing of political campaigns, its never-ending pursuit of a freewheeling exchange of ideas, and its goal of creating a better-informed citizenry.

The Court upheld the contribution limits and public financing of presidential campaigns, but it flatly rejected all attempts to limit the amount of money candidates spend on campaigns. It also rejected any limits on what individuals could spend on their own campaigns.

The Court was blunt and emphatic when it ruled unconstitutional any attempts to limit spending on federal campaigns.

A restriction on the amount of money a person or group can spend on political communication during a campaign necessarily reduces the quantity of expression by restricting the number of issues discussed, the depth of their exploration, and the size of the audience reached. This is because virtually every means of communicating ideas in today's mass society requires the expenditure of money.

The distribution of the humblest handbill or leaflet entails printing, paper, and circulation costs. Speeches and rallies generally necessitate hiring a hall and publicizing the event. The electorate's increasing dependence on television, radio, and other mass media for news and information has made these expensive modes of communication indispensable instruments of effective political speech.

The expenditure limitations contained in the Act represent substantial rather than merely theoretical restraints on the quantity and diversity of political speech.

It's impossible to overstate the Court's declaration that spending limits inhibit free speech. As the Court said in its preamble, federal campaign spending limits would not only inhibit free speech, they would hobble a process that is "integral to the operation of the system of government established by our Constitution."

The Court cited precedent in no fewer than seven First Amendment cases in deciding the case. The law is clear on this point: limiting the amount spent on political campaigns violates the First Amendment. Politicians who propose laws to limit campaign spending, regardless of how sincerely they believe this will strengthen democracy, must explain how America profits from laws that reduce First Amendment rights and inhibit an individual's right to express political opinions freely and without government interference.

The Court stated:

Given the important role of contributions in financing political campaigns, contribution restrictions could have a severe impact on political dialogue if the limitations prevented candidates and political committees from amassing the resources necessary for effective advocacy. . . . Making a contribution, like joining a political party, serves to affiliate a person with a candidate. In addition, it enables like-minded persons to pool their resources in furtherance of common political goals.

The Act's contribution ceilings thus limit one important means of associating with a candidate or committee, but leave the contributor free to become a member of any political association and to assist personally in the association's efforts on behalf of candidates.

In other words, the Court said the only reason contributions of individuals were constitutionally defensible was *that individuals were free to join PACs.* The Court accepted and amplified the presumed ethical and legal superiority of PACs by preserving the $5,000 limit compared to the $1,000 limit on individual contributions.

The Court seemed to be saying: PACs serve the public good.

Last, it's important to study what the Court said about attempts to limit the amount an individual can spend on his or her own campaign. The 1974 law set a ceiling on individual expenditures as follows: $50,000 for a presidential and vice presidential campaign, $25,000 for a senatorial campaign, and $15,000 for a House campaign. The Court summarily rejected these limitations, arguing they served no rational government purpose and trampled a candidate's First Amendment rights.

The candidate, no less than any other person, has a right to engage in the discussion of public issues and vigorously and tirelessly to advocate his own election and the election of other candidates. Indeed, it is of particular importance that candidates have the unfettered opportunity to make their views known so that the electorate may intelligently evaluate the candidates' personal qualities and their positions on vital public issues before choosing among them.

The [law's] ceiling on personal expenditures by a candidate in furtherance of his own candidacy thus clearly and directly interferes with constitutionally protected freedoms.

The 1974 law also tried to limit the amount outside groups could spend on advertisements addressing issues related to an upcoming federal election—ads known as "independent expenditures." (An example would be an advertisement paid for by pro-choice citizens highlighting a congressman's vote to limit abortion rights.) So long as such an advertisement does not specifically call for the election of another candidate or the defeat of the incumbent, it is legal. Politicians hate independent-expenditure advertising because it usually forces them to discuss issues they would just as soon avoid. Granted, political commercials funded through independent expenditures can quite often be distracting or, worse, destructively negative. But do we really want to subject all political speech to a government-sponsored filtration process that strives for such nebulous criteria as "balance" and "positive tone"? Political speech should flow freely, even if that means political speeches, commercials, handbills, or other communications that are inflammatory or negative. One of the burdens of citizenship is for voters to separate truth from hyperbole during a political campaign. Coauthor Penny has devoted much of his time in 1996 and again in 1998 to promote clean campaigns by increasing civic involvement, not by proposing legislation placing restrictions on campaign content.

Independent expenditures attracted a lot of attention in the 1996 campaign because politicians were furious that outside groups (such as labor unions, corporations, and think tanks) were pouring money into advertisements that discussed their votes in Congress. Imagine that! Citizens paying for radio and television spots that shined a light on a lawmaker's record in Congress. How dare they?

But the high court held that independent-expenditure advertising was vital to a full airing of issues important to the public. The Court said:

> While the independent expenditure ceiling thus fails to serve any substantial governmental interest in stemming the reality or appearance of corruption in the electoral process, it heavily burdens core First Amendment expression. For the First Amendment right to "speak one's mind . . . on all public institutions" includes the right to engage in "vigorous advocacy" no less than "abstract discussion."

Here the Court is quoting heavily from the landmark *New York Times v. Sullivan* case. This case allowed publication of the Pentagon Papers (the Defense Department's secret assessment of the government's flawed strategy to win the Vietnam War). The Court also said:

> Advocacy of the election or defeat of candidates for federal office is no less entitled to protection under the First Amendment

than the discussion of political policy generally or advocacy of the passage or defeat of legislation. It is argued, however, that the ancillary governmental interest in equalizing the relative ability of individuals and groups to influence the outcome of elections serves to justify the limitation on express advocacy of the election or defeat of candidates imposed by [the law].

But the concept that government may restrict the speech of some elements of our society in order to enhance the relative voice of others is wholly foreign to the First Amendment, which was designed to "secure the widest possible dissemination of information from diverse and antagonistic sources," and "to assure unfettered interchange of ideas for the bringing about of political and social changes desired by the people."

Here the Court is again quoting from *New York Times v. Sullivan.* (Emphasis added.)

To summarize, the Court said emphatically that the Constitution forbids spending limits on campaigns and limits on what an individual can spend on his or her own race. The Court allowed contribution limits because, it said, they helped minimize the appearance of possible corruption and through the creation of PACs gave individuals an alternate venue to make political contributions.

So any future proposal that seeks to limit campaign spending or prevent individuals from spending as much as they wish on campaigns should similarly be found unconstitutional. The same should be true of laws that seek to limit the amount individuals or groups can spend on advertisements related to pressing issues in a federal campaign. All of this spending is emphatically protected by the First Amendment. There is no gray area.

There are more than seventy pieces of legislation floating around Congress intended to reform the campaign-financing system. Nearly all violate the constitutional protections of free speech outlined in the high court's 1976 ruling. That's because nearly all tinker with the existing assumptions about money and politics. Some set lower contribution limits; some try to impose spending limits; others try to limit what outside groups can spend to publicize issues relevant to an approaching election. Still others try to eliminate PAC contributions.

As mentioned before, a constitutional amendment debated in 1997 would allow Congress and state legislatures to "adopt reasonable regulations of funds expended, including contributions, to influence the outcome of elections provided that such regulations do not impair the right of the public to a full and free discussion of all issues." Even if you agree with the concept of limited campaign spending, the long-range implications of this amendment should frighten you.

One piece of campaign-reform legislation before the 105th Congress that does not violate First Amendment standards set by the Supreme Court calls for a radical change in financing federal campaigns.

Like most radical ideas, this one is very simple.

Authored by California Representative John Doolittle, the bill would lift all contribution limits but require instantaneous disclosure of all contributions. This would include so-called hard contributions, those regulated under existing law, and so-called soft contributions, which are not regulated by existing law.

Under the Doolittle legislation, there would be no limits on what any donor could give. If an individual wanted to give a House candidate $1 million, that would be OK. Ditto a labor union, a corporation, or a PAC. The bill would continue to forbid contributions from foreign nationals. It would also end public financing of presidential campaigns, which would save taxpayers nearly $200 million every four years. All contributions received by political candidates and political committees within ninety days of an election would have to be disclosed to state election officials within twenty-four hours of their receipt. State election officials would then have to transfer information about each contribution to a candidate or a political committee on the Internet within twenty-four hours.

The best innovation in the 1974 laws was the requirement that politicians disclose from whom they raised money. This was also the *only* section of the new law that was not challenged in court.

After Watergate, it became clear to all Americans that voters simply had no idea who was giving what to whom and in what amounts. No one outside of Congress or the presidency had any idea how much money was flowing into the political system or where it was coming from.

The politicians knew, of course. Their reaction to this element of the law is most instructive when considering what the political class thought was most threatening to it. Most politicians were more than willing to live with spending limits and found little to quibble with over contribution limits (only 5 percent of all donations in 1974 exceeded $1,000 anyway).

What politicians *did* resent was having to disclose the sources of their contributions. Wilbur Mills, then chairman of the House Ways and Means Committee, which writes all tax laws, so detested disclosure that he resisted releasing his campaign-finance documents until the very last day. When reporters arrived to inspect the documents, Mills said they would have to pay him $1 in cash per page to cover his copying costs. The Federal Election Commission (FEC), created to enforce the 1974 laws, overruled the powerful chairman and forced him to make the documents available at no cost.

Kent Cooper, who is now the executive director of Citizens for Responsive Politics, well remembers Mills's antagonism. Back then, Cooper was helping to enforce the new campaign laws at the FEC. He left the FEC in 1996 to lead Citizens for Responsive Politics.

After more than twenty years of examining the effects of the 1974 laws, Cooper has concluded that only one part of the law worked as the reformers imagined: disclosure.

Contribution limits did not reduce the cost of campaigns. Creating PACs did not diminish the perceived influence of special-interest groups. But disclosure did give the public and the press tangible evidence of the role money played in politics. We regret that so many in the media have drawn hysterical and utterly unfounded conclusions about money and politics, but we're delighted that the debate has been joined. It would not have been without disclosure.

As we've said, we'd like to take disclosure even farther.

In 1974 there was no practical way to disclose campaign contributions quickly. The flow of paper from a congressional campaign committee to the FEC was slow. The processing of the information at the FEC was even slower due to the agency's small budget and staff. As a result, information on campaign contributions was released every quarter in election years. The most-revealing details about contributions, such as those that arrived in the last three weeks of a campaign, were not released until after the election. Consequently, the public knew less than it needed to know about the flow of money to a candidate until *after* it had cast its vote. For years, the limitations of the FEC staff and technology made swift disclosure an unreachable goal.

That's no longer true.

Thanks to the power of computers, candidates should now be able to report contributions instantaneously to the FEC. The FEC could move with equal speed to post them on Web sites on the Internet that would be available to any citizen with a computer and at every public library in the nation. This rapid-fire disclosure would, of course, be available to all reporters covering politics in Washington. More important, the information would be available to reporters covering politics in any senator's home state or the district of any congressman. As it is now, local reporters have quite a difficult time accessing FEC files and obtaining information about the lawmakers and candidates they cover. And even Washington-based reporters have a hard time plowing through all of the FEC documents on campaign contributions. The agency has never had the budget necessary to create databases that are easily searchable and capable of processing cross-referencing requests to follow, for example, the trail of one big contributor or one particularly active PAC.

If the law required full and instantaneous disclosure, we are willing to bet the marketplace would quickly respond with computer software that would catalogue, cross-reference, and track campaign donations with the same precision and accuracy that Turbo-Tax and its cousins have brought to the United States tax code.

In such a world, curious voters and investigative reporters would know instantly who gave what to whom. Evidence of foreign contributions to the Democratic National Committee in the 1996 election would have surfaced *before the election, when voters could have processed the information before deciding whom to vote for.* Learning of this money after the fact doesn't stir the public's anger, because voters know it's too late to do anything about it.

But before the election? Talk about a deterrent.

The no-limits-full-disclosure system is based on the core assumption of this chapter: *there simply are not enough fat cats in American politics.* By "fat cats," we mean big donors who give to politicians because *they want them to win and are willing to donate lots of money to help make that happen.*

That's the way politics worked in America for all the years leading up to Watergate. The problem wasn't the presence of big donations, but the fact that the public didn't know anything about them. When the public learned that a powerful industrialist gave $100,000 to Nixon's reelection campaign, it was as if a meteor landed on the Ellipse. Who knew so much money could come from one person? And to the president of the United States? It was a scandal all by itself. Why? Because until then, the public had no idea how much politicians needed and how much certain contributors were willing to give. In White House tapes from the Nixon years released in 1997, it was learned that Nixon demanded sums of up to $250,000 for those petitioning his administration for ambassadorships. It was also revealed that Nixon sought more than $1 million from three dairy groups in exchange for granting them price controls. Under a system of predisclosure it would be much more difficult for politicians to apply such pressure to potential donors—and much easier for an aggressive media to spot problems *before* the next election.

Now we can know. As Voltaire observed, "Knowledge is power."

Voters should have the knowledge of who gives the most money to politicians. But contributors should have the right to give as much as they want. Disclosure can protect the public against undue influence by giving voters the chance to confront a candidate about the size of his contributions before the election. If they are dissatisfied with the answers, they can vote against the candidate. It's that simple. If a contribution leads to a political favor, a crime has been committed and the corrupt politician will be prosecuted. Again, it's that simple.

"It would be interesting to look at," Kent Cooper says. "I would not toss it out as an option. Disclosure has worked well."

What else would be gained by such a system?

Well, first we would diminish the advantage incumbents have in raising money from PACs. PACs were created as a way to reform campaign financing. Their contributions were given higher legal status than those coming from individuals. And we've also learned that PACs represent the will of one constituency and, as such, tend to favor incumbents over challengers.

Lifting the limits on individual contributions would give challengers more leverage in raising money from sympathetic individuals. Individuals now are limited to donations of $2,000 per election (ten thousand for the primary and general election). Freeing individuals to give as much as they wish would allow challengers to tap sources outside of PACs. Under a "no-limits" system, individuals and PACs might be accused of trying to "buy" a politician, but that's exactly the point: There would be plenty of publicity about each and every large contribution. If a candidate cannot explain why he or she accepted a contribution, then he or she will have to deal with the voters' wrath on Election Day.

Think of what a campaign might look like under these circumstances: A senator from Louisiana decides to accept only three donations for his reelection campaign: $2 million each from Exxon, Standard Oil, and Shell. His rationale is that these oil companies employ vast numbers of Louisiana voters; he was going to fight for their interests in Washington anyway, so he might as well accept their generous contributions and ignore the forty thousand other Washington-based PACs. The senator could tell the voters that these contributions will allow him to view all other national issues with a completely open mind.

He or she could make that argument. His or her opponent might call the contributions obscene and an abrogation of a senator's obligation to view all issues from a national perspective, despite the economic needs of a powerful home-state industry. The challenger might also try to attract big contributions from outside donors who dislike big oil's influence over national energy policy. He or she might attract several contributions of $1 million from wealthy environmentalists. He or she might also solicit very small contributions from voters across the country infuriated by big oil's attempt to "buy a seat in the Senate." This challenger could similarly appeal to voters whose jobs are not tied to the oil industry, seeking only their votes to counteract the power of "big oil."

This scenario could play out in hundreds of ways. The most-important fact is that every single step in the process would be conducted in public. Voters would see the money up front and evaluate the candidate's rationale for accepting it. After that discussion, they would cast their vote, *fully informed of their candidate's fund-raising tactics.*

Here's another benefit of a wide-open financing system. It offers the possibility of sparing the nation from millionaires who want to run for president or Congress. We have nothing against wealthy people running for office, but we suspect that at least two who've recently run for president might have been better off giving their money to others more adept at the political arts.

Who knows whether Ross Perot's policies might have carried the election in 1992 or 1996 if he could have passed along his millions and his message to another candidate. Might a candidate with Perot's ideas but not his, er, *eccentricities* have made a better showing? It's hard to say. Perot was lightning in a bottle in 1992—a rarity who captured the hearts of millions of Americans. But Perot was never going to be president. His conduct proved that. How much different the campaign of 1992 would have been if a candidate with Perot's message and his millions had stayed the course. Now, it's quite possible that Perot would have become the issue anyway, since he was bankrolling the campaign in the first place. We say, "So what?" We all would have been party to that debate. No harm there.

Perot clearly did not want to run in 1996. Suppose he had given his millions to another candidate—someone like former New Jersey Senator Bill Bradley, or former Connecticut Governor Lowell Weicker? Both would have brought an entirely different message to an otherwise boring presidential campaign.

Ditto Steve Forbes. He wanted to give the millions he spent on his campaign to Jack Kemp. But he couldn't. He wanted his progrowth, supply-side economic message debated during the campaign, so he did the only thing the law would allow—he ran himself. Why shouldn't Forbes or anyone else with wealth give to a candidate willing to articulate a message they believe is vital for the nation to hear? As long as everyone knows about the source of the money, who would be harmed? No one. And the range of debate in presidential and congressional elections would open up dramatically.

How do we know?

Well, we can make an educated guess based on the story of the 1968 presidential campaign.

Senator Eugene McCarthy ran against President Lyndon Johnson in 1968's New Hampshire primary, assailing his prosecution of the war in Vietnam. McCarthy had almost no money to run a campaign and was desperately trying to force the issue of Vietnam into the debate over the Democratic nomination for president. It was assumed that Johnson would run again and win the party nomination; early in 1968 there was no other credible challenger but McCarthy. But the antiwar senator had no money and little means to raise it. Sure, he got by with small contributions from college students opposed to the war. But that wasn't enough to mount a serious effort in the New Hampshire primary, the first primary in the nation and the one in which McCarthy decided to take a stand.

McCarthy got the help he needed from two wealthy Americans: Stuart Mott and Jack Dreyfus Jr. Mott gave McCarthy about $210,000, and Dreyfus, a Wall Street banker, gave as much as $500,000. These donations gave McCarthy more than enough resources to challenge Johnson in New Hampshire and force his continuation of the war to the forefront.

With the help of these two wealthy donors, McCarthy won 42 percent of the vote (to 49 percent for Johnson, a stunning repudiation of

Johnson's continuation of the war). Shaken by the narrowness of his victory, Johnson announced one month later, on March 31, that he would not seek or accept nomination as president.

The candidacy of Eugene McCarthy, propelled by two wealthy donors, changed the direction of the American presidency, the direction of the American war effort in Vietnam, and the entire course of American history—all due to the contributions of a couple of fat cats nobody in America knew anything about.

Under current law, the donations to McCarthy would have been illegal. That's why McCarthy joined in the lawsuit that reached the Supreme Court and resulted in the *Buckley v. Valeo* repudiation of limits on political contributions. Later, Mott complained in the book *Independent Fundraising for an Independent Candidate* that the new laws forbade him from bankrolling John Anderson's independent presidential candidacy in 1980, just as he had helped bankroll McCarthy's 1968 campaign.

Think about it.

THE EIGHTH LIE

◆

THE BUDGET WILL BE BALANCED
BY THE YEAR 2002

O F ALL THE lies that will be told this election year, none will be told more frequently than this one.

Republicans will tell it. Democrats will tell it. The media will tell it. But don't believe it.

Depending on the performance of the national economy—not anything Congress or Clinton did or will do—the federal government this year will generate the first surplus since 1969. On the basis of the brittle nature of the so-called balanced-budget law's economic assumptions and its reliance on unidentified spending cuts in the years 2001 and 2002, it's evident to us that this year's budget numbers might be as good as we're going to see for some time.

If the economy dips into a mild recession, the deficits will increase dramatically. It will soon become clear to this nation that Congress and Clinton missed a once-in-a-lifetime opportunity to draft new policies that would have made deficits far less likely in the future. Instead, they passed a law that marginally reduces deficits now, makes them quite likely to surge again in the near future, and guarantees terrifying and potentially catastrophic deficits early in the twenty-first century.

But you'd never know it judging by what Congress and Clinton said about their balanced-budget law as it was passed and signed into law last summer. "We have put America's fiscal house in order again," Clinton said at a July 29 ceremony on the South Lawn of the White House to celebrate his signing of the law. He described it as "an historic agreement that will benefit generations of Americans."

"We are eliminating the deficit while investing more in our future and cutting taxes for the middle class," said Vice President Gore, eager to associate himself with the balanced-budget chic Clinton wisely brought to the Democratic Party after Republicans won control of Congress in 1994.

For their part, Republicans were equally enthusiastic and hyperbolic. "Today we celebrate the beginning of a new era of freedom," said Majority Leader Trent Lott of Mississippi, one of the Republicans who gathered on the Capitol steps on July 29 to pat themselves on the back. The new law, he said, would "lead us to less Washington spending, to tax relief for working Americans, to security for our senior citizens and less dependency on government."

So proud of themselves were Congress and Clinton that they orchestrated three separate made-for-television celebrations to laud their "historic" achievement. On August 5, congressional leaders and Clinton gathered at the White House for another ceremony marking the signing of the balanced-budget law. Congress and Clinton had celebrated the new law separately a week earlier; now they stood together, praising each other effusively and cooing over the triumph of bipartisanship. "I believe," Clinton said, "that together we have fulfilled the responsibility of our generation to take America into a new century where there is opportunity for all who are responsible to work for it, where we have a chance to come together across all of our differences as a great American community. We can say with pride and certainty that those who saw the sun setting on America were wrong. The sun is rising on America again."

Speaker Newt Gingrich, beaming in the atmosphere of choreographed self-congratulation, said the law proved "that the American constitutional system works, that slowly, over time, we listened to the will of the American people, that we reached beyond parties." Gingrich said he hoped the new law would lead to deeper bipartisan cooperation so that congress and Clinton could achieve "progress at home" and "leadership across the planet."

Did we miss something?

The ceremonies celebrating the so-called balanced-budget law are case studies in political hyperbole. There are three rules of thumb about public ceremonies celebrating new budget legislation. Number One: When the rhetoric is lofty, the accomplishment is probably puny. Number Two: If Republicans and Democrats are there and everyone is *smiling*, it's because everyone got what he or she wanted.

Number Three: If everyone got what he or she wanted, the nation's in trouble.

You see, new budget laws that actually cut spending or raise taxes are inherently unpopular. Such deals were cobbled together and passed in 1990 under President Bush and in 1993 under Clinton. The ceremonies marking the announcement of these laws had all the frivolity and high spirits of a police lineup. There was no signing ceremony for the 1990 budget law that included tax increases Bush promised he would never impose; Bush signed the bill privately. (And let history note: supposed budget-balancer Newt Gingrich voted against both the 1990 and the 1993 bills.)

Neither one of us was very impressed with the 1990 and 1993 budget laws. We felt both failed to reduce spending adequately on discretionary programs Congress funds every year, and on entitlements such as Social Security and Medicare. But we do applaud these laws because they required *some* sacrifice—and did, in fact, reduce federal deficits. We also remember how hard it was for Congress to approve these new budget laws. A Democratically controlled Congress rejected the first version of the 1990 budget law because its spending cuts were too steep and its tax hikes too high (considerations that united liberal Democrats and conservative Republicans). The second version had much-lower spending cuts and the same tax increases. Liberal Democrats got on board, and Congress passed this version after the nation endured a four-day government shutdown. The 1993 budget law passed by one vote in the House (Tim's included) and one vote in the Senate. Not one Republican voted for it.

The 1990 and 1993 budget laws passed by narrow margins, divided the parties, antagonized special-interest groups, and cost Presidents Bush and Clinton precious political support.

In stark contrast, the 1997 balanced-budget law passed Congress in two phases. The House supported the bill calling for $121 billion in spending cuts over five years by a vote of 346 to 85. The Senate passed it by a vote of 85 to 15. The bill providing $96 billion in tax cuts over five years passed the House by a vote of 389 to 43. The Senate approved it by a vote of 92 to 8.

The 1997 law prevailed with huge bipartisan margins, antagonized no special-interest groups, and bolstered the standing of Congress and Clinton. Congress and Clinton threw their parties, and America watched with barely any sense of what was really going on.

As someone famous and brilliant once said, the past is prologue.

That is definitely true with this balanced-budget law. Just as they did last summer, congressional Republicans and Democrats have agreed this election season to *say the same things about the budget.* The have all agreed to tell you that it will be balanced—that America's long and tortuous struggle with the deficit dragon is over, thanks to the diligence and hard work of your elected leaders in Washington.

Congressional Republicans love this pro-incumbent strategy. They hope the sonorous, optimistic sounds of their campaign commercials will tranquilize all anxiety about the budget, the deficit, and the national debt. They want you upbeat and confident about the nation's balance sheet, and they want you to reward Republicans by trudging to the ballot box and pulling the lever *for them* on Election Day. Over and over again you will hear this Republican proclamation: Republicans balanced the budget, Republicans cut taxes, Republicans kept their promises. Reelect the Republican Congress!

As sloganeering goes, it's pretty good. And it will be very enticing to believe. That's because no one will actively disagree. Clinton will nod approvingly, in the belief that progress achieved in reducing deficits and moving the nation toward a balanced budget will go far in cementing his legacy as a top-flight president. Democrats running for reelection in the House and Senate will also campaign on having balanced the budget. Most of them voted for the deal, and even those who didn't are unlikely to spoil all the other politicians' fun by pointing out the rude truth that the budget won't, in fact, be balanced in 2002.

So everyone will be saying more or less the same thing . . . and everyone will be lying. Here's why.

The fact is, in their efforts to achieve a balanced budget, Congress and Clinton have agreed to some very dubious assumptions about the future of the United States economy and their own ability to cut spending at a later date. Both of us are battle-scarred veterans of the federal budget process. Tim wrestled with deficits on the floor of the House, and Major covered the budget battles of 1990, 1993, and 1995. We've learned through experience that long-term assumptions about the direction of the economy are fanciful—and assumptions about Washington's willingness to cut spending in the future are worthless.

In reality, the prospect of a balanced budget in 2002 is nothing more than a dream. Congress and Clinton are dreaming of an America where no recessions ever occur and where legislators and the White

House summon the courage to cut government spending in ways they never have before. Congress and Clinton did *nothing* in the deal to fundamentally alter the size, scope, or intrusiveness of the federal government.

Now, there are a lot of variables in budgeting and projecting economic growth, but there is one immutable truth about any multiyear budget deal written in Washington: the first year is the only one that matters. That's because things change from year to year and Congress and the president can adapt next year's budget laws to these changes. When evaluating what Congress and Clinton actually did in their "balanced budget," it's most important to understand what they did in year number one.

In the first year, the balanced-budget law actually increases government spending by tens of billions of dollars. The logic has a Vietnam-like quality to it. In order to decrease the deficit, Congress and Clinton had to increase spending.

This spending is of the utmost importance, because the balanced-budget law requires Congress to reduce government spending dramatically in the years 2001 and 2002. How willing do you believe Congress is going to be in 2001 and 2002 to tell voters—the ones they seduced in 1998 with higher federal spending and tax cuts—that now it's time to cut spending if you all still want the budget to stay balanced?

We all know the answer: it's not going to happen.

If the 1997 budget didn't produce this year's surplus, what did? Two things: declining defense spending and an expanding economy. Defense spending has declined every year since 1985, when it accounted for more than 6 percent of the national economic output. This year (1998) it will account for barely 3 percent of national economic output. If America's superpower status is to be maintained, defense spending cannot decline much more. Federal Reserve Chairman Alan Greenspan, in testimony on October 8, 1997 before the House Budget Committee, placed the peace dividend America has reaped since the end of the Cold War in proper context:

> Much of the fiscal improvement of recent years is much less the result of a return to the prudent attitudes and actions of earlier generations, than the emergence of benevolent forces largely external to the fiscal process. The end of the Cold War has

yielded a substantial peace dividend, and the best economic performance in decades has augmented tax revenues far beyond expectations while restraining (recession-induced) outlays.

The payout of the peace dividend is coming to an end. Further cuts may be difficult to achieve, for even if we are fortunate enough to enjoy a relatively tranquil world, spending will tend to be buoyed by the need to replace technologically obsolescent equipment, as well as by the usual political pressures.

But this is only part of the story.

The truly fascinating tale is how Congress and Clinton found their way so easily to a "balanced budget" without significantly cutting spending or making any politically painful decisions about Social Security and Medicare. In fact, Congress and Clinton found a way to create a "balanced budget" by *increasing* welfare spending and transportation funding.

In the spring of 1997 Congress and Clinton were girding for battle over the budget. Both sides had already reached an informal agreement that the government would not shut down again, but animosity and mistrust were the concierge and butler for all of their formal White House talks about the budget.

Neither side had any idea about how to get what it wanted. Congress wanted lower taxes—specifically a $500-per-child tax credit and lower estate and capital gains taxes. Clinton wanted more spending for education and for environmental cleanup, and tax breaks for college tuition. At the time, the Congressional Budget Office, Congress's budgetary scorekeeper, was projecting a 1997 deficit of $115 billion. The 1998 deficit was projected to be $122 billion, and deficits were projected to rise steadily for the next decade, topping out at $278 billion in 2007. With projected deficits that high, it didn't seem plausible to objective observers that Congress and Clinton could get all the things they wanted—higher spending and a variety of tax cuts—and still balance the budget early in the twenty-first century.

And then something was found.

Late one night in April, economists at the Congressional Budget Office began recalculating receipts of tax revenue generated by the surprisingly robust and resilient United States economy. In 1997 alone, the government collected $71 billion in unexpected tax revenue—a whopping figure that allowed the Congressional Budget Office to revise downward its 1997 deficit projection from $115 billion to $34 billion (helped along by the fact that Congress actually spent $10 billion less than expected).

The astonishing performance of the economy led these and other government economists to revise their long-term projections for national economic growth. The Budget Office economists began projecting stable, long-term growth for the next five years, growth only slightly less robust than in the previous five years.

Just as the economic growth of 1997 produced an unexpected burst of tax revenue, these long-term projections produced even more tax revenue.

How much?

More than $225 billion over five years.

This torrent of projected tax revenue suddenly made balancing the budget much, much easier. Congress and Clinton could do it without significant cuts in any federal programs and by providing modest tax cuts. As it turned out, these optimistic revenue projections provided enough money to pay for even more generous benefits to those on welfare and recent immigrants.

We respect the Congressional Budget Office economists. They could be correct about the future growth of the economy. If they are, then the government might collect all the revenue in its projections. Under these conditions, Congress would be in position to maintain a balanced budget *if it made dozens of billions in spending cuts early in the twenty-first century.*

As much as we respect the Budget Office, though, we must observe that Congress and Clinton basically found an extra $225 billion in the bottom of the nation's economic sock drawer and used it to make all the numbers add up in their balanced-budget program. Upon making the discovery, Congress and Clinton conveniently forgot all about their familiar old rhetoric calling for a streamlined government and joint sacrifice on behalf of future generations.

This entire process does a disservice to the American taxpayer. Congress and Clinton did not create a balanced-budget law by doing anything to change the fundamental spending habits of the federal government. They made no hard choices. They denied nothing to anyone. This is no way to balance the budget. On the basis of our long experience with economic and budget projections, we have absolutely no confidence that American taxpayers will ever see the dreamlike world Congress and Clinton imagined last spring and summer when they concocted this plan.

The Congressional Budget Office itself is dubious. In its September 1997 report to Congress about the outlook for the federal budget and the United States economy, it offers these cautionary words on the first page of its introduction.

> Setting the budget on a course to balance is a significant achievement. Still, some words of caution are required.
>
> First, the economic and other assumptions on which the budget projections are based could prove to be too optimistic. Just as favorable economic developments have caused the deficit outlook to improve rapidly in recent months, unfavorable developments could similarly cause a quick deterioration. In particular, the onset of a recession could push the deficit above current projections by $100 billion or more for several years.
>
> Second, achieving budgetary balance in 2002 depends on adhering to new statutory limits on discretionary spending, which are quite restrictive after 2000. Discretionary spending has been squeezed since 1991, and it may be difficult for Congress and the President to make the further real (inflation-adjusted) reductions required to live within the limits set by the new [spending] caps. In short, the tough decisions on appropriated spending have yet to be made.

To expand upon the CBO's message: The five-year budget deal contains economic projections that do not account for the possibility of a recession. For those of you who have forgotten the technical definition of a recession (it's been so long since we've seen one we actually had to look it up), it is two consecutive quarters of negative economic growth as measured by the gross domestic product. The current economic expansion began in the third quarter of 1991 and is now in its seventh year. For the budget projections to hold, the economy must avoid a recession for another four years. That would make this cycle of economic growth the longest in American history. We're not guaranteeing it will not happen. We're not saying it cannot happen. We *are* saying it is very unlikely.

One mild recession and the budget's out of balance.

Why?

Because the new budget's revenue projections are built upon a foundation of continued economic growth. Since Congress and Clinton delayed what few spending cuts are in the balanced-budget law until the years 2001 and 2002, there will be no budgetary cushion should the economy slide into recession.

To be fair to the Congressional Budget Office, it has not drawn up wild-eyed projections of economic growth; in fact, they are conservative. The office projects economic growth of 2.1 percent on an annual basis from 1988 to 2002. The office's projections for this year (1998) are not dramatically different from those of the Federal Reserve Board or the fifty leading private economic forecasters who produce the Blue Chip Economic Indicators report. But neither the Budget Office nor the Federal Reserve Bank nor the Blue Chip Economic Indicators produce hard economic projections for more than one year. Economic instability being what it is, none of these groups feel confident about long-term economic prognostications they know will be used by legislators, world financial institutions, or private investors.

Economic projections are a huge part of the balanced-budget law. If they come true, that still will not guarantee a balanced budget by 2002. Why? Because Congress and the president will have to agree to deep discretionary spending cuts in 2001 and 2002 to meet the law's savings targets. Discretionary spending is what Congress and the president agree to spend each year on all sorts of government functions, chief among them defense. In 1997 discretionary spending was about $550 billion. It routinely accounts for one-third of the annual federal budget, which in 1997 totaled $1.6 trillion. Of the $550 billion in discretionary spending, about $271 billion went to the Pentagon. The rest paid for federal education programs, environmental protection, law enforcement, space exploration, health research, conservation, and the building of roads, bridges, and mass-transit systems. As the Congressional Budget Office said, this spending has been squeezed since 1991. It hasn't been cut significantly (except for the Pentagon), but it hasn't grown much either.

The 1997 balanced-budget law set spending limits, or caps, on discretionary spending for each year from 1998 to 2002. Congress must adhere to those caps or violate the law. If Congress needs to spend more than the spending caps call for, though, it can simply change the law (something that has happened many times before). These spending caps are tightest in the years 2001 and 2002. The law now calls for

Congress to reduce discretionary spending by $14 billion between this year (1998) and in 2000. Then it calls on Congress to cut spending by $16 billion in 2001, and $22 billion in 2002. In other words, 71 percent of the spending cuts required to keep a balanced budget are delayed until the final two years of the five-year deal.

Entitlements: these include but are not limited to Social Security, Medicare, Medicaid, and food stamps. In 1997 the nation spent $902 billion on all entitlement programs. Of this amount, $362 billion was for Social Security, $209 billion for Medicare, $96 billion for Medicaid, and $23 billion for food stamps. These programs are governed by eligibility requirements, and all Americans who qualify receive benefits. Congress does not have to approve the amounts paid out in benefits each year. Entitlement spending is often thought of as being on automatic pilot. That's because neither Congress nor the president can change the funding levels unless they agree to change the eligibility requirements. In the 1997 balanced-budget law, Congress is required to reduce the rate of growth in entitlement spending by $153 billion. Almost all of these savings are to come by means of lower reimbursements paid through Medicare to doctors and hospitals.

Discretionary and entitlement spending are the two largest components of the nation's budget.

The other big line-item is interest paid on the national debt. In 1997 the national debt exceeded $5.3 trillion. Interest paid on that debt totaled $245 billion, just slightly less than the nation spent on national defense.

In that same October 1997 testimony before the House Budget Committee, Alan Greenspan spoke the following prophetic words about the future of discretionary and entitlement spending:

On the outlay side, the recently enacted budget agreement relies importantly on significant, but as-yet-unspecified, restraints on discretionary spending to be made in the years 2001, 2002, and thereafter. Supporters of each program expect the restraints to fall elsewhere. Inevitably, the eventual publication of detail will expose deep political divisions, which could make realization of the budget projections less likely.

In addition, while the budget agreement included significant cuts in Medicare spending, past experience has shown us how difficult Medicare is to control, raising the possibility that savings will never be realized.

By now, it's clear that the so-called balanced-budget law has plenty of holes in it. The Congressional Budget Office and the Federal Reserve Board chairman fear that the economy will not perform as well as projected. If this happens, deficits will rise. The Budget Office and the Reserve Board chairman also doubt that Congress will find the political courage required to cut spending as much as is required to bring the budget into balance early in the twenty-first century.

We share their apprehension.

But that's not all that's wrong with this "historic" budget law.

Congress and Clinton had a glorious opportunity to address the nation's long-term deficit problems, ones that a peace dividend or a persistently perky economy could help to erase. Congress and Clinton were sitting atop the best-performing economy in decades, one with low unemployment, inflation, and interest rates, one in which prosperity was rampant, one in which sacrifices for future generations could scarcely be easier.

Congress and Clinton were given a golden opportunity to use the prosperity of today to ensure the prosperity of generations to come.

But they didn't.

Congress and Clinton did almost nothing to address this nation's headlong rush to insolvency, driven by Social Security's and Medicare's obligations to the baby-boom generation. As a careful analysis shows, the number of working Americans in the next thirty years will be insufficient to provide enough tax revenue (collected through wage-suppressing, growth-choking payroll taxes) to finance current benefits through Social Security and Medicare. According to the Social Security Administration, in thirty-five years the number of Americans 65 and older will double, while the number of people between ages 20 and 64 will increase by only 20 percent. Do the math: Americans between ages 20 and 64 will increase by only 20 percent. Do the math: Americans between ages 20 and 64 pay the payroll taxes that finance Social Security benefits and Medicare health insurance. It stands to reason that, in a nation with twice as many retirees collecting twice as many benefits as were being paid out in 1995, there will be substantial pressure on working Americans to pay for these benefits.

In 1996 America spent $630 billion on Social Security and Medicare benefits. That amounted to 8.4 percent of the nation's annual economic output. By 2030 the costs of Social Security and Medicare are expected to consume 16 percent of the nation's annual economic output. Sixteen percent! It would be slightly easier to pay for this enormous increase in benefits if the number of workers paying payroll taxes were to keep pace with the number of eligible Social Security and Medicare beneficiaries. But it won't. If changes aren't undertaken now, the nation's work force will face the following drastic choices very early in the next century:

1. Dramatically higher payroll taxes to finance Social Security benefits and Medicare health-insurance reimbursements to baby-boom retirees. The current tax rate of 15.3 percent might have to rise as high as 20 percent or 25 percent.

2. Drastically slashed Social Security benefits and Medicare health-insurance coverage. Monthly Social Security checks would have to be smaller, and annual cost-of-living-adjustments would likely disappear. Medicare insurance coverage would shrink to the point where patients would have to pay for at least half and possibly as much as three-fourths the cost of out-patient care. Patients would also see an end to Medicare reimbursements for many surgical and diagnostic procedures or be forced to pick up a substantial portion of their costs.

3. Both sides could share the burden of financing less-generous retirement and health-insurance benefits. Retirees would see smaller reductions in Social Security benefits, pay higher Medicare premiums, and lose coverage for certain medical procedures. Workers would still see their payroll taxes increase, but probably not by more than 25 or 30 percent above current rates.

These are the choices every American taxpayer will face early in the next century. It's no exaggeration to contend that these budgetary choices will be the most difficult America has had to make in its history. For the first time since the Great Depression and the Great Society, taxpayers will have to choose between drastically lower wages for themselves or drastically lower benefit and health insurance levels for the elderly. Even if option number three is chosen and taxpayers pay more and retirees get less, both sides will suffer as they never have since Social Security and Medicare were instituted.

Social Security and Medicare have only been growing since their inception. Not once has either program's benefit schedule contracted in real terms. Social Security benefits have never been cut in any way, shape, or form. Medicare benefits to patients have never been cut either. The government has reduced the rate of annual growth of reimbursements to doctors and hospitals, but reimbursements have never been cut in real terms.

A national commission to study the future of Medicare is now in place and its chairman, Senator John Breaux, a Democrat from Louisiana, this year (1998) wisely dismissed a Clinton proposal to extend Medicare coverage to Americans aged 55 to 64. Breaux said it was unwise to expand access to Medicare when the existing system was facing imminent insolvency.

On another front, Clinton has, at the prodding of congressional Republicans, begun a national dialogue on the future of Social Security. For now, it's not a debate on the specific reform proposals because Clinton is unwilling to propose any of his own.

These steps, timid though they may be, are better than no steps at all. Maybe, just maybe, our political leaders will get it right. We must point out, however, that the best ideas to reform Medicare and Social Security still get short shrift.

And there's a further important side note to this depressing but very real glimpse of our not-too-distant budgetary nightmare. While taxpayers and retirees are fighting (and we do mean fighting) over who pays higher taxes and who receives fewer Social Security and Medicare benefits, there will be almost no money left to pay for national defense, medical research, road and bridge construction, space exploration, environmental cleanup, education, or conservation. That's because the cumulative cost of Social Security and Medicare benefits, by the year 2020, will squeeze out from the federal budget these other forms of so-called discretionary spending. That is, of course, unless taxpayers have already agreed to pay higher income taxes to finance these government functions. If they haven't, then the requirement for higher income taxes will only add tension to this debate. A lot of tension.

Just listen to Federal Reserve Board Chairman Alan Greenspan, again from his October 1997 testimony before the House Budget Committee:

> We should view the recent budget agreement, even if receipts and outlays evolve as expected, as only an important down payment on the larger steps we need to take to solve the harder problem—putting our entitlement programs on a sound financial footing for the twenty-first century.
>
> I have been in too many budget meetings in the last three decades not to have learned that the ideal fiscal initiative from a political perspective is one that creates visible benefits for one group of constituents without a perceived cost to anybody else, a form of political single-entry bookkeeping.

We have an obligation to give those who will retire after the turn of the century sufficient advance notice to make what alterations may be necessary in their retirement planning. The longer we wait to make what are surely inevitable adjustments, the more difficult they will become. If we procrastinate too long, the adjustments could be truly wrenching. Our senior citizens, both current and future, deserve better.

Did you notice how often the word *inevitable* cropped up in Greenspan's testimony? Greenspan is no politician. He doesn't have to pander or sugarcoat. He can see the future, and it alarms this legendarily unflappable financial titan. Greenspan is not a man prone to use words such as *staggering* and *wrenching*. He can see the future, and he has spoken the truth about it.

In this coming campaign many incumbents seeking reelection will not tell you this truth. If they are seeking your vote, you might want to ask them, borrowing Greenspan's phrase, why the nation doesn't "deserve better."

THE NINTH LIE

◆

SOCIAL SECURITY IS A SACRED GOVERNMENT TRUST

SOCIAL SECURITY IS as good a government program as has ever been created. Would that all other federal programs matched its clarity of mission, service to beneficiaries, and efficient use of federal tax dollars.

Thanks to Social Security, elderly Americans and their children now enjoy a level of financial independence their ancestors could only dream of. Unlike generations of families before them, American families today no longer have to make boarders of impoverished parents or relatives. Scandal-free and virtually immune from political manipulation, the program has served the nation better than its drafters could have imagined.

Social Security did precisely what it set out to do: provide what President Franklin Roosevelt described as "some measure of protection . . . against poverty-ridden old age."

Social Security has functioned exactly as predicted. Thanks to Social Security, old-age poverty has been nearly eliminated.

In 1962 the median income for married couples on Social Security was $14,062 (in 1994 dollars), and the median income for individuals was $5,527. In 1992 the median income for couples on Social Security was $25,045 (in 1994 dollars), and the median income for individuals was $10,405. This increased prosperity is due to Social Security and the increasing number of investment portfolios now held by America's elderly. In 1962 only 69 percent of eligible elderly Americans received Social Security benefits. That figure was 91 percent in 1994. In 1994 more than two-fifths of America's elderly population was lifted out of poverty by Social Security. In that year the poverty rate among the elderly was 12 percent. Without Social Security it would have been 54 percent.

These are among the wonderful things Social Security has accomplished. We acknowledge them and salute the unique insight and judicious planning that went into the creation of this program. With all respect to Shakespeare, we seek to praise Social Security, not to bury it.

But we have no interest whatsoever in praising the way politicians discuss Social Security. Which leads us to the title of this chapter. The slogan we describe as a lie is the favorite among politicians of both parties who want to prove their commitment to Social Security and, most important, to its 43 million beneficiaries.

A good number of Americans believe Social Security benefits are guaranteed no matter what else happens to the nation's economy. Still other Americans believe their benefits are kept safe and secure in a "trust fund" with their name on it, and that that trust fund will magically pop open when they reach sixty-two, the age at which partial Social Security benefits may first be collected. These Americans believe that over the course of a normal retirement, they will collect about as much in benefits as they contributed in payroll taxes, plus accumulated interest.

All these widely held beliefs are false.

We don't blame you for believing some or all of them. Politicians have plied voters with distortions about Social Security for years. Each new distortion has been designed to calm any anxiety about the future of *your* benefits. While these distortions have served the short-term interests of the nation's political class, they have created a fog of misunderstanding that makes serious discussion about the future of Social Security unnecessarily difficult.

And believe this: there needs to be a serious discussion about Social Security's future. The decisions we make in the next five years about the program will go far in determining our economic health for the next three generations. Very soon this nation will be asked to do something it's never done before: reduce Social Security benefits and shift some of Social Security's resources from the government into the private sector. Along the way some Americans are going to have to sacrifice to preserve Social Security's promise of providing a minimum pension for all elderly Americans. The choices will not be particularly easy to propose or accept. The coming debate is in its infancy, and many Americans are blissfully unaware of the difficult choices they must soon confront. Yet even Social Security's staunchest defenders have concluded that the current system cannot survive. In this regard, we applaud Clinton for accelerating the national dialogue on this critical issue.

First, a prediction: Social Security will be privatized in your authors' lifetimes (Major is thirty-six, Tim forty-six). No one yet knows how this will be accomplished, though some of the early options are outlined later in this chapter. Before we as a nation can decide what to do about Social Security, though, we must all understand what the program is, and what it is not. This will be a painful process. Most Americans have a distorted view of Social Security, one fed for years by politicians who have pandered to voters for political support instead of dealing honestly with the program's built-in limitations and its very real march toward insolvency. Like most political liars, your leaders did not deceive you to hurt you but to help themselves.

The time has come to dispel the myths—to look squarely at Social Security's problems and what will become of this nation if they are not dealt with promptly and courageously.

So let us begin anew, if you will, in our efforts to rescue Social Security from its fragile future and to deliver to future generations the "measure of protection . . . against poverty-ridden old age" that the program was always meant to provide.

Social Security Myths

Myth Number One: Social Security is a "sacred government contract."

Nothing in the Social Security law requires that the government provide a fixed amount of benefits if the actuarial tables fall out of balance. There are no provisions in the Social Security law to raid other parts of the budget if there is insufficient payroll-tax revenue to provide the stipulated Social Security benefits. In this regard, Social Security is just another government program. It has not one bit more and not one bit less legitimacy or permanency than the Environmental Protection Agency, the National Endowment for the Arts, or the Appalachian Regional Commission.

Social Security is a pay-as-you-go pension program whereby the nation's workers pay taxes to finance benefits for current retirees. The system is built around actuarial tables that have always kept taxes collected and benefits paid out in rough balance. That changed in 1983 when Congress and President Reagan passed a Social Security bailout plan that called for gradual increases in payroll taxes to create surpluses in the so-called trust fund. The actuarial tables for Social Security are not sacred. Neither is the programs underlying mathematics.

Both are subject to the irrepressible forces of demographics. Social Security is only as secure and permanent as the mathematics that applies to the actuarial tables: the number of workers *multiplied* by the individual payroll-tax rate *divided* by the number of beneficiaries. There is no legally protected right to Social Security benefits. Shielded for generations by sound actuarial calculations, Social Security is about to enter the world of hardball politics and compete toe-to-toe with every other line item of the federal budget. That is because by the year 2012 annual payroll taxes will be insufficient to cover annual benefit payments.

Myth Number Two: Social Security benefits are kept in a special trust fund.

Social Security benefits are, for accounting purposes only, registered in the federal budget as belonging to a Social Security trust fund. Currently, though, payroll-tax revenue far exceeds benefits paid out. Last year (1997), Social Security collected $438 billion in payroll taxes assessed at 12.4 percent on wages up to $68,400. The Social Security Administration paid out $362 billion in benefits, leaving a surplus of $76 billion.

Politicians discuss this surplus as if it were something the government sets aside for future retirees. But nothing of the kind is being done and all politicians who suggest otherwise are lying. In fact, the Social Security surplus is used to minimize the size of the federal budget deficit—another reason that the budget won't be truly balanced in 2002. All deficit figures are based on the difference between tax-revenue receipts and annual spending *plus funds in the Social Security "trust fund."* In other words, the 1997 deficit figure of $34 billion should be reported as *$110 billion.* That's the amount that government programs (aside from Social Security) are spending beyond general tax revenues collected.

Several cynical politicians have lied about this mythical Social Security trust fund to defend a flip-flop vote on the Balanced Budget Amendment. In 1997 efforts to pass the amendment fell one vote short for the second time in three years. Both times Democrats in the Senate who originally supported the amendment reversed field because, in their words, the amendment failed to protect the Social Security "trust fund." We repeat: *Social Security is not a trust fund.* Congress uses the reserves built up in Social Security to mask the real size of the federal deficit. Congress does this because it is unwilling to reduce spending enough to balance the budget *even when tax revenues, due to an unexpectedly long economic expansion, have never been higher.* A popular bumper sticker among seniors with a funny bone reads "We're spending our children's inheritance." As far as the Social Security "trust fund" is concerned, that's exactly what Congress is doing.

Myth Number Three: Social Security beneficiaries collect what they put into the system.

Under current law, retirees can collect limited benefits at age 62 and full benefits at age 65. Elderly Americans who keep working receive full benefits unless their earnings exceed certain levels. In 1996 workers aged 65 to 69 could collect full benefits with outside earnings of up to $11,280. For those younger than 65, the wage limit was $8,160. Social Security benefits are designed to replace a portion of the worker's former earned income, measured as a percentage of wages or salary. The benefit is slightly progressive in that the less a worker earned, the higher the percentage that is used to calculate his or her annual stipend. All beneficiaries receive cost-of-living adjustments (COLAs) designed to keep their annual benefits in line with the prevailing national inflation rate.

According to the Congressional Research Service, it would take the average worker who retired in 1996 at age 65 more than fourteen years to recover, with interest, the value of his or her payroll-tax contributions. In 1980 it took the same worker less than three years to recoup his or her payroll-tax contributions with interest.

These statistics underscore one of Social Security's many problems. Because payroll taxes (which depress wages and reduce economic growth) rose sharply in the 1970s and 1980s, it takes retirees longer and longer to recoup their contributions. This trend will continue as payroll taxes rise and the number of beneficiaries increases. According to the Social Security Administration, it will take twenty-three years for the average retiree in 2025 to recoup his or her payroll-tax contributions with interest.

One of the reasons for this, of course, is that the surplus amounts in the mythical Social Security trust fund are invested in hypersafe

Treasury bonds that pay annual interest of less than 3 percent. And even those paltry returns are used to hide the size of the real federal deficit. Instead of investing pension reserves to create higher later returns, as most privately financed pension plans do, Social Security employs a take-no-risks strategy that ensures the safety of the "trust-fund" surpluses but does little to increase their value. This strategy keeps benefits lower than they might otherwise be and hastens the program's sad rendezvous with insolvency.

OK, enough myth-busting. Let's deal with some basic questions about Social Security and its future.

What kind of trouble is it in?

Right now, Social Security is in fine fettle. As we mentioned, it racks up annual surpluses of more than $70 billion, and its short-term future is quite bright indeed. But Social Security is, to use a nautical metaphor, the budgetary equivalent of an oil supertanker. It carries more freight than any other program in the federal government. It collects payroll taxes from nearly 130 million Americans and provides benefits to another 43 million. As in the case of a supertanker, it is hard to change the direction of Social Security. The system nearly collapsed before Congress and President Reagan pulled together to bail it out in 1983. Since then, proposals to change its benefit structure or eligibility requirements have drowned in its wake. Yes, Social Security is sailing confidently right now, but it's heading straight for an ice flow sure to crack its hull in half and pitch millions of unwitting elderly Americans into icy financial waters in which retirement benefits will be a fraction of what they expected.

The 1994–1996 Advisory Council on Social Security—the first since 1979 to examine the program's long-term financial health—reached the following conclusions:

> While the Council has not found any short-term financing problems with [Social Security], there are serious problems in the long run. Because of the time required for workers to prepare for their retirement, and the greater fairness of gradual change, even long-run problems require attention in the near term.
>
> Under their intermediate assumptions, the Trustees of the Social Security Funds estimated that income (the sum of the revenue sources plus interest on accumulated funds) will exceed expenses each year until 2020. The trust fund balances will

then start to decline as investments are cashed in to meet the payments coming due. The trustees estimated that although 75 percent of costs would continue to be met from current payroll and income taxes, in the absence of any changes full benefits could not be paid on time beginning in 2030.

That last clause is a backbreaker: *"in the absence of any changes full benefits could not be paid on time beginning in 2030."*

Such a possibility has never before occurred. Social Security came close to insolvency in 1983, but that problem was relatively easy to fix because the number of available workers was much larger than the number of eligible beneficiaries.

But we won't be so lucky the next time. Here's how the numbers break down.

In 1995 the Social Security Administration said there were 160 million Americans aged twenty to sixty-four. Those are the prime earning years, when payroll-tax receipts are highest. In that same year, there were 34 million Americans sixty-five and older. In other words, there was one Social Security beneficiary for every 3.5 workers. This is the lowest the ratio has ever been. In 1960 there were about 5 workers to every retiree. The decline will grow ever steeper after the turn of the century.

Take a look at these alarming numbers:

In 2030 there will be two workers paying payroll taxes for every Social Security beneficiary. In 2050, when your school-age children become eligible for Social Security, there will be about 55 beneficiaries for every 100 workers.

What this means is that there will be more and more Social Security recipients chasing fewer and fewer benefits. The squeeze will force something or someone to give. Recipients will have to accept lower Social Security benefits, workers will have to pay higher payroll taxes, or both sides will have to give up a little of both.

Unlike many problems in the modern world, this one cannot be solved or even softened by technological inventions. The mathematics of Social Security has always been very simple. From the beginning the program has needed lots of workers paying payroll taxes to finance benefits for America's elderly. As the baby-boom generation reaches retirement age, there simply will not be enough workers to pay for the benefits the current law promises.

According to the Social Security Administration, the average rate of growth in the labor force—which was 2 percent per year from 1960 to 1989—will slow to 1 percent from 1989 to 2010. Now, a drop from 2 percent to 1 percent may not sound like much, but when applied to a work force of 153 million people, it's a staggering statistical change. Remember, we're talking about a 50-percent shrinkage in the annual growth rate of America's work force until 2010. A contraction of this magnitude is especially hazardous to Social Security because it pays today's benefits with today's payroll taxes—not with any trust fund revenue.

As bad as the work-force shrinkage will be from now until 2010, it's only going to get worse. Between 2010 and 2050 the rate of growth in America's labor force will decline to a microscopic *2/10 of 1 percent per year.*

Liberalized immigration laws might to some extent alleviate this problem, but they cannot solve it entirely. To raise the rate of labor-force growth to 1 percent per year after 2010, America would have to import millions upon millions of new workers, an influx that would dwarf the immigrant influx at the dawn of this century. During the great waves of central and southern European immigration to America from 1900 to 1910, more than 8.7 million immigrants arrived in America. That translated to 10.4 immigrants per 1,000 residents, the highest immigration rate in this century. From 1911 to 1930 another 9.8 million immigrants arrived in America, whereupon Congress sharply restricted legal immigration to allow time for the economy to absorb the new workers and for the immigrants to assimilate.

To compensate for the shrinkage of the American labor force in the next century, America would have to attract far more than the 800,000 to 900,000 immigrants who legally and illegally enter the country each year. While no hard numbers exist, it's safe to assume the nation would have to triple or quadruple its annual quota for legal immigration, raising it to more than 2.5 million. We would have to find jobs for and assimilate more than 2.5 million immigrants each year from 2010 to 2050 just to minimize *but not erase* the structural shortfall in Social Security compensation. Even if the nation decided to dramatically increase legal immigration, which it is by no means certain to do, there is no clear evidence that enough skilled workers would be available to fill available job slots.

So you see, all of this makes it inevitable: Social Security will have to undergo some serious changes in the near future. If it does not, all of these problems will intensify, and the solutions will be even more jarring to elderly beneficiaries and workers financing the system.

We now have the wealthiest elderly population in the history of the world. But the price of that affluence is lower pay for today's workers due to the ravages of the payroll tax. Workers who have seen wages stagnate since the late 1970s will be unlikely to accept even-higher payroll taxes to bail out Social Security. That means future recipients will have to give up benefits to save the system. If the poorest of America's elderly are shielded from any benefit reductions, Social Security will become what it has never been and what it was never meant to be—a welfare program. The day Social Security loses its universality is the day middle-class and wealthier retirees revolt.

The evidence should be very clear now.

Ignore all platitudes about Social Security. Demand that your representatives and senators tell you what they intend to do about Social Security's impending doom. This is one of those questions that simply must receive an answer. Politicians who fail to provide an answer are disserving you and betraying their vaunted fidelity to Social Security and its current beneficiaries. The time for blandishments is over. For far too long politicians have harvested the votes of America's elderly by giving them the impression that Social Security was a sacred government commitment, an unbreakable bond linking one generation to the next, and a system that would live as long as the republic. As Harry Truman would say, this was and is a lot of bosh.

And it's done tremendous damage. While some politicians are showing surprising courage in discussing these fundamental problems, no new ideas have been put to a real political test. As we pointed out in an earlier chapter, the recent balanced budget deal which Congress and Clinton contend does so much to guarantee future prosperity, punted the Social Security issue.

That's too little, and pretty soon it's going to be too late.

If Congress and Clinton care as much about Social Security as they profess to, it's time for them to face these problems and figure out what can be done about them. Most important of all, politicians must start telling us what *they believe is the right path toward solvency for the system and equity for current workers and future recipients.*

This is the next big issue, folks.

Forget about free trade, race relations, tax reform, or health care. As we've already shown, Social Security is the biggest program in the federal government. Every adult is part of it, either as a contributor through payroll taxes or as a beneficiary. Dealing with Social Security's perilous future will require a degree of courage, vision, leadership, and determination this nation has not seen since the advent of the Cold War.

We're not demanding that politicians produce the perfect solution to Social Security's problems. We are only asking them to put some possible solutions on the table—to help their constituents understand the choices that soon will confront us all. Until this process begins in earnest, all the campaign rhetoric you hear about Social Security will be a pack of lies, and those who spin them should be ashamed for treating so valuable a program with such cavalier indifference and cowardice.

We shall devote the rest of this chapter to possible ways to improve Social Security.

RAISE PAYROLL TAXES, KEEP CURRENT BENEFITS: According to Social Security Administration data, current benefits can be maintained if workers are willing to see their payroll taxes increased from the current 12.4 percent (excluding Medicare) to 14.57 percent. This higher tax rate would cover Social Security obligations for the next seventy-five years. (But this calculation assumes that we can draw upon the "trust fund," which represents money that isn't really there.) Raising payroll taxes had been the preferred method for bailing out Social Security, but political tolerance for such taxes has reached its limit. Economists now recognize the costs these taxes impose and have warned lawmakers to resist the temptation to cover Social Security's looming shortfall with still-higher taxes on labor.

When the program was born, Treasury Department actuaries estimated that the highest practicable payroll-tax rate would be about 6 percent. Above that level, the actuaries calculated, workers would need to be compensated for their lost wages. When Medicare taxes are included, today's payroll-tax rate is 15.3 percent—already much higher than government economists thought advisable. Raising it higher will further suffocate wages and inhibit economic growth. While once a viable political option, raising payroll taxes to cope with Social Security's problems will do far more harm than good. What's more, to pay for the estimated long-range costs of Social Security *and* Medicare (a program we will dissect in our next chapter) workers will have to endure a payroll-tax rate of 28 percent. You read that right. *Twenty-eight percent.* That's nearly twice what you pay now. This rate is positively unacceptable, and all economists know that. That's how serious these funding shortfalls will be if structural changes are not made, but it should be abundantly clear by now that higher payroll taxes simply are not the answer.

REDUCE SOCIAL SECURITY BENEFITS: Well, as we've already seen, this is a trend that has been going on for some time—not in the sense that the benefit formula has reduced benefits, but in that it takes longer and longer for beneficiaries to recoup what they paid into the system in payroll taxes and interest. In reality, Social Security is becoming an increasingly poor investment and it cannot become a better one if its benefits are reduced. But reducing benefits across the board is a way of guaranteeing solvency; as a recent bipartisan commission recommended, this could be accomplished by reducing the Consumer Price Index in order to shield the government from the hefty costs of providing cost-of-living adjustments (or COLAs) to Social Security beneficiaries. Political pressure in 1997 swiftly killed that idea. Groups representing the elderly resented sacrificing annual inflation adjustments simply because a handful of economists told them inflation wasn't as high as they previously thought. The mere mention of cutting Social Security benefits in such a way sent congressional leaders from both parties scurrying for cover.

Another idea that has been floated is to tie Social Security benefits more directly to income. Benefits are already skewed in favor of workers who earn less; current formulas reward them a higher percentage of their monthly earnings than higher-paid workers receive. While this scheme favors low-income workers, everyone still receives Social Security benefits. Some have suggested abolishing Social Security benefits for the wealthiest beneficiaries; the problem is, there just aren't enough such recipients to produce meaningful savings—and such a change would destroy Social Security's universality. Americans have supported the program vigorously because benefits flow to all workers regardless of their incomes. Retirees who worked hard and shrewdly saved and invested aren't punished by having their benefits withheld just because they managed to save money while they were working. What's more, the day Social Security prohibits wealthier Americans from receiving benefits is the day it becomes another welfare program. From that point forward, the program will lose its widespread political support and fall prey to intense political pressures. Under this scenario, resentful seniors kicked out of the program could join forces with workers unwilling to subsidize a system that will deny them benefits once they cross an arbitrary level of affluence.

All these reasons make dramatic reduction in Social Security benefits another dubious political option.

PRIVATIZE THE SYSTEM: The authors believe that converting Social Security to a system of personally controlled retirement accounts is by far the best option. Under a system that allowed taxpayers some discretion to invest a portion of their payroll taxes, Social Security would be able to survive and thrive.

Social Security is a compulsory system that provides universal benefits. These have always been its pillars of political strength. For obvious reasons, retirees think of their monthly Social Security check as *their* money—a return on the investment taken out of their paychecks throughout their working lives. While this was never true in a technical sense, millions believe in the idea even today. Until recently, Social Security was a reasonably good deal as a pension program, and it had the added benefits of being remarkably easy and risk free.

But now the program isn't such a good deal. A worker who earns forty thousand dollars annually will collect a 2 percent return on his or her contributions. Workers are now paying exorbitant payroll taxes they won't recoup when they retire. How can our society condemn an entire generation of workers to lives of artificially suppressed wages and artificially suppressed economic growth so that they can participate in a compulsory pension system that cheats them once they retire?

It can't.

What should the new Social Security look like?

We'd like to float some ideas, many of which have been developed by distinguished economists and endorsed by a tiny minority of courageous politicians.

First, the new system simply must have a built-in bias toward investment freedom. Right now, Social Security is the only game in town. Payroll taxes are mandatory. It may be OK to stick everyone in a system that works (as Social Security did) but it's criminal to chain them to a system that has as many problems as Social Security will have. However, because of the needs of current Social Security beneficiaries, we obviously cannot allow today's workers simply to opt out.

But we can imagine a system in which workers can set aide a certain percentage of their payroll taxes and invest them on their own. If we wish to increase national savings, this is really our only option. Tax incentives for investments in Individual Retirement Accounts have proven helpful only to those workers with plenty of disposable income. Those at the lower end of the wage scale simply do not have the means to set aside $2,000 each year on a tax-free basis, as current law allows.

No, to help these workers Social Security simply must allow them to set aside some of their payroll taxes, so that they too will have the means to invest for their future. Let's look at a few numbers. A worker born in 1970 who always earned a low wage of $13,000 and retires at the full benefit level at age sixty-seven would receive a monthly Social Security stipend of $770. But if that same worker had been allowed to invest his or her entire payroll contribution in the stock market and reaped a 10-percent gain—close to the historic average—then his or her monthly stipend would be $2,400. While Social Security guarantees that few Americans will slide into poverty, it also guarantees that most Americans will never have substantial wealth in their retirement years.

The new Social Security system must provide flexibility for workers who want to segregate some percentage of their payroll tax for personal investment. It's clear to us that those individuals who opt out of the system and invest wisely will do far better in the stock market than they've done within Social Security. Perhaps a system could be created in which those who opted out would agree to reduced Social Security benefits in the future. A sliding scale could be created by which the more payroll taxes workers withheld, the less they could claim upon retirement. As for those workers who did very well with their investments, perhaps a new system could allow them to transfer their Social Security benefits to tax-free retirement investment accounts for their children. That would strengthen private pensions and further reduce the next generation's need for Social Security benefits. Another option, proposed by Democratic Sen. Bob Kerrey of Nebraska, is to establish a $1,000 account for every newborn child. As earnings on the investment compound, each child would be on his or her way to creating a nice retirement nest egg.

Social Security's most-important contribution—financial independence—is now threatened by demographic forces beyond anyone's control. Politicians cannot wish away the baby boom. No budgetary shell game will help them find the resources necessary to cover a temporary and miniscule shortfall of payroll-tax revenues. The shortfall in payroll taxes won't be temporary, and it won't be miniscule. On both counts it will be the exact opposite. Young Americans must now be given more freedom to invest their payroll taxes as they see fit.

Allowing partial exemption from payroll taxes would give young workers a hedge against future losses in Social Security and instill in

Americans of the next generation stronger incentives to plot their own financial destinies. Within a generation, the program can be returned to the modest monthly stipends of its earliest days, and workers can have their payroll taxes to invest.

Maintaining the current system is less defensible than having no Social Security at all. Without Social Security, all workers would know they're on their own. As it is now, workers have been deceived into believing their payroll taxes will actually leave them with a retirement nest egg. That simply will not be true in the future. So Social Security is really a double lie. It is not a sacred government contract and, as currently constructed, is not a reliable retirement system for the coming generations of retirees.

It's time for a change.

MEDICARE WORKS

MEDICARE DOES NOT work—not by any rational standard. Yes, Medicare provides health care to 37 million elderly and disabled Americans.

But the way the system works is a travesty.

Here are the main problems:

• The program is rife with fraud. Two reports last year offered these sobering facts: Fraud in the exploding area of home health care—which Medicare covers—is rampant, but punishment is almost nonexistent. Medicare paid $18 billion in home health-care reimbursements in 1996, up from $2.7 billion in 1989. Medicare approves licenses for one hundred home-health companies a month—and almost no applicant is turned down. According to the General Accounting Office, a cabdriver, a pawnshop operator, and an individual with a felony drug conviction have all received permission by Medicare to provide home-health services. Only ³⁄₁₀ of 1 percent of the licensed home-health providers were disciplined for misuse of funds in 1996. What's worse, Medicare hasn't even drafted rules to sanction poor home-health services that provide inadequate care. The overall Medicare program is also overrun with fraud and waste. The inspector general of the Department of Health and Human Services reported that in 1996 Medicare issued $23 billion in improper payments. Twenty-three billion dollars! That was more than we spent that same year to run the Environmental Protection Agency, the National Aeronautics and Space Administration, Congress, and the federal judiciary. This fraud and waste accounted for 12 percent of Medicare's $194 billion in layouts. Previously, auditors had estimated that fraud and waste accounted for 3 to 10 percent of Medicare's annual outlays. In truth, the problem is much, much worse.

• The system by which reimbursements are set for Medicare services is arbitrary and cannot possibly account for regional differences in the cost of these services, such as the frequency with which the service is provided. The system tries to account for all these variables, as well as others, but remains a one-size-fits-all, command-and-control bureaucracy incapable of appropriately setting prices for health-care services.

• The system is so rigid that 88 percent of its participants obtain health care through a fee-for-service system. Meanwhile, health-care services for all other Americans use several different delivery systems: health-maintenance organizations, preferred-provider networks, medical savings accounts. Fully 70 percent of American workers receive health-care coverage through these alternative delivery systems. The 12 percent of seniors enrolled in health-maintenance organizations are receiving a wider array of services (because HMOs, unlike Medicare, keep an eye on costs), but this trend is not saving taxpayers very much. That's because Medicare basically pays HMOs what it would pay, on average, to a fee-for-service doctor or hospital for care they would provide.

• Medicare pays for approved procedures, regardless of their cost or medical necessity. The reimbursement scheme provides no incentive for doctors or hospitals to reduce costs or provide more-efficient, cost-effective care.

• Medicare needlessly shields elderly Americans from the true cost of their health care. Medicare Part B, which pays for doctor's visits, covers 80 percent of all costs of approved procedures after a patient has reached the $100 deductible. Participants who enroll in Part B—about 35.5 million Americans—pay a monthly premium of $42.50, which covers only 25 percent of the program's cost. The rest of the costs are absorbed by all taxpayers through general tax revenue. When Medicare began in 1965, the premium for participants in Medicare Part B was 50 percent of the total cost. Gradually Congress has reduced this premium to "protect" Medicare beneficiaries from the costs of their own medical care. A compassionate goal, to be sure, but one that puts other taxpayers in the position of subsidizing this care while seniors grow less and less aware of the true costs of their care. This distorts the marketplace, for neither the doctor nor the patient has an incentive to monitor costs. The doctor is reimbursed for his costs, while the patient pays the same low premium regardless of how much his or her treatment costs.

- All of this contributes to runaway costs. In 1985 Medicare cost $72.2 billion. It cost $110.9 billion five years later. Five years after that it cost $176.8 billion. This year (1998) it is projected to cost $239.7 billion, more than three times what it cost only twelve years ago. In 1995, Medicare Part A (hospitalization) cost $87.5 billion and Part B (doctor's visits) cost $40.3 billion. The remainder paid for, among other things, skilled-nursing facilities ($9.1 billion), home-health care ($14.8 billion), and hospice care ($1.8 billion).

Payroll taxes of 2.9 percent per worker pay for Medicare Part A (hospitalization) costs through a special trust fund. But that trust fund is running out of funds and will lapse into insolvency in 2007. It was headed for insolvency by the year 2001, but cost-saving legislation enacted in 1997 (and which we will discuss in greater detail shortly) extended the trust fund's life. All taxpayers covered 75 percent of the cost of Medicare Part B (doctor's visits) because that share is paid out of general revenue. The other 25 percent, as mentioned earlier, was covered by a premium of $42.50 per patient.

As the cost of doctor's care rises, there will be less money to spend on other federal priorities such as defense, environmental protection, border patrol, space exploration, and conservation. In 1975 Medicare spending accounted for 5.1 percent of the federal budget and 1.2 percent of the total value of all the goods and services the United States economy produced (otherwise known as the gross domestic product). In 1995 Medicare spending consumed 11.3 percent of the federal budget and accounted for 2.6 percent of the gross domestic product.

This is the sorry state of Medicare. We can't afford to continue down this path.

We suppose things could be worse, but it's hard to imagine how. Costs have already begun spiraling out of control—even before the first wave of the baby-boom generation becomes eligible for Medicare coverage. Even if there were no baby-boom surge, Medicare would be facing financial ruin, and the health care of America's elderly and soon-to-be-elderly would be in peril. But the baby boom will begin claiming Medicare benefits in 2010, three years after Medicare is due to lapse into bankruptcy. Unlike Social Security, which has larger financial obligations but more time to prepare for the baby-boom onslaught, Medicare's problems are immediate and dire.

It won't do any of us any good to debate Medicare's intentions. Medicare is full of good intentions and has provided millions of elderly Americans and their families guaranteed access to all but the most exotic health-care services. The security that comes with this guarantee knows no price, and we salute the commitment to providing such care and the security it has brought to two generations of Americans. But saluting these good works won't help us solve Medicare's very real problems.

During this campaign year you're going to hear a lot of pleasantries about Medicare. If incumbents discuss the subject at all, which is doubtful, they will commend themselves for bravely intervening to spare Medicare from immediate insolvency. They will applaud the "bipartisan spirit" that led Congress and Clinton to make the purportedly historic and fundamental changes that will extend Medicare solvency for about a decade. They will also congratulate themselves for extending Medicare coverage to diagnostic services such as mammography, Pap smears, and screenings for prostate cancer, colorectal cancer, and osteoporosis. Lastly, incumbents will remind you that they achieved all of these wonderful things *without increasing anyone's Medicare premiums.*

All these statements, dear friends, sound too good to be true. That's because they are.

For future reference, you can safely use the following axiom whenever politicians discuss Medicare: whatever a majority of them tell you is bad is almost certainly good, and whatever they tell you is good is almost certainly bad.

For starters, Medicare's insolvency was not extended by a decade. It was extended by six years. The trust fund that pays for Medicare Part A (hospitalization) was due to lapse into insolvency in 2001; the changes *may* keep it going until 2007. The assertion that Medicare will remain solvent for another decade is technically correct, but Congress can rightfully claim credit for only six years of extended solvency.

The changes Congress and Clinton passed were minuscule when viewed in the context of what must be done to stabilize Medicare and give the next wave of seniors (baby boomers) any realistic hope of receiving basic health-care services. We assure you, there was nothing revolutionary, brave, or innovative about how Congress agreed to change Medicare.

How did they do it?

Instead of fundamentally altering the incentives for patients or health-care providers to economize, Congress and Clinton fell back on the oft-tried but never successful strategy of reducing payments to hospitals and doctors. This approach, of course, does nothing to change the habits of Medicare patients and only inflicts a financial penalty on hospitals and doctors who treat them. Also, of course, an arbitrary reduction in Medicare reimbursements does not suddenly make the underlying health-care services *any cheaper*. Overnight hospital stays don't suddenly become cheaper simply because Medicare has cut the amount of money it will give to the hospital treating the patient. Syringes and gauze do not become any cheaper. Neither, of course, do X-rays, mammograms, CAT scans, or any of the myriad other services hospitals and doctors provide to Medicare beneficiaries.

And there is another problem. Paying doctors less does not make elderly patients healthier. If doctors refuse to treat patients (as many have because of reduced government reimbursements), many patients simply forego treatment. Later, they are treated—typically at higher cost—for systemic disorders that might have been treated less expensively had they been discovered earlier.

In other words, the government refuses to do anything to encourage healthier behavior among seniors. Since their benefits remain the same, they need only find the physicians available to treat them. If they're not willing to treat them for minor ailments, then they tend to let the problem fester—a decision that typically leads to higher costs later on. So projections of $115 billion in Medicare savings are unrealistic, because the same policy changes have never before produced the projected savings.

For example, in 1990 Congress and President Bush agreed to reduce Medicare payments to hospitals and doctors by $44.2 billion for the next five years. This hard-fought budget deal, which forced Bush to raise taxes and spawned a short-lived government shutdown, was meant to bring Medicare's soaring costs under control. The following chart represents what Congress and Bush *thought* Medicare would cost in the four years after 1991, and what it *actually* cost. The amounts are in billions of dollars.

Congress-Bush Projections (in billions)

1992	1993	1994	1995
$116	126.5	140.1	156

Actual Medicare Cost (in billions)

1992	1993	1994	1995
$132.3	145.9	162.5	180.1

Even with the $115 billion in projected savings passed by Congress and Clinton last year (1997), here are the projected spending totals for Medicare from 1998 through 2007 in billions of dollars:

1998	1999	2000	2001	2002	2003	2004	2005	2006	2007
$221	233	246	270	279	307	333	370	384	427

Under the most-optimistic scenario, one in which projected Medicare spending ultimately resembles *actual spending,* Medicare will cost nearly twice as much in a decade (2007) as it does now. Remember, the first wave of baby-boom retirees will not begin to lap onto Medicare's craggy and desolate budgetary shores until 2010. In other words, Medicare's costs will nearly double in ten years—before a single baby boomer goes to Medicare-funded doctor with the flu.

And this nightmarish world is one we can only hope to see. As we've shown, projected Medicare expenses typically bear no relation whatsoever to actual costs, frequently falling below them by a factor of $10 billion to $20 billion each year.

These numbers explain why the *Wall Street Journal,* on May 9, 1997, editorialized: "Anyone with a week of budget experience knows that Medicare spending predictions are worse than meaningless. They do damage because they always claim 'savings' or 'cuts' that turn out to be illusory. What matters is policy—in particular, whether Medicare will retain a command and control bureaucratic nature that is hurtling toward bankruptcy, or else be opened up to more private competition and choice."

Congress and Clinton also added services *without asking anyone to pay for them.*

The new Medicare law will provide reimbursements for mammograms, Pap smears, and tests for prostate cancer, colorectal cancer, and osteoporosis. All of these diseases afflict elderly patients at a much-higher rate than they do the general population, and it's quite possible that, over time, early diagnosis of such ailments could accelerate detection, improve treatment, and lower overall costs. We hope this is exactly what happens. But we also understand that theses new tests cost money and nowhere in the new law does Congress or Clinton ask anyone to pay for these new services. It does not raise Medicare Part B (doctor's visits) premiums even though these are precisely the services patients will receive on an out-patient basis. Medicare beneficiaries should be willing to pay since they will benefit enormously from early detection of any diseases.

It's important to point out that successful use of these and other diagnostic tests will, we all hope, lead to longer lives for Medicare beneficiaries. Naturally, longer lives means longer use of Medicare. While life-saving health care is good news, we must also admit that increased use of Medicare by beneficiaries who live longer inevitably raises the cost of the program over time. So it's wrong for Congress and Clinton to suggest, as they have repeatedly and will do again this campaign season, that Medicare has been saved from insolvency for a decade and that new services will be provided at no cost to beneficiaries. The cost will come due—for someone—sooner or later.

There is one word for this situation.

Unsustainable.

It may seem hard to understand why Congress and Clinton have been so timid in their approach to Medicare reform.

The answer is simple: politics.

Few issues have been as distorted and exploited as Medicare. Certain politicians, starting with Clinton and including most but not all Democrats in Congress, have capitalized on the fears of elderly voters to punish politicians who have suggested changing Medicare in ways that would force wealthy beneficiaries to pay more for their health care.

But politicians are not the only ones to blame. American's elderly bear some responsibility as well. When Congress passed a cata-strophic-health-insurance package in 1988, it required Medicare ben-eficiaries to pay higher premiums in exchange for the new insurance benefits providing prescription drugs and coverage for catastrophic ill-nesses.

Wealthy and politically active Medicare recipients protested the new premiums of this new benefit package and demanded that Con-gress repeal the insurance program entirely. One year later, that's ex-actly what happened. Congress learned a valuable political lesson: don't expect seniors to pay more for additional Medicare benefits. Since then, Congress has done nothing to increase the out-of-pocket expenses for Medicare beneficiaries, preferring instead to continue their ruse of projecting imaginary savings gained by reducing what Medicare pays doctors and hospitals for health-care services.

The lessons learned in 1989 are only marginally relevant to today's politics. That's because the vast majority of members of the House and Senate did not serve in the Congress that passed and repealed the cat-astrophic-health insurance package. In fact, former House member Bill Gradison, who now is a lobbyist for the health-insurance industry, often carries a picture with him when he meets members of Congress to talk about Medicare. The picture is of President Reagan and Dan Rostenkowski, then the chairman of the House Ways and Means Committee, celebrating a new catastrophic-health-care program dur-ing a White House signing ceremony.

At the time, the new law enjoyed broad public support and the backing of the nation's biggest lobby for seniors, the American Asso-ciation of Retired Persons. Months later, when the premiums came due, angry seniors began to protest. A group with placards and canes even pummeled Rostenkowski's car, an act of civil disobedience that chilled the blood of the average legislator. (If the elderly will do that to the baronial Rostenkowski, what will they do to me back home?) As Gradison told the *Wall Street Journal:* "Sometimes when I go over to the Hill, I take it [the picture] with me as a reminder."

It was just such a reminder that led House Republicans to reject a Senate move in 1997 to actually impose some modest new costs on Medicare beneficiaries. The Senate voted to increase premiums for Medicare Part B (doctor's visits) for the wealthiest 5 percent of benefi-ciaries. This small group includes individuals who earn $50,000 (and couples who earn $75,000) in annual retirement income. The Senate also voted to extend the eligibility age for Medicare gradually from sixty-five to sixty-seven (to become fully effective in 2007) and to charge a $5 copayment for home-health-care visits.

Let's pause for a minute to chew over the implication of one of these changes—increasing premiums for Medicare Part B for beneficiaries whose annual retirement income exceeds $50,000 ($75,000 for couples). Under current law, Medicare Part B premiums are the same for these beneficiaries as for beneficiaries whose income is at or below the poverty line ($7,309 in 1995).

Stop and think about this, please. An elderly person who earns $7,000 has to pay the same premium for doctor's visits as an elderly person with an income of more than $50,000. The annual premium equals $510, which translates into 7 percent of the annual income of the poor Medicare beneficiary and 1 percent of the annual income of the beneficiary who earns $50,000 a year. We have two questions: Is this fair? Is it rational?

We don't believe it is, especially when you consider that poor workers are paying taxes to subsidize the cost of doctor's visits not paid for by these nominal monthly premiums. So the poor on Medicare pay much more as a percentage of their annual income for doctor's visits than do wealthy Medicare recipients. And poor workers lose wages they might otherwise earn in order to subsidize doctor's visits for the wealthiest 5 percent of Medicare beneficiaries.

This is mass madness. It makes no sense as social policy. It makes no sense as budget policy. It makes no sense as economic policy. Why should the poor of this county—the elderly on Medicare and those earning the lowest wages—have to suffer the financial hardships this system inflicts? They shouldn't. Doctor's visits are not a constitutional right. They are a perk this society generously provides to elderly Americans through the Medicare system. But generosity has its limits, and the system currently financing these doctor's visits is about to shrivel up and die unless we make some sensible changes—and start requiring the wealthiest seniors to pay a bigger portion of their health-care expenses. The Senate tried to take a step in this direction in 1997, but political trepidation in the House foiled even these trivial steps towards fiscal sanity, social equity, and economic reality.

That the Senate moved to make these small changes led some with Pollyannaish tendencies inside the Beltway to declare gleefully that a new era had begun in Medicare politics, one in which legislators could confidently reduce benefits without fearing an immediate voter backlash. Well, the House never signed on, and there is ample evidence to

suggest it never intended to—which made all those supposedly courageous votes in the Senate utterly meaningless. After all, virtually all of
America supported the 1988 catastrophic-health-care bill *until the bill
came due*. We applaud the Senate's efforts. They were an important
step in the right direction. Having cast a vote in favor of these changes
once, the Senate is much more likely to do so again. Momentum is important in politics, and we congratulate Senators Bob Kerrey of Nebraska and Daniel Patrick Moynihan of New York for persuading
their colleagues to take these baby steps toward more-comprehensive
Medicare reform.

But the good work of these two senators were insufficient to persuade skittish House Republicans to go along. While many of them
were not around when Congress repealed the catastrophic health plan
in 1989, most of their leaders were.

More important, all of them remembered the savage, misleading,
and destructive demagoguery that accompanied the debate over Medicare in 1995 and 1996.

You remember: That was the debate about Medicare "cuts"—the
"cuts" Republicans supposedly proposed. The "cuts" at the center of
a protracted budget dispute with Clinton that eventually led to two
government shutdowns.

Clinton called them "devastating." At one point in his confron-
tation with Congress, Clinton said he would not "discuss the destruction of Medicare." At another, he said that Republican plans
for Medicare would deprive the elderly of the opportunity to "live
out their last years in dignity." Still another time, Clinton said he
would not allow Republicans to "slash Medicare." Clinton also called
the Republican proposal "the biggest [set of] Medicare cuts in history."

Clinton leaned heavily on three adjectives to describe the Republicans' plans for Medicare: *slash, devastate,* and *destroy.*

By comparison, the sycophantic underlings in the Democratic cau-
cus on Capitol Hill were far more imaginative. Their repertoire included:
"shameful," "outlandish," "disgraceful," "ridiculous," "extreme,"
"chilling," "bogus," "mean-spirited," "phony," and "a monstrosity."

Oh, really?

If this was all true in 1995 and 1996, than why did Clinton and the
vast majority of Democrats in Congress agree to a package of Medicare "cuts" that in many ways resembles exactly what the Republicans
originally proposed?

That's right. Those horrible "cuts" that Clinton and congressional Democrats went to such rhetorical extremes to denounce are almost identical to those in the hollow balanced-budget law they signed on to with Republicans in the summer of 1997.

The only major difference between the Republicans' 1995 budget and the one Clinton and congressional Democrats signed on to in 1997 is that in the second case the proposed tax cuts are 50 percent smaller and domestic spending is much, much higher. In other words, Clinton and congressional Democrats willfully misled America about the consequences of the Republican Medicare proposals so they could force the GOP to retreat on tax cuts and force it to spend more on domestic programs. Whether or not you agree with this eventual outcome, it's obvious that the partisan tactics have seriously hampered a truthful discussion of Medicare's bleak future.

The truth? No politician (Republican or Democrat) has ever proposed cutting Medicare benefits. They never have, and in all likelihood they never will. Not real cuts, anyway. We define real cuts the way anyone who lives outside of Washington would define them: a cut is when you spend less on something than you did the year before. If times were tight in the family budget and fifty dollars less were spent than the year before on fast food, that would be a cut of fifty dollars. Washington, on the other hand, defines cuts quite differently. A cut in Washington is when the government spends less next year than it *intended* to spend.

That's Washington for you, though, to be fair, it's not exactly as crooked as it seems. By law Congress has to estimate each year how much it will spend the next year. Sometimes that's a difficult job, and estimating the cost of medical expenses is particularly tricky. Lots of things drive up medical costs, and as long as Congress maintains Medicare's command-and-control bureaucracy, there is not much any of us can do about them.

Still, there are discernible patterns in medical expenses, particularly among the elderly, and it is these patterns that policymakers rely upon to calculate the magnitude of increased federal spending for Medicare each year. When the nation heard so much about "draconian" Republican cuts in Medicare during the great 1995–96 debate over the budget, what it was really hearing about were *reductions in the projected increases in federal spending each year for Medicare*.

But why are Medicare costs rising so rapidly?

Three reasons: beneficiaries are living longer (that's good), Medicare insulates patients and health-care providers from the true cost of health care (that's bad), and new high-tech medical services are very expensive (that's the way it is).

OK, what can we do about it?

The first thing, of course, is to deal seriously with the facts of Medicare and disregard the political double-talk you will doubtless hear this year. It's our hunch that most politicians will not discuss Medicare at all this election season because the balanced-budget law they are so proud of came with an unspoken political cease-fire agreement. In contrast to 1996, when Democrats savaged Republicans across the country for proposing Medicare "cuts," during this campaign Democrats are likely to ignore the issue entirely. Both parties will take credit for their part, Republicans are likely to discuss Medicare only in the context of the wonderful and amazing contributions they made to extending its solvency and to conferring more benefits. We've already shown you the hollowness of this rhetoric.

So it's up to you (and maybe the media) to demand a clearer-eyed discussion of Medicare this campaign season. You must force politicians to discuss the choices they believe we must make to protect Medicare now and in the future. Each and every choice will inflict sacrifice on someone—today's recipients, future beneficiaries, or current or future workers. But if we don't do something soon, the cost of fixing Medicare in the future will be much higher, and the range of options will be more limited. This isn't a problem the country wants to solve at the last minute. Laws born in an atmosphere of crisis are typically the worst ever written. That will surely be true if we wait too long to deal with Medicare.

What are the options worth debating *now*?

The first thing we all have to remember is that there is no market incentive for patients to use Medicare economically. Not every trip to the doctor is necessary. Not every diagnostic test is valuable. Sometimes patients see their doctors for reasons utterly unrelated to illness, such as a need to socialize or just to have their nerves calmed about their health. Sometimes doctors perform tests to protect themselves from malpractice claims and not because they are medically necessary. On other occasions doctors treat patients they know are not sick simply because the patient comes to see them and demands *some* service. If the doctor doesn't provide a service, he or she might lose the patient as a client, which might affect his bottom line. Anyone who has explored the underlying reasons behind the 10 percent annual growth in the cost of Medicare knows that some very complex psychological forces are at work with some patients—and that there are equally odd financial incentives that encourage doctors to provide costly services they know are unnecessary.

Until patients and doctors are required to confront the true cost of the health care they request and provide, the system will continue to cost more than it should. The longer it costs more than it should, the sooner it will lapse into bankruptcy. Lawmakers will have precious few options:

- Raise payroll taxes that pay for Medicare Part B (doctor's visits).

- Raise premiums on Medicare beneficiaries.

- Reduce the rates Medicare pays to Medicare providers through Part A (hospitalization) and Part B.

- Raise the age of eligibility for Medicare.

If the crises is acute, Congress may have to do all four. Without a doubt, the changes will impose abrupt and painful costs on taxpayers and Medicare beneficiaries.

And there are problems with each of these solutions:

- Raising payroll taxes merely inflicts higher costs on today's workers by transferring more of their income through taxes to current Medicare beneficiaries. This does nothing to discourage excessive use of Medicare services on the part of the beneficiaries. Costs per beneficiary would continue their upward spiral, and workers would lose more economic ground as a higher percentage of their wages is siphoned off to sustain the same inefficient Medicare payment scheme.

- Raising premiums on the wealthy would address problems of social equity and may in the short run extend the solvency of the Medicare Part A (hospitalization) trust fund. Currently premiums cover only 10 percent of the average benefits paid by Medicare. But Congress cannot solve the trust fund's long-term budget problems without significantly increasing Medicare premiums on all but the poorest beneficiaries. That's because focusing higher premiums on only the wealthiest seniors raises relatively little revenue: only 5 percent of all seniors earn more than fifty thousand dollars (as individuals) or seventy-five thousand dollars (as a couple) per year.

- Reducing reimbursement rates to health-care providers typically creates an incentive for doctors and hospitals to find more procedures to bill to Medicare. In other words, they make up for the lost revenue by simply increasing the number of procedures performed. With the number of Medicare beneficiaries rising steadily for the next fifty years, this option will be used extensively—count on it. Also, these arbitrary payment cuts often distort Medicare payments from state to state or city to city. The reimbursement price is typically too low in rural regions and too high in large metropolitan areas. When prices are higher than true costs, however, no one complains. Doctors and hospitals receive more than they are spending to provide the service—which adds to their bottom line.

- Extending the eligibility age for Medicare would not address the systemic problems of overconsumption. It would only delay the inevitable onset of Medicare costs.

While, for the time being, some of these approaches may need to be instituted, the best solution is to move Medicare gradually toward a system that more closely resembles a two-tiered package of medical benefits: catastrophic health insurance and a basic package of physician services. The system must be opened up to competition among all types of health-provider systems, including health-maintenance organizations and preferred-provider networks. Congress did begin the process of opening up Medicare to market-based competition in the recent balanced-budget plan, but serious reform must build aggressively on this approach. Future Medicare beneficiaries must be weaned off the notion that Medicare will pay for all things forever. It cannot.

THE ELEVENTH LIE

◆

TAX CUTS ARE GOOD

WHAT DO YOU mean?
Of course tax cuts are good.
For goodness' sake, everyone in Washington finally agrees on that. Wasn't that 1997 budget deal all about both sides coming together on tax cuts while they balanced the budget at the same time? Well, yes, tax cuts *were* what the deal was really about. It certainly was not about balancing the budget.

Not since 1981 have Republicans and Democrats agreed so much on tax policy in America. That was the last time there was a bipartisan tax bill meant to stimulate economic growth and balance the budget. For reasons we shall soon outline, the 1997 tax cuts are far worse than those enacted in 1981.

These tax cuts, targeted with excruciating political precision, reward certain taxpayers while doing nothing for others. The cuts make precise value judgments about which kind of behavior the government likes and reward people who do what the government wants (thereby punishing those who do not).

In other words, the new tax laws are an exercise in economic discimination—discrimination designed to capture votes.

The new tax cuts were not engineered to increase economic growth, equalize wage disparities, or improve the competitiveness of the United States economy vis-à-vis its international trading partners.

Most important, the tax cuts were not written to simplify the tax code, or improve taxpayers' ability to file their returns with full confidence that they are paying what they actually owe (and not more, as so often happens under so complex a code).

The 1997 tax cuts are a schizophrenic jumble of social engineering and special-interest favoritism.

Economists frown on tax subsidies meant to alter social behavior because they inherently divide taxpayers into winners and losers, needlessly pitting one sector of the economy against another and distorting economic fundamentals. Politicians, especially Republicans, used to loathe social-engineering tax cuts for the same reasons. They wanted the government to reduce taxes *for all taxpayers* and let the people themselves decide how best to spend the windfall.

This is why the 30 percent federal income tax cut of 1981 applied to all taxpayers, regardless of their standards of living. Reagan contended that all Americans should benefit from tax cuts. He argued the government had no business denying wealthy Americans the same tax breaks as the rest of America. To do so, he said, would be to institutionalize government hostility toward wealth, and to inflame "class-warfare" sentiments.

Similarly, the tax reforms of 1986 stripped away hundreds of tax benefits that had been carved out by special interests and others seeking to involve the government in the dicey business of determining marketplace winners and losers. The 1986 bill was a reaction against the forces of special-interest favoritism and social engineering that had distorted the nation's economy. The bill dispensed with most tax shelters and reduced the number of tax brackets from fifteen to three. Whether or not you agree with the underlying economic philosophy of these tax measures, both tax bills undeniably expressed a core economic philosophy that favored individual liberty over government-sponsored social engineering, and simplicity over complexity.

The 1997 tax bill did precisely the opposite. It chose social engineering over individual liberty, and complexity over simplicity.

Allow us to cite two examples.

Thanks to the new tax bill, the government is now in the business of subsidizing children. Starting this year, families can receive a $400 deductible tax credit for each child aged seventeen and younger (a break that will rise to $500 per child under seventeen in 1999). When families compute their annual federal income tax burden, they are to multiply the number of children who qualify for the break by $400 and subtract that amount from what they owe the federal government.

Did we say families receive this tax credit? We're sorry. We meant *some* families.

The government wants to subsidize children and families, but not *all* children and families—only certain types.

Which types? Middle-class, mostly.

Individuals or married couples who earn too much money each year ($75,000 for individuals and $110,000 for couples) do not qualify for the tax credit. Their children are worth less to the government than are the children of individuals and couples with less annual income. These income limits were billed as a necessary strategy to help keep the tax code progressive—to ensure that the wealthy pay higher taxes than middle- and lower-income earners both in aggregate amounts (sheer dollars paid) and as a percentage of earnings. Of course, the wealthy already pay much higher taxes in aggregate terms than the middle class and poor; as it happens, they *also* pay a higher percentage of their income in taxes. In other words, the tax code is already quite progressive, thank you. The 1997 tax bill did nothing to change the progressive tax increases imposed through higher federal income taxes on America's wealthiest wage earners.

The family tax credit is far different from the kind of tax cut that can improve the lives of all Americans or help stimulate general economic growth. It's a segregated tax cut, designed to encourage one social behavior—having children. So, if tax writers are already segregating tax cuts, why segregate them further by denying benefits to some families simply because they have crossed an arbitrary threshold of affluence?

Politics.

When they wrote the 1997 tax bill, Republicans were terrified of appearing to favor the "rich," an accusation that Democrats hurled with gusto (and limited success) in the 1996 campaign. Republicans also feared a veto showdown with Clinton and were worried that an unlimited family tax credit might provoke just that. To defang Democrats and keep the president's veto pen idle, Republicans jumped aboard the class-warfare bandwagon. They wrote a tax law that makes the legal distinction that any child born to to a middle-class family is of greater value to society than a child born to a wealthy family.

And there was another purely political consideration: the tax credit was designed to curry favor with social conservatives within the Republican coalition. The idea arose from GOP discussions with leaders of the Christian Coalition and the Family Research Council, powerful constituency groups within the Republican Party. Both groups wanted the tax code to affirm the contributions of families by providing a special tax break to parents raising children or those contemplating raising children. The political allure was too great to resist. Republicans imagined the cumulative effect of hundreds of thousands of middle-class families calculating their taxes and deducting their family tax credit in a new box on their 1040 and 1040 EZ forms. House Speaker Newt Gingrich said it best when he remarked that the Republican Party would make sure those Americans knew who put that family tax credit box on their tax form.

Tim is the father of four children, Major the father of two. We are sympathetic to the high costs of raising children. We understand that families are having a hard time juggling the costs of health insurance, day care, and the bite of taxes at the local, state, and federal levels. Nevertheless, the family tax credit seems to us an illogical and economically spurious means of addressing these meat-and-potatoes hardships. The real economic problem facing most American families is that wages are stagnant or rising only modestly. The tax credit does nothing to alleviate this problem or, more important, strike at the systemic causes of wage stagnation.

Let's analyze the vaunted tax breaks that Republicans and Clinton hailed as a means of helping families to defray the cost of college tuition.

Alas, if it were only true.

The new tax code provides something called a HOPE scholarship that gives taxpayers a nonrefundable tax credit worth 100 percent of the first one thousand dollars of tuition expenses and 50 percent of the next one thousand dollars of tuition expenses during the first two years of college. The model for this program came from Georgia, where the state required scholarship recipients to maintain a B average. That inevitably led to grade inflation, as professors were pressured by parents, students, and administrators to keep the money flowing by adjusting grades upward. The federal law has no such requirement, eliminating the need for a national academic police force to confirm students' grade performance before approving scholarships. What's the trouble with that?

These HOPE scholarships will have one inevitable, self-defeating byproduct: tuition inflation.

Tuition inflation is the great scandal of American higher education. Colleges are likely to increase tuition, secure in the knowledge that even-larger sums of federal tax money will be heading their way. Tuition inflation has deprived most American families of the benefits they thought they would have enjoyed through Pell grants and direct federal student loans. These earlier means of federal assistance for higher education helped students to pay for college but did nothing to lessen the tuition load on cash-strapped families. That's because most colleges simply raised tuition to keep pace with the rising availability of federal student loans and grants. Since 1980, the average tuition at public universities has increased 234 percent—while household inflation has increased 80 percent.

The same will happen now.

In fact, the provisions of the 1997 tax bill achieved something none of its predecessors could: it united economists across the country in the opinion that it would not do very much good. Higher-education experts believe the tax credits will assist only parents who were going to send their children to college *anyway*—and assist them only slightly.

If that isn't bad enough, arbitrary income thresholds bedevil the HOPE scholarship. To qualify, individuals sending their children to school must earn between $40,000 and $50,000, and couples must earn between $80,000 and $100,000. Again, the law doesn't make a universal statement that higher education is important for all Americans—only for those who fit into specific financial categories drawn up by political draftsmen trying to assemble voting blocs for their party.

So the great bipartisan agreement on taxes leaves in its wake selective subsidies meant to appease key constituency groups. These subsidies will further complicate a hopelessly complex tax code and do almost nothing to stimulate economic growth or broaden access to higher education.

Which leads us to our broader point about tax policy, particularly as it was drafted in 1997: politicians use tax cuts to manipulate voters with promises of new subsidies (the family tax credit or college "scholarships") or with vows to eliminate an irksome tax currently being levied. Frequently these offers are meant to achieve a short-term political gain rather than to enhance economic freedom or simplify the tax laws (the only compelling reasons to cut taxes in the first place).

So much of what goes on in Washington with the tax code amounts to shuffling deck chairs—moving one set of subsidies, scaling back another. The amount of tax revenue rarely changes; the tax code remains as dense as it was or, worse still, gets even gummier. As for economic growth and individual liberty, well, Republicans and Democrats bow in ritualistic homage to both principles, but the true measure of their dedication can be found only in their shoddy handiwork.

By any measure the 1997 tax bill offers less liberty because it's riddled with subsidies for government-approved behavior. Subsidies punish those who do not meet the government's social-engineering goals.

Such subsidies only whet the appetites of special interests hungry for their own gain, confirming the notion that the tax code is a political piggy bank to reward friends and, by definition, punish enemies. With each convoluted page, the thickening United States tax code becomes the enemy of the average person and the friend of the politician. With each new subsidy, people adjust their behavior to take full advantage of the new subsidies. These behavioral changes are not easily reversed, and new constituencies grow up around the new subsidies. It's worth observing that there have been dozens of tax bills this century, but only one that actually reduced the number of shelters, subsidies, and politically crafted tax emoluments.

A cynic might wonder if politicians wanted to complicate the tax code so that you would be more inclined to support their efforts to dismantle it. Republicans themselves drafted many of the tax cuts that make the tax code so obscure—which now sets the stage for a Republican-led revolt to abolish the code entirely, replacing it with a national sales tax or a flat tax.

Just months after passage of the 1997 tax cuts, the Senate convened hearings into the criminal conduct of, and misapplication of tax laws by, the Internal Revenue Service (IRS).

Before we go any further, let's make one thing clear. The hearings were enormously valuable and illuminated long-ignored problems within the IRS. Republicans deserve credit for uncovering thuggish and sometimes criminal IRS tactics. It's worth noting that many of the Republicans involved in the hearings bemoaned the code's complexity and sympathized with taxpayers brought down by an innocent misreading of IRS hieroglyphics. They did this after drafting laws that will make the new tax code far more complicated than Republicans found it when they won control of Congress in 1994. Republicans evidently hope voters will find the new code so intimidating and incomprehensible that they will join in the GOP revolt to abolish the IRS and substitute a national sales tax or a flat tax for the new code. Republicans hope to use the punishing power of the tax code to push voters over the brink and into their sack-the-IRS camp.

Talk about cynical.

To review: Republicans and Clinton wrote new tax laws that doled out a select few breaks to prized political constituencies, with no realistic hope that these changes would fundamentally alter the nation's economy or education for the better. With these changes, they are rewarding certain behaviors that the government likes and concurrently punishing others it doesn't like. By encroaching on the liberty of individuals and foisting a dizzying array of new tax regulations on the populace, Republicans now hope to inspire a national mass movement to obliterate an entire system of taxation politicians wrote to "serve" the taxpayers in the first place.

Our biggest gripe with all of these tax machinations is that they ignore the kind of tax reform that would do more to increase wages and spur economic growth than *any* tax cut in the 1997 bill—or any others currently being debated.

Yes, friends, there is one tax that does more to retard wage growth than any other government policy. This tax, which hits lower- and middle-class families the hardest, has been rising steadily since 1983. With each and every increase, workers have seen their wages fall or stagnate.

Are you wondering what stealth tax Congress has increased over and over without your knowledge, without roll-call votes, and without media fanfare?

The tax is your payroll tax.

Its current rate is 15.3 percent, of which the biggest component is the Federal Insurance Contributions Act (FICA) tax. This tax pays for Social Security benefits (12.4 percent) and applies to all wages up to $68,400. The second component is the Medicare Part A tax that pays for hospitalization costs incurred by Medicare recipients. The Medicare tax rate is 2.9 percent and applies to all wages. Employers deduct half of the tax; employees pay the other half through straight payroll deductions. The self-employed pay the entire 15.3 percent.

Take a good look at your paycheck next time you receive it. If you're like most Americans, the combined cost of your Social Security and Medicare taxes is larger than your income-tax deductions. The vast majority of Americans pay more in payroll taxes than in income taxes.

Payroll taxes suppress wages, suffocate job creation, and pit young wage earners against well-off retirees. What's more, the working poor and middle class pay a disproportionate share of these taxes, because of the $68,400 cutoff for FICA taxes. Those who earn more than this princely sum (four times the poverty rate for a family of four) pay no FICA taxes on each additional dollar earned, which reduces the percentage these taxes consume of their wages.

Consider the following example: A worker who earns $30,000 a year pays $4,590 in payroll taxes ($3,720 in Social Security taxes). Payroll taxes consume 15.3 percent of this worker's wages *before a single cent is deducted for income taxes or state and local taxes.* A worker who earns $300,000 pays $16,809 in payroll taxes (but only $8,109 in Social Security taxes). Payroll taxes consume only 5.6 percent of this worker's wages.

This punitive system forces workers paid the least to sacrifice the most in providing Social Security benefits. To compound the damage, current retirees paid far-lower payroll taxes than today's workers and yet reap the most-generous benefits in the history of Social Security. Worse still, the current payroll taxes are *not high enough* to provide for today's workers the Social Security benefits current retirees enjoy. The poorest American workers are paying disproportionately high taxes to provide disproportionately high Social Security benefits to today's retirees and yet have little realistic hope of receiving retirement benefits commensurate with their contributions.

What a mess! And it gets worse: federal and state income taxes are applied to the *total wages paid*—not the amount workers have left after payroll taxes.

The worker who receives $30,000 a year is taxed on that entire amount, with a 15-percent income tax levied, plus his or her own state's income tax to follow. And yet the income taxes are applied to an amount the worker never has a chance to spend. The income taxes from the federal government and his or her state apply to the $4,590 he or she lost immediately to payroll taxes. This is a double tax on money the worker *never has a chance to see, never has a chance to spend, and never has a chance to invest.*

Payroll taxes are like the Tasmanian Devil from the Bugs Bunny cartoons—ravenous, terrifying, and reckless.

When we contend that tax cuts are no good, what we really mean is *the tax cuts politicians talk about are no good.*

Politicians, you see, refuse to discuss payroll taxes and their debilitating effect on wages, job growth, and personal savings. This is because payroll taxes are tied to Social Security and Medicare benefits, both of which, as we've seen, are protected by powerful blocs of voters.

Refusing to discuss the ravages of payroll taxes doesn't soften their blow, but it does insulate politicians from criticism. It also allows them to dazzle unsuspecting voters with proposals to cut other taxes that have far less impact on wages, job creation, and individual savings.

Since politicians refuse to discuss the truth about payroll taxes, let's take a closer look at the payroll tax and how it has gobbled up more and more of your wages over the years.

In 1937, when the payroll tax was first enacted, the rate was 2 percent of wages and salaries.

In 1960 the rate was 6 percent; by 1980 it was 12.3 percent.

In 1980, the government collected $157 billion in payroll taxes.

In 1990 it collected $380 billion, more than twice the 1980 figure.

Last year the government collected an estimated $550 billion in payroll taxes—three and a half times more than in 1980.

Now let's examine how payroll taxes fit into the big picture of federal taxation.

In 1950 payroll taxes, then assessed only on the first $3,000 in wages and salaries (about $19,000 in inflation-adjusted dollars), accounted for 11 percent of federal tax revenue. In 1980 payroll taxes accounted for 30.5 percent of all federal tax revenue. In 1996 that figure was 35.1 percent. No other form of taxation rose as much—and many forms have grown smaller—as a percentage of federal tax revenue. In the mid 1950s payroll taxes consumed 1.5 percent of the median two-earner income. In 1998, payroll taxes consumed 7.3 percent of the median two-earner income.

Income taxes constituted 47.2 percent of all taxes paid in 1980 and 45.2 percent in 1996—a 4-percent decrease. Corporate income taxes accounted for 12.5 percent of all taxes paid in 1980 and 11.8 percent in 1996—a 6-percent decrease. Excise taxes accounted for 4.7 percent of all taxes in 1980 and 3.7 percent in 1996—a 21-percent decrease.

Interestingly, payroll taxes now generate nearly as much revenue ($550 billion in 1997) as the income tax ($670 billion). Three quarters of American workers pay more in payroll taxes than in income taxes, because they can shield parts of their wages and salaries from the income tax through deduction and exemptions. The payroll tax takes its bite out of every dollar.

Payroll taxes impose huge burdens on the creation of new jobs. Small businesses find this particularly troubling. To create a new job, a small business must find revenue sufficient to pay the new employee's wages and his or her payroll taxes (which cost the employer 7.6 percent). Payroll taxes discourage creation of the lowest-paid jobs—the ones Americans on welfare must be able to find to comply with new federal and state rules setting hard limits on time spent on welfare.

Payroll taxes also suppress wages. Employers must calculate the 7.6 percent in payroll taxes first when they calculate wages. If they can afford to pay a worker $30,000, what they must offer him or her is $27,720 (the $30,000 allotted for the new hire minus the $2,280 cost of paying the employer's share of the payroll tax). The new employee then takes the job at $27,720 and immediately sees the payroll tax consume $2,106 of these wages.

Thanks to the payroll tax, a job that the employer can provide at a wage of $30,000 pays only $25,614 in *real* wages. Of course, federal and state income taxes are applied to the gross wage, which is $27,720.

For those of you looking to unlock the mystery of stagnant wages in America, look no further than the payroll tax. Payroll taxes are Washington's dirty little secret. Politicians will have you believe all variety of treacherous forces are to blame for wage stagnation: the Japanese, unfair trading partners, corporate downsizing, NAFTA, the Federal Reserve, a low national savings rate, and high income taxes.

So the answer to the persistent question among wage earners— Hey! Where's my raise?—can be answered as follows: America's politicians are giving some of it to retirees in the form of Social Security and Medicare benefits and are keeping the rest to make the budget deficit look smaller than it really is.

The bottom line is this: "tax reform" that does not address the systemic inequity of the payroll-tax system is not worthy of the name.

EDUCATION—MORE MONEY EQUALS BETTER RESULTS

E DUCATION . . . WHERE to begin?
There are so many problems with the way we educate our children. As a culture, we obsess over them, demanding answers from school boards, state superintendents, congressmen, senators, even the president. We cast about aimlessly in search of solutions to these problems, which appear to threaten the very existence of our civil society.

We know test scores are lower than they should be. We know our high-school graduates can barely describe the American Revolution, explain how a bill becomes law in Washington, name a single member of the Supreme Court, or identify their congressman or one of their state's two senators.

Too many high-school graduates typically require remedial mathematics and English instruction when they arrive in college. A fair percentage of those who do not attend college may not read or write well enough to complete a job application form adequately. And even those who can fill out the application and do, in fact, land a job may not possess the fundamental math skills required to balance a checkbook or solve rudimentary algebra problems. A fair percentage of those who do enter college will never finish, and many of those who do finish will be saddled with huge student loans because the cost of a college education has risen at twice the rate of inflation.

We know many of our schools are unsafe and that many of our children and their teachers feel menaced on and off the school grounds, placing a psychological strain on them utterly alien to students and teachers even a generation ago. We know these problems exist across America and vary in magnitude from school district to school district, rising and falling in lockstep with each district's relative affluence. And though wealth is a common denominator in suggesting which school districts perform well and which do not, affluence has not spared any district from the ravages of violence, from stagnant test scores, or from a decline in education quality.

These truths stare us in the face each and every year. We scan newspapers for the latest statistics on college test scores that measure achievement in reading comprehension, mathematics, writing, and science. Though we search in vain for hopeful signs, the message every year is the same. We are not educating our children nearly as well as we were thirty years ago, despite spending hundreds of billions more now than we did then.

And yet we demand more spending on education at the local, state, and federal levels because we know the high-tech economy of the twenty-first century will demand that our children attain high levels of proficiency in reading, writing, mathematics, and science. Those of us who can pay higher college tuition do so for much the same reason. Ditto those who take out student loans.

Our willingness to spend is a defensive gesture because, as a society, we really don't know what else to do. With sour, schoolmarmish seriousness, politicians and educators lecture us about a theorem they appear to believe with an ardor and certainty typically reserved for Pythagoras. The theorem, as best we can determine, goes something like this:

$$S(x) + B = R$$

In this equation the variable S represents public spending. The (x) factor is the amount by which S is increased annually. The variable B represents the education bureaucracy. And R represents positive educational results. In layman's terms, the theorem reads as follows: increased public spending, funneled through the existing education bureaucracy, should produce positive educational results.

But politicians and educators do not leave taxpayers with this theorem to ponder. They explain the benefits of higher education spending with laudable precision. If taxpayers spend more, class sizes will shrink to appropriate levels, teachers' salaries will rise enough to attract the best and the brightest, and schools will be equipped with the high-tech tools children will need to prepare for the twenty-first century.

This argument sounds so plausible, and the risks of ignoring it seem so dire: crowded classrooms, lackluster teachers, antiquated schoolrooms, a lost generation. Given this choice, is it any wonder legions of parents have trooped to the ballot box for two generations in support of local and state bond issues for education and have supported state and national politicians who called for increased spending on education?

No.

And yet the amount of money poured annually into our education system never seems to be quite enough. We always appear to be falling just short of the requisite multiplier, just shy of that magic amount by which we need to increase our "investment" in education before we will see results.

In August of 1997 the National Assessment of Education Progress offered the following summaries of the trends in student proficiency in science, mathematics, reading, and writing. This annual diagnosis of the American education system is considered superior to standardized tests such as the Scholastic Aptitude Test (SAT) and the American College Test (ACT), because the National Assessment measures the performance of students aged 9, 13, and 17. We have chosen to focus on the assessment's report on the "progress" of America's 17-yer-old students for two reasons: their progress was not measurably different than that of younger students, and their performance gives us the clearest understanding of the quality of contemporary high-school students.

To quote from the National Assessment's report:

- Science: "Among 17-year-old students, declines in performance that were observed from 1969 to 1982 were reversed, and the trend has been higher average science scores since that time. Despite these recent gains, the *overall trend was negative, and the 1996 average score remained lower than the 1969 average.*" (Emphasis added.)

- Mathematics: "Among 17-year-olds, declining performance during the 1970s and early 1980s was followed by a period of moderate gains. Although the overall pattern is one of increased performance, *the average score in 1996 was not significantly different from that in 1973."* (Emphasis added.)

- Reading: "At age 17, the pattern of increases in average reading scores from 1971 to 1988 was not sustained into the 1990s. Although the overall pattern is one of improved performance across the assessment years, the average score of 17-year-olds in 1996 *was not significantly different from that of their counterparts in 1971."* (Emphasis added.)

- "Among eleventh graders, an overall pattern of declining performance is evident in the average writing scores across the assessment years. In 1996, *the average score attained by these students was lower than that in 1984."* (Emphasis added.)

With results such as these it would be easy for an outsider to assume the nation had devoted scant attention to improving elementary and secondary education from 1969 to the present.

But a quick review of federal and state education spending over these years reveals that taxpayers spent lavishly on education, equating this spending with the creation of a better-educated citizenry. That, after all, is the equation politicians and educators frequently represent to the public, as summarized in a popular bumper-sticker slogan: *If you think education is expensive, try ignorance.*

As the following statistics show, however, America may not be spending a lot for education, but rather just spending a lot.

Let's first take a look at the trends in education spending in America since 1960, the first year a presidential election was influenced by the question of education. America at the time was consumed with the idea that it had fallen behind the Soviets in terms of technical skill and know-how, a conclusion drawn almost entirely from the Soviet's successful launch of Sputnik, an unmanned satellite that successfully orbited Earth in 1957. America decided it had to address what appeared to be a gap in its technical and engineering acumen, and the electoral contest between Vice President Richard Nixon and Senator John Kennedy was the first in which the national role in education was seriously and strenuously debated.

In 1960 this nation spent $831 billion on elementary and secondary education, including all federal, state, and local allocations. That amount rose to $1.6 trillion in 1970; to $1.9 trillion in 1980; to

#2.7 trillion in 1990. In 1995 the nation spent $3 trillion on elementary and secondary education. (These figures are all in constant 1993–94 dollars.)

Behind this string of mind-boggling numbers is this central fact: this nation tripled its "investment" in elementary and secondary education from 1960 to 1990. And we are on a pace to quadruple that investment by the year 2000.

And what are the trends in federal spending on education?

In 1962 the federal government spent $1.2 billion on all education programs. In 1997 it spent $51 billion. Federal support for elementary and secondary education rose from $482 million in 1962 to $16.2 billion in 1997. Federal spending on higher education rose from $323 million in 1962 to $9.1 billion in 1997. And federal support for training and employment increased from $189 million to $6.8 billion. In 1962 federal education spending accounted for less than 0.8 percent of the entire federal budget. In 1997 it will account for 1.7 percent, a twofold increase. Perhaps it's time for taxpayers to start asking politicians of both parties when they can expect to see a commensurate return on the trillions they have invested in the cause of better educating the citizenry.

What do we have to show for this noble investment? What do we have as a return on an investment urged upon us by nearly two generations of politicians who have promised greater returns for substantially higher federal, state, and local spending on elementary and secondary education?

As the statistics from the National Assessment of Educational Progress show, test scores for children in all grades in the core curricula of reading, mathematics, and science *have fallen or remained constant* even though we have tripled our local, state, and federal support for elementary and secondary education.

Consider the following scores on standardized tests:

- In 1967 the average score on the verbal portion of the Scholastic Assessment Test (SAT) was 466. In 1995 the average verbal score was 428—a 38-point decline.

- In 1967 the average score on the mathematics portion of the SAT was 492. In 1995 the average mathematics score was 482—a 10-point decline.

- In 1967 the composite score on the American College Test (ACT) was 19.9. In 1995 it was 20.8. English scores rose from

18.5 to 20.2, mathematics scores from 20.0 to 20.2, and science scores from 20.8 to 21.0.

At a very basic level, it just does not make sense. How can the wealthiest, most-innovative, and most-productive nation on the planet consistently produce mediocre results in its public education system? How can so many people at the local, state, and federal levels who obviously care deeply about the education of our children find themselves perpetually bewildered by the difficulties in translating higher public spending into better results in the classroom?

It is time for voters and their elected leaders to reject the rigid, one-dimensional notion that more spending is the only route to better learning.

Beyond that, we offer the following observations about the national education debate:

- Albert Einstein defined insanity as doing the same thing over and over while expecting a different result. Using this as a measurement, our current debate over education is insane. We keep debating how much to put into the system—*without asking fundamental questions about the system itself.*

- Unless this system strengthens its emphasis and improves its ability to prepare students for the rigors of the twenty-first-century workplace, the disparity in wages among workers will only increase.

- America's racial divisions cannot be solved unless all children, white, black, Hispanic, Asian, and others, receive a quality education. Those who want to abolish affirmative action must concede, as some do, that the real problem in the American workplace is no longer institutional discrimination, but the appalling gap between the skills of the average white and the average black and Hispanic high-school graduate.

LOOKING FOR ALTERNATIVES

With very little help from Washington or many state legislatures, families are trying to force school districts to change their habits. For most parents, this means leaving the system entirely by sending their children to private schools or by educating them at home. This choice is being increasingly exercised by upper-income and middle-income families who simply refuse to accept the public-school status quo. Many families who have stayed within the system have developed charter schools, learning centers that receive taxpayer support but create their own specialized curriculum and teaching methods.

According to the Department of Education, 1.2 million students were taught at home in 1997, up from 480,000 in 1990. Enrollment in Catholic private schools was 2.7 million in 1997, up from 2.5 million in 1990. And enrollment at Christian schools was 797,000 in 1997, up from 523,000 in 1990.

An article by Rene Sanchez in the October 1, 1997 *Washington Post* summarized the trend as follows:

> In a movement flustering schools across the nation, more parents than ever are choosing alternatives to public education for their children, so much that what once seemed only a fad to many educators is instead starting to resemble a revolution.
>
> Those migrating from public education say the roots of their disenchantment vary. Some parents are frustrated with bureaucracy, others fear student violence. Some want their children to spend more time learning values, others call the one-size-fits-all model of most large public schools an ineffective and impersonal way to learn.
>
> Not long ago, many public school officials virtually ignored . . . and scoffed at the growth of other options in education. But today those trends have begun to send a powerful message to public schools, even prompting some of them to acknowledge a threat of competition for the first time.
>
> The migration is transcending race, class and geography. Charter schools are being opened in wealthy suburbs and in the poorest urban neighborhoods. Christian schools, often a refuge a generation ago for whites fleeing desegregated public schools, have growing appeal to black families. Home schooling, once widely perceived as a dubious form of education used most by religious zealots, is going mainstream, embraced by an array of professionals who are working at home and taking advantage of new computer technology that helps children learn.

Frustration with the status quo has fostered a "bottom-up" revolution in which many parents have decided to seize their children's education destiny from a system they no longer believe is interested in or capable of meeting their children's needs. And lest we forget, families who send their children to private schools or home school pay twice for education—they continue to subsidize the public system they left behind through taxes, even as they pay private-school tuition or pay for the materials required to operate a school at home.

When these ideas first surfaced at the state level, the education bureaucracy responded with unremitting hostility. Over time educators have become begrudgingly tolerant of charter schools. But they continue aggressive campaigns against public support—either through subsidies or tax breaks—for private school or home schooling.

Similarly, at the federal level a Democratic filibuster smothered a pilot project in which two thousand students attending schools in the District of Columbia would have received vouchers to attend private school. The District of Columbia spends more than $9,000 per pupil (the 1995 national average was $5,907), and yet its schools are among the worst in the nation. They are dilapidated. Teachers and students live in fear of thugs inside and outside school grounds. Textbooks are in short supply, as are tutors and counselors. In 1997 a federal judge ordered a three-week delay in the opening of the school year because forty-three schools needed extensive roof repairs. Again, few school districts in America spend more per pupil than the District of Columbia (it ranked fifth in per-pupil expenditures in 1995). Yet test scores for District students are routinely among the lowest in the nation, and the city's schools lag far behind those of similarly sized municipalities in graduation rates and college attendance.

Literally thousands of children and their parents feel trapped because tuition to attend excellent private schools in the District of Columbia or in neighboring Virginia or Maryland is simply too expensive. Many District of Columbia parents hire professional tutors to provide basic reading, mathematics, and writing instruction that their children should be receiving in school but are not. For those who can't afford to pay, volunteer tutors are available, but the waiting lists are lengthy, and the quality of the tutors is uneven. Democrats refused to allow federal support for a voucher program because they feared it would undermine support for the public-school system and set a dangerous precedent for federal support of private education.

It's time for a wake-up call, though: support for schools in the District of Columbia has already been undermined by their abysmal performance. As for the precedent of setting aside federal funds for private education, we wish to ask these two rude questions: why do we provide billions in federal grants and loans for students attending private and church-affiliated colleges and universities? Why are these subsidies appropriate for a college education but inappropriate for students in grades kindergarten through 12?

The point we want to make is this: not that this piece of legislation alone would have been a cure-all for D.C. schools. Rather, we argue the status quo is not working and those who perpetuate it must be held accountable.

So, what can make a difference? Let us introduce you to LeRoy Koppendrayer, a member of the Minnesota House of Representatives, who sponsored the nation's largest tax-credit program for alternatives to public-school education. Koppendrayer, a dairy farmer and agricultural consultant, became a believer in alternatives to the education status quo while working in Indonesia from 1987 to 1989. There, on the island of Java, his three children, ages nine through fifteen, attended the same school. Actually, they attended school in the same room. One of your authors, Tim Penny, had a similar experience, attending a two-room county elementary school in rural Minnesota.

"There were 50 kids from 13 countries in two rooms that sat on a concrete slab that had paper-thin walls on three sides," Koppendrayer recalled in an interview. "But the students were motivated, the parents were caring, and the teacher was energized. All of my children learned as much as, if not more than, they had in the States. I don't care if you have a Taj Mahal or a palm tree, education can happen."

So Koppendrayer joined forces with Republican Governor Arne Carlson to push through a set of tax credits for low-income parents and tax deductions for all Minnesota parents to defray educational expenses. After a long fight with the Democratically controlled legislature, Carlson had to drop his insistence that poor families be allowed to use the tax credits for private-school tuition, but he got everything else he wanted. Minnesota is now home to a two-year, $160 million program that will allow parents to use their own tax dollars to pay for computers, computer software, tutors, and summer educational camp. In the case of wealthier taxpayers, these dollars defray some costs at private schools their children attend.

Carlson's plan attracted strong support throughout the state, and eventually Democrats accepted most of his proposals and passed them into law with huge majorities, making them political shareholders in the largest publicly funded school-choice program in America.

Every large institution in this country has undergone a transformation triggered by three dynamic outside forces: new technology, global competition, and harried customers. American industry has retooled, increased worker productivity, and improved customer service to respond to these changes. Government at the local, state, and federal levels has begun to dismantle some of the bureaucracies erected to fight the Cold War, and to use new technology to provide more information and nominally better services to taxpayers.

Despite modest successes in states such as Minnesota, by and large our public education system has not yet retooled. It has not yet shown a commitment to giving taxpayers good value. More important, it has not risen to the challenge posed by increased competition in the "intellectual marketplace." The public education system in America looks remarkably similar to the one created at the turn of the century as America completed the transition from an agrarian to an industrial society.

In his best-selling and breathtakingly prescient 1980 book, *The Third Wave,* futurist Alvin Toffler described the rise of the public-education system at the dawn of the Industrial Revolution.

As work shifted out of the fields and the home, moreover, children had to be prepared for factory life. If young people could be prefitted to the industrial system, it would vastly ease the problems of industrial discipline later on. The result was another central structure of all Second Wave [industrial] societies: mass education.

Built on the factory model, mass education taught basic reading, writing, and arithmetic, a bit of history and other subjects. This was the "overt curriculum." But beneath it lay an invisible or "covert curriculum" that was far more basic. It consisted—and still does in most industrial nations—of three courses: one in punctuality, one in obedience, and one in rote, repetitive work. Factory labor demanded workers who showed up on time, especially assembly line hands. It demanded workers who would take orders from a management hierarchy without questioning. And it demanded men and women prepared to slave away at machines or in offices, performing brutally repetitious operations.

Thus from the mid-nineteenth century on, as the Second Wave cut across country after country, one found a relentless educational progression: children started school at a younger and younger age, the school year became longer and longer (in the United States it climbed 35 percent between 1878 and 1956), and the number of years of compulsory schooling irresistibly increased.

Second Wave schools machined generation after generation of young people into a pliable, regimented work force of the type required by electro-mechanical technology and the assembly line.

Public education remains centralized and wedded to the practice of warehousing students for set periods of time, training all of them under a set of lowest-common-demoninator standards, and forbidding teachers and principals to develop more-flexible and innovative ways of meeting the various needs of their customers.

When, as the *Washington Post* pointed out, parents begin fleeing the bureaucracy and the "inefficient and impersonal, one-size-fits-all" education system, it's safe to assume they are fed up with precisely the Second Wave mass-education model Toffler described in 1980.

THE RELATIONSHIP BETWEEN SKILLS AND WAGES

American companies can no longer rely upon a high-school diploma as a guarantee of proficiency in mathematics, reading, and English comprehension. In their 1997 book, *Teaching New Basic Skills,* economists Richard Murnane of Harvard University and Frank Levy of the Massachusetts Institute of Technology argue that American industry is hiring college graduates to perform skills that require only ninth-grade math and reading skills.

"Doing math at a ninth-grade level means the ability to manipulate fractions and decimals and to interpret line graphs and bar graphs," Murnane and Levy wrote. "It requires only a bare minimum of algebra."

Murnane and Levy argue that companies chose to hire more-costly college graduates over high-school graduates because they can no longer trust a high-school diploma to guarantee "this level of mathematical skill," since "many recent high-school graduates don't have it."

As a result, high-school graduates are being left behind, and high-school dropouts are almost guaranteed substandard wages for many years.

Consider these statistics:

- In 1975 the mean (average) yearly income in America was $8,552, and a high-school dropout earned $6,198 or 73 percent of the mean income. A high-school graduate earned $7,843 or 92 percent of the mean income.

- In 1995 the mean annual income in America was $26,792, and a high-school dropout earned only $14,013 or 52 percent of the mean income. A high-school graduate earned $21,431 or 80 percent of the mean income.

- In twenty years high-school dropouts have lost 28 percent of their earning power as it relates to average income. High-school graduates have lost 12 percent of their earning power.

In his 1990 book *Power Shift,* Toffler explained the effect the new, technology-driven Third Wave economy was having on the relationship between skills and work and, more important, on the relationship between skills and joblessness.

The old Second Wave factories needed essentially interchangeable workers. By contrast, Third Wave operations require diverse and continually evolving skills—which means that workers become less and less interchangeable. And this turns the entire problem of unemployment upside down.

In Second Wave or smokestack societies, an injection of capital spending or consumer purchasing power could stimulate the economy and generate jobs. Given one million jobless, one could, in principle, prime the economy and create one million jobs. Since the jobs were either interechangeable or required so little skill that they could be learned in less than an hour, virtually any unemployed worker could fill almost any job. Presto! The problem evaporates.

Yet it is no longer possible to reduce joblessness simply by increasing the number of jobs, because the problem is no longer merely numbers. Unemployment has gone from quantitative to qualitative.

Thus, even if there were ten new want ads for every jobless worker, if there are 10 million vacancies and only one million unemployed, the one million will not be able to perform the available jobs unless they have skills—knowledge—matched to the skill requirements of those new jobs. These skills are now so varied and fast-changing that workers can't be interchanged as easily or as cheaply as in the past. Money and numbers no longer solve the problem.

EDUCATION AND RACIAL DIVISIONS

At a forum on race relations in America in early December of 1997, President Clinton sparred with social scientist Abigail Thernstrom over the role affirmative action plays in American society. Thernstrom believes that affirmative action needlessly pits whites and minorities against one another and ignores the true cause of inequality in the workplace—the skills gap we have referred to.

Skeptical, Clinton asked Thernstrom the following question: "Abigail, do you favor the United States Army abolishing the affirmative-action program that produced [General] Colin Powell?

"Yes or no," the president demanded. "Yes or no."

Thus provoked, Thernstrom replied: "I do not think it is racial preferences that made Colin Powell. Let us have real equality of education. These preferences disguise the problem. The real problem is the racial skills gap."

The president's suggestion that General Powell would never have risen through the ranks of the army but for the intervention of affirmative action policies is very troubling. But the fact of affirmative action makes Clinton's argument plausible in Powell's case, just as it does in any other question of employment anywhere in the nation. Whether he intended to or not, Clinton legitimized the oft-spoken water-cooler lament: Yeah, he/she got that job because he/she is black/Hispanic/Asian.

Attributing all career success for Powell and members of other minorities to affirmative action diminishes appreciation for the talent, initiative, and exemplary performance *demonstrated* by these successful men and women.

It doesn't have to be this way.

But let's be honest with ourselves. Though many of us would prefer to live in a world without racial preferences, unless we address this skills gap between whites and minorities, we shall remain a racially divided nation.

Whether we like it or not, the workplace of the early twenty-first century will brutally discriminate between workers with skills and those without them. It is our belief that race, sex, and sexual orientation will be of far less interest to employers in this decentralized and regenerative economy than the relative skill levels of competing applicants. Currently, the opportunities for black, Hispanic, and other minority children to develop the skills needed for this high-tech economy are far behind those available to the average white child. Until these inequities are appreciably narrowed, our nation will be unable to solve the economic divisions among races—divisons that intensify feelings of isolation and separateness that lie at the heart of racial suspicions and, eventually, racial hatred.

As Toffler indicated, the promise of the twenty-first century is that economic forces will penalize those who discriminate on the basis of race, sex, and sexual orientation. Employers who hire workers on the basis of their personal characteristics instead of their skills will be at a competitive disadvantage with rivals who base their hiring decisions entirely on skills. Unlike assembly-line managers earlier in this century, who suffered no loss in production by giving more of their "interchangeable" jobs to whites than to minorities, the managers in the Third Wave economy will lose market share if they discriminate against better-qualified applicants.

So our nation can begin to heal its racial divisions and increase average wages if it thoroughly alters the structure of public education to emphasize teaching skills relevant to the Third Wave economy. Just as society rebuilt its public education system to assist the Second Wave industrial economy, we can build a new system that teaches skills and habits applicable to the information-based Third Wave economy.

We cannot begin this process as long as we allow politicians to answer our pleas for better education with the same hackneyed more-money-equals-better-outcome equation. America's taxpaying parents have a right to demand policies that lead to appreciable improvements in the quality of our educational system. The debate should not be about money. It should be about results.

THE ENVIRONMENT—IT'S MOTHER EARTH OR MOTHER LODE

THIS LIE IS used in politics to demonize either side of any environmental debate. Conservatives denounce certain environmental laws—those protecting endangered species, for example—by dredging up rare and largely unrepresentative stories about the regulations running amok. Environmentalists charge that those seeking to strike a balance between competing economic and environmental interests are, in fact, hungry to abolish all environmental regulations.

Since this debate so frequently follows a predictable partisan pattern—Republicans in favor of free-market solutions, Democrats in favor of greater environmental regulation—it's important to quickly review each party's credibility on environmental policy.

Republicans and their allies in industry have routinely sought to circumvent environmental regulations. They have attacked many attempts to improve air and water quality as "too costly" or riddled with "too many regulations." Conservatives have long resented the very presence of the Environmental Protection Agency (EPA), and Reagan carried out a successful campaign to reduce its budget. When Reagan ran for president in 1980, the EPA budget of $5.6 billion accounted for 0.9 percent of all federal spending. In Reagan's first budget, which was for fiscal year 1982, the EPA budget was cut to $5 billion. The next year it was cut to $4.3 billion. The year he ran for reelection, the EPA budget was down to $4 billion and accounted for 0.5 percent of all federal spending. By 1989 the EPA budget had dropped to 0.4 percent of total federal spending, a percentage that prevails today and is projected to persist until 2002. Make no mistake: Reagan reversed the nation's commitment to using federal resources to enforce environmental laws.

President Bush made a significant contribution to environmental policy by breaking a decade-long legislative logjam over the Clean Air Act, the principal means by which the federal government regulates air pollution. Ironically, Bush teamed with Senate Democrats led by Majority Leader George Mitchell, an archenemy on so many other domestic issues, to shatter an opposition led by Representative John Dingell, a Democrat from Michigan. Bush drew withering criticism from conservative Republicans for passing the Clean Air Act. Many said the new regulations would cripple industry, cost the economy jobs, send wages plummeting, and do nothing to actually improve air quality. They were wrong on all counts.

Interestingly, conservatives now fighting a worldwide treaty to reduce air pollution cite the decline in air pollution in America as a reason to reject the treaty. Why do we need a new treaty, they argue, when the air is already so much cleaner in America? What they forget to mention, of course, is that the air is cleaner *precisely because* of the new air-pollution standards that Bush signed into law and they so vigorously opposed.

This sorry record continued when the Republican Congress arrived in 1995. When it came time to write the EPA's budget, the GOP's first instinct was to prevent it from enforcing regulations on oil- and gas-refinery emissions, raw sewage, arsenic, and radon in drinking water. The Republicans did not try to change these regulations but instead used a behind-the-scenes legislative maneuver to deprive the EPA of the money needed to enforce them. One would think that if the regulations were too onerous or constituted an inefficient means of reducing pollution, Republicans would have conducted public hearings to study better alternatives and given their colleagues in the House and Senate the opportunity to devise better regulations or take a completely fresh approach. But the GOP decided against presenting this case to the public and chose instead to wage a secret war against the EPA. It hoped that by depriving the EPA of the means to enforce certain arcane environmental regulations, it could achieve its aims while attracting scant public scrutiny.

It didn't work.

Republicans from northeastern states teamed with Democrats and President Clinton to block these changes, and the entire House Republican leadership suffered a public-relations black eye in the process. And deservedly so. While it's difficult to change laws that already exist, the legislative process and sound political strategy demand that those who want change should state their cases publicly and persuade members of Congress and the public at large that a new approach is required. We would have applauded Republicans had they attempted this strategy, and we venture to say the public would have been far more supportive. We believe the time has come for a serious inquiry into the effectiveness of EPA regulations, because more and more evidence suggests that Washington's one-size-fits-all rules are woefully inefficient. But the sneak attack on the EPA only furthered the longstanding suspicion among environmentalists in Congress and the public at large that conservative Republicans (who dominate the party's leadership) cannot be trusted to rewrite pollution laws.

Ultimately, though, environmentalists cannot escape blame. They deserve a similar dose of scorn for their adamant refusal—or, at least, extreme reluctance—to use market forces and simple common sense to address some of the nation's most-severe environmental problems. Numerous scholars, many of them leaders in the environmental movement of the 1970s, now complain that the EPA's command-and-control bureaucracy cannot adequately address the nation's myriad and technologically diverse pollution problems.

The best example of this failure is the Superfund law—by far the most-expensive and most-important effort the EPA has ever undertaken to protect Americans from pollution.

This law is the poster child for everything that is wrong with our national environmental policy. All anyone needs to know about the limits of Washington's one-size-fits-all regulations can be found in this law's dismal record. Virtually all of the flawed assumptions about how to improve environmental conditions—the state of the air or the water, of endangered species, or of topsoil or wetlands—are inherent in this law and its results.

Our story begins in 1977, when investigators discovered that the Love Canal subdivision in Niagara Falls, New York, was built atop a chemical dump operated by Hooker Chemical Facility, even though the company had warned the city the site was unsuitable for a housing development. Eventually chemicals from Hooker's discarded drums began to leak into the soil and poisoned the residents. About the same time, a seven-acre site in Kentucky strewn with seventeen thousand drums of chemical waste was dubbed the "Valley of Death." In Elizabeth, New Jersey, at a Chemical Control Corporation facility, forty thousand rusting drums full of (among other things) nitroglycerin, TNT, phosgene, and other unidentified chemicals exploded and caught fire. Clearly, there was a serious problem with the disposal of hazardous and potentially hazardous chemicals.

In a lame-duck session in 1980, the Democratically controlled Congress passed and President Carter signed the Comprehensive Environmental Response, Compensation and Liability Act. The law imposed new taxes on the chemical and oil industries to create a pool of money, known as the Superfund, to clean up toxic-waste sites. The law placed the EPA in charge of discovering such sites and supervising the cleanup.

The law was less ambitious than original versions that gave individuals and families the right to sue for damages in federal courts and provided compensation for the victims' out-of-pocket medical expenses. Opposition from the chemical industry forced lawmakers to drop both of these provisions. Nevertheless, the law gave the EPA the power—known in legal jargon as joint and several liability—to force a single business or businesses responsible for toxic pollution to pay for the cleanup. The philosophy underlying the law was simple: polluters and not the government should pay to clean up toxic-waste sites. What's more, the law said that companies would have to pay for the cleanup—even if they broke no laws when they originally dumped the toxins.

This concept is known as retroactive liability.

This is how former congressman Dennis Eckhart, a Democrat who represented northeast Ohio from 1980 to 1992, described what this concept, when applied to Superfund, meant in the real world:

> Under retroactive liability it doesn't matter if you put one pound or one ton of waste in the dump; it doesn't matter if you are the only company still in business and others who dumped more are long gone; it doesn't even matter if you were told to or had a permit to dispose of the waste in a certain way—you are still liable for the total costs of the cleanup.

When Congress passed the Superfund law, it promised that the $1.6 billion in new taxes levied against the oil and chemical companies would pay to clean up all of the nation's toxic waste sites in five years. As he signed the legislation, President Carter said the law was "landmark in its scope and in its impact on preserving the environmental quality of our country."

Senator Robert T. Stafford, a Republican from Vermont, called it "the major preventative health bill to come before the Congress in the last four years."

And Congressman James Florio, a Democrat from New Jersey, said the law "set in motion the mechanics to begin removing the threat of harmful and dangerous waste sites."

We don't doubt that Carter and these lawmakers had high hopes for Superfund. But it's interesting now to read these prophetic comments from the president of the Chemical Manufacturers Association, Robert A. Roland, quoted in a December 3, 1980 dispatch from the Associated Press. Roland said he was concerned how the industry would react to the law's "unfortunate precedents" and was worried that the Washington bureaucracy created to enforce the law might prove ineffective.

"The test of any new law, of course, will come during its implementation, and our industry will participate actively and constructively in the process of perfecting the legislation," Roland said.

Now, it would be unrealistic to assume that any new federal program could achieve 100 percent of its goals in the time allotted. No one could have predicted, however, how far short Superfund would have fallen from these modest goals.

As of last year (1997) the federal government had spent more than $30 billion on Superfund but had cleaned up fewer than 10 percent of the toxic-waste sites identified by the EPA. According to congressional auditors, 30 percent of this $30 billion had been consumed by what are euphemistically known as "transaction" costs, in other words, payments to lawyers and environmental consultants. Thus, roughly $10 billion was squandered on lawyers and consultants instead of ridding America of toxic waste.

The American Academy of Actuaries estimates that $900 million of the $2 billion now spent annually on Superfund pays legal fees.

According to a General Accounting Office (GAO) report issued in March 1997, the number of years required to clean up a Superfund site has increased from 2.3 in 1986 to 10.5 in 1996. The report also revealed that only 44 percent of Superfund's annual $1.4 billion budget pays to clean up toxic wastes. The remainder, the report said, is spent on questionable "outreach," "travel," "lawyers," "job training," and other dubious bureaucratic costs. The report also found that it's taking the EPA longer and longer to place toxic-waste sites on the Superfund list, whose goal is to find sites and evaluate whether they deserve Superfund designation. This process, which was supposed to take only 4 years, on average, now takes more than 9.

As of the summer of 1997, the EPA has designated 1,208 Superfund sites. The EPA has tinkered with its administrative procedures, but none of those changes has done much good. The General Accounting Office (GAO) found that only six of the EPA's forty-five administrative reforms produced measurable benefits. As the *Washington Times* said in a June 9, 1997 editorial: "So for the time being at least, putting a site on the Superfund list remains just about the only surefire way of ensuring that nothing ever happens to it."

Now here's a Superfund story straight out of a *Saturday Night Live* script: Meet Barbara Williams, whom we got to know through a story in the March 19, 1997 *Wall Street Journal* by reporter John Fialka. Barbara owns the SunnyRay restaurant in Gettysburg, Pennsylvania. Barbara sells an addictive lemon sponge pie and other traditional coffee-shop fare that attracts customers throughout eastern Pennsylvania. Conscientious and courteous, Barbara does her part to spare the environment by recycling these restaurant waste products: glass, metal, plastic, cardboard, newspapers, even her cooking grease. As Fialka put it in his story, "What she puts in her dumpster is usually nothing more harmful than yesterday's mashed potatoes."

So you can imagine what a surprise it was to Barbara in October 1995 when a postman delivered a lawsuit the United States Department of Justice had filed against her. The charge? Disposing of toxic wastes in a local dump. Incredulous and afraid, Barbara broke down and wept on the spot. As Fialka relates the story, the postman then offered that he had "been handing out all these things all morning."

As it turns out, Barbara was one of more than eight hundred people sucked into the voracious maw of the Superfund law through a case known in legal circles as *U.S. v. Keystone*. As Fialka explains, the *U.S. v. Keystone* precedent "functions as a kind of legal black hole run by Philadelphia lawyers that could absorb as much as $30 million." Under this legal wrinkle individuals and businesses three times removed from the source of pollution can be held liable for it in federal court. Many are forced to settle with powerful and heavily financed big-city law firms because they don't have the time or money to fight back.

Here's how this insidious process works.

The EPA wants to clean up the Keystone Sanitary Landfill near Philadelphia. To do so, the Justice Department filed suit against 13 large businesses who used the dump and are thought to be the major polluters. Through a tricky legal maneuver, those 13 large businesses blamed 120 midsized businesses that also used the dump for contributing to the contamination. Those 120 businesses then used the same tricky legal maneuver to snare businesses such as Barbara's SunnyRay restaurant. Lawsuits were also filed against a Gettysburg bowling alley, a motel, and a Lutheran home for the elderly.

The main problem at the landfill is the presence of heavy metals and, according to Fialka, "other nasty stuff" that the EPA wants to prevent from "leaching into the ground water." The problem is, no one currently knows (or, more probably, is willing to admit) who put the heavy metals and the other "nasty stuff" in the dump in the first place.

But it's a safe bet that Barbara's restaurant did not do it. And neither did the bowling alley, or the Lutheran home for the elderly.

Nevertheless, the suit filed against Barbara seeks seventy-five thousand dollars in damages, which, she told the *Wall Street Journal,* is more than she makes in an entire year.

We mentioned that Barbara's lemon sponge pie is addictive, and that's where this story begins to grow slightly brighter. Barbara has an attorney now, one who agreed to take the case while discussing Barbara's woes over a wedge of the aforementioned pie. Gary Hartman has taken on Barbara and thirty other clients who have found themselves in the same boat, even though he had never handled Superfund litigation before. As we said, he likes the pie.

The law is not hospitable to defendants such as Barbara, even if they have legal representation. The Superfund law says that if a dump has toxic waste in it and there is proof that a defendant used the dump, then the defendant is guilty *whether he or she contributed to the pollution or not.* Barbara cannot argue her case before a judge because judges don't handle Superfund litigation. Negotiations are supervised by "liaison attorneys" from big-city law firms—in Barbara's case, big shots from Philadelphia. "It's like practicing law on Mars," Hartman told the *Wall Street Journal.*

The big defendants ensnared Williams and others because their legal costs are insured. That gave them the wherewithal to hire expensive lawyers to search for small-fry defendants such as Barbara in hopes that they would settle and thereby help defray their liability costs. Barbara cannot settle, however, because her insurance company says it will not pay as she is not covered for toxic-pollution liability. How many coffee shops are?

For the second time in as many sessions of Congress, Republicans have tried to rewrite the Superfund law to protect victims such as Barbara from this type of daisy-chain litigation. The EPA has also stepped in to cut some fourteen thousand defendants from Superfund lawsuits. But that does not change the underlying law, and other victims are being sucked into this terrifying legal whirlpool every day. At last count, the EPA estimates twenty-five thousand small businesses have been caught in this type of Superfund hell because they used a municipal dump now designated a Superfund site. Such sites comprise roughly one quarter of all Superfund cases.

Fears of liability claims such as these have brought Superfund to a screeching and destructive halt. Not only has the program failed to clean up more than one thousand designated toxic-waste sites, it has also idled thousands of acres of commercial property that developers fear may at some point in the future receive a Superfund designation. These areas are called "brownfields," and there are more than 450,000 of them across the country. But developers are afraid to tread there, fearing to get caught in the Superfund liability whirlpool. So developers put new industrial sites atop "greenfields"—a dopey, bureaucratic word for pastures, forests, and farmland.

Now stop and consider this insanity: Abandoned industrial sites sit amid urban decay. Developers who want to use them don't because they are afraid of being trapped in a litigious tar pit, one created to make sure toxic-waste sites would be cleaned up. Except the law that created the litigious tar pit has failed to clean up the site. This same law contains idiotically strict guidelines on what constitutes a "clean" industrial site: the soil must be so free of contamination that it would not cause cancer in a child if he or she ate a teaspoon of dirt a day *for seventy years.*

Ridiculous as it might seem, this is the law, and the liability risks that come with it pose a real threat to today's developers, who flee urban areas to develop their new industrial sites on pastures, in forests, and atop farms. This new development increases surburban sprawl, which necessitates the building of more roads and the destruction of still-more pastoral land. Meanwhile, the old industrial sites rot, creating eyesores, depressing real-estate values, and denying potential jobs for inner-city residents.

Does this make any sense to you?

Well, it doesn't to many big-city mayors.

"We agree that far too much money is being spent on lawyers and not enough on cleanup," said Robert Ingram, president of the National Conference of Black Mayors. "Our primary concern is that tens of thousands of abandoned properties in urban areas lie contaminated and unproductive because developers and business fear Superfund's far-reaching liability system."

In 1991 a prominent business attorney, George Clemon Freeman Jr., at the time chairman of the business-law section of the American Bar Association, described Superfund's retroactive liability as being "without any precedent in the civilized or uncivilized world."

In May of 1996 Superfund's retroactive-liability standard was ruled unconstitutional. United States District Judge William Brevard Hand ruled that the Department of Justice could not punish companies or individuals for violations of law that occurred before the law took effect. His ruling nullified all Superfund litigation for offenses that occurred before passage of the law on December 11, 1980. The Justice Department immediately appealed Judge Hand's ruling.

This nation has imposed retroactive liability rarely, and only in those cases when the courts were absolutely sure that this was Congress's intention and that the potentially harmful consequences of such a policy had been fully debated. This is not entirely clear with the Superfund law.

Nevertheless the Eleventh Circuit Court of Appeals ruled unanimously in March 1997 that the retroactive liability provisions of the Superfund law *were* constitutional after all. The court said that it believed Congress's intent was to impose costs retroactively on known polluters.

Responding to the verdict, Lois J. Schiffer, who argued on behalf of retroactive liability for the EPA, said: "With this ruling we can continue our commitment to faster and more efficient cleanups in every area of the country."

Fast and efficient are clearly not words that accurately describe the Superfund program. Schiffer might want to check these statistics on the pace of Superfund cleanups.

- 1992 = 88 sites
- 1993 = 68 sites
- 1994 = 61 sites

- 1995 = 68 sites
- 1996 = 64 sites

It's important at this juncture to point out one of the many lessons the law has taught us and how it should inform our judgment about future environmental laws. Unless our society accepts its role in the creation of pollution and agrees to share the cost of paying for its removal, our efforts at reducing future pollution or getting rid of it will be less productive and just as shamefully ineffective.

Imagine how much safer we would have been if the Superfund legislation had imposed a small tax on all Americans to pay for the immediate cleanup of all Superfund sites without wasting time on legal witch-hunts. Our itch to punish big, bad industry was then, and is now, highly hypocritical. Industry survives only through our own use of its products. As consumers, we share in the problems of pollution and of diminishing natural resources because we create the demand. As long as we're unwilling to pay the true cost of our consumptive habits, we are far less likely to address our environmental problems effectively or efficiently. We are not averse to collecting some of the costs from actual polluters, but we cannot see the logic of the government spending billions in legal costs instead of devoting more time, energy, and tax dollars to cleaning up toxic waste.

For four years the Republican Congress and some sympathetic Democrats have wrestled with the Clinton administration over how to reform Superfund. One of the requirements Republicans sought in their bill was to eliminate "retroactive liability." For this they were accused in the 1996 congressional campaigns of doing the bidding of "big polluters."

A compromise Superfund-reform bill died in the final days of the first year of the 105th Congress. Few in Washington expect the bill to be resurrected in an election year because this issue, like so many others in the environmental debate, is simply too easy to demagogue.

Federal control of environmental regulation needlessly isolates citizens from the process of swiftly and efficiently addressing pollution problems in their backyards. Anyone who has tried to deal with the EPA to address a local pollution problem knows firsthand of its inhospitable and lethargic ways. A centralized pollution-control bureaucracy will never be as responsive to local concerns as municipal and state pollution-control agencies.

In fact, it may surprise you to learn that states took the lead in regulating air pollution in the 1960s, long before pollution control was federalized. We came upon this fascinating anecdote in an article in the CATO Institute's quarterly magazine *Regulation*. The writer was David Schoenbrod, a law professor at New York Law School and former senior attorney for the Natural Resources Defense Council, one of the nation's most influential environmental organizations.

Schoenbrod first points out that aggressive efforts at the state level to regulate air pollution resulted in a reduction of air pollutants in the 1960s that was three times the magnitude of the reduction achieved in the 1970s. These new laws alarmed the auto industry, which began to inquire about how it could protect itself from similar regulations in other states. We pick up Schoenbrod's anecdote here:

> In the early 1960s, the automobile manufacturers, concerned that many states might impose strict and differing emission limits on new cars, sought advice from Lloyd Cutler, an eminent Washington lawyer, former New Dealer, and later counsel to President Carter [and Clinton]. Cutler suggested that the manufacturers get Congress to give the secretary of Health, Education and Welfare (this was before the creation of the EPA in 1970) the authority to regulate emission standards for new cars. He reasoned that the companies would be able to keep the secretary from imposing expensive pollution-reduction measures and that this national authority would be a powerful argument against state regulation. Congress obliged the manufacturers in 1965 and in 1967 it actually prohibited most states from regulating new-car emissions.

Congress changed course in 1970. Responding to mounting public concern about air pollution, Congress passed the Clean Air Act, which regulated new-car emissions and required that states regulate industrial air pollution by means of achieving national air-pollution–reduction goals. As Schoenbrod observed: "The belief that it took the federal government to make the states act comes from federal officials who claim credit for what states officials had already been accomplishing." There is logic to federal intervention. After all, air and water pollution impose costs and diminish the quality of life for people living hundreds of miles from the source of the pollution. Nonetheless, the approach taken by the federal government to ameliorate these "orphan costs" has often proven ineffective and expensive.

In several areas of environmental policy—protecting endangered species, cleaning up water, air, and toxic pollution—environmentalists and their federal-government allies rely on inefficient, costly, and arrogant centralized bureaucracies to achieve their goals. Environmental programs often emphasize intimidation and litigation over negotiation and cooperation. More often than not, the laws advocated by environmentalists and implemented by Washington-based bureaucracies have turned potential private-sector allies into sworn enemies.

Schoenbrod also refers to this assessment of current environmental regulation offered by Professors Henry N. Butler of the University of Kansas and Jonathan R. Macey of Cornell University. In it, Schoenbrod argues that professors encapsulate the flaws many "liberal and conservative scholars" see in the EPA's centralized and sclerotic regulatory schemes:

> [The EPA's] command and control regulatory strategy . . . has not set intelligent priorities, has squandered resources devoted to environmental quality, has discouraged environmentally superior technologies, and imposed unnecessary penalties on innovation and investment.

Environmental regulations are pervasive and expensive. Current estimates suggest that environmental regulations impose costs on the private sector that average $1,800 per household. Authoritative estimates place the cost of environmental regulations imposed since 1970 at $1.5 trillion. So it's important to realize the true expression of the EPA's power is not its annual budget, but rather the number of regulations it promulgates and their costly effect on the private sector. Clearly, when the EPA's budget shrinks, it finds itself unable to monitor all of its regulations. And there are plenty of regulations. For the Superfund program, the EPA wrote a set of regulations dealing with only one portion of the project, and yet these "guidance documents" filled thirteen (13!) loose-leaf notebooks.

So it might be time to ask whether the EPA's regulations work well for the environment and the economy. We don't believe they do. But the answer is not simply to reduce the EPA's budget or to reduce funding surreptitiously for enforcement of select regulations. The answer is to conduct a full-scale congressional investigation into EPA regulations. Congress must bring before the public environmental scholars (many of whom are critical of EPA procedures), state and municipal government leaders (many of whom are frustrated by the EPA's un-willingness to grant them the flexibility they need to clean up their own pollution problems), and private-sector entrepreneurs (many of whom have new ideas about how to address old pollution problems).

What we're talking about is a public inquest into the current state of environmental regulation. We'd like to see hearings similar to those conducted in the summer of 1997 on the Internal Revenue Service. Those hearings highlighted horrific abuses of power within the agency and prompted a significant revision in IRS practices. The House swiftly approved the taxpayers'-rights legislation it spawned in the fall of 1997; the Senate followed suit in April of 1998 and Clinton signed the bill into law soon thereafter.

And, speaking of the IRS, we must offer one last piquant observa-tion on the EPA from Schoenbrod as he destroys one of the EPA's cen-tral defenses—that states are incapable of writing effective antipollution laws or of cracking down on powerful industries within their borders.

EPA loyalists argue that state governments are not competent to produce sound regulations. But, being the folks who took part in writing the EPA's contributions to the *Federal Register,* they were throwing stones from a glass house. The language that the EPA produces is—and I mean this—worse than the babble that comes from the Internal Revenue Service. It is opaque, arcane, elliptical, repetitive, and evasive. The policies are often dumb and sometimes perverse. EPA staffers explain that such problems derive in part from the legislative and ad-ministrative constraints under which they operate. True enough, but the federal house is still glass, regardless of who built it. In the downsized EPA that I propose, the EPA, stripped of its fiat power, could retain its leadership role only by convincing states to adopt its regulations by the quality and sensibility of its poli-cies. That is how the private organization that proposes the Uniform Commercial Code and other uniform laws to the states attains its influence. We need an EPA that succeeds by earning its leadership, not by bringing the states down to mind-numbing mediocrity.

It's the EPA's turn to be brought to the rail. America should hear from witnesses whose property has been seized by zealous regulators needlessly enforcing wetland statutes under the Clean Water Act. We should hear from farmers and ranchers whose property was seized without due compensation under powers given the federal government under the Endangered Species Act. We should hear from municipal leaders who have had to wait years for the EPA to address pollution problems in their own communities while they were forbidden by law from taking proactive steps on their own. We should also hear from governors who are eager to write their own environmental regulations and compete for business and residents on the basis of the "cleanliness" of their states. These governors might also make a case for using their powers to create innovative solutions to pollution problems in their own backyards, much the same way governors are using new approaches to deal with another problem Washington used to try to "solve" through central planning and a one-size-fits-all federal mandate—welfare.

THE FOURTEENTH LIE

REPUBLICANS BELIEVE
IN SMALLER GOVERNMENT

THIS LIE IS central to the Republican Party's appeal for American voters. Sure, Republicans have used the promise of tax cuts effectively as an issue against Democrats, but the core message behind tax cuts has always been that they would contribute to smaller government.

Smaller government is the cause for which Republicans say their party exists. Almost every domestic policy they propose—whether it's abolishing affirmative action, shrinking welfare payments, eliminating regulations, or eliminating government agencies—arises from the belief that the government that governs best governs least. According to their rhetoric, Republicans want a smaller federal government because it will be less intrusive, less prone to regulatory excess, and, most important, less expensive.

When Republicans rhapsodize about the value of returning power to the states, they are calling for a smaller federal government. When they decry the regulatory hyperactivity of the Environmental Protection Agency or the Occupational Health and Safety Administration, they are arguing for smaller government. When they propose tax cuts, they are seeking to reduce the size of government by gradually reducing the revenue it collects.

If the rhetoric is to be believed, the central mission of the Republican Party is to make government less expensive and less meddlesome, and at the same time more effective. This is the central organizing principle of the Republican Party and has been since at least since the closing days of Herbert Hoover's campaign for president in 1928 against Democrat Alfred E. Smith. It was then that Hoover declared that the choice before America was one of "the American system of rugged individualism" put in place by Republicans after World War I and "doctrines of paternalism and state socialism" that were then all the rage in Europe, and increasingly attractive to Democrats in America.

Throughout the New Deal and the Truman presidency, Republicans clamored for smaller government and paid a hefty political price for it, claiming only one majority in Congress from 1930 to 1994. The majority they won in 1946 was short-lived; America had seen enough of Republican austerity and threw them out in 1948, in the election that saw President Truman score his stunning upset over Republican Thomas E. Dewey.

Even after that defeat, Republicans held firm to their "smaller-government-is-best" mantra. While domestic spending grew through the fifties, sixties, and seventies, Republicans lamented that they had no mandate from the people to reverse the steady increases in social spending, federal regulation, and taxes imposed by the Democratically controlled Congresses. Then Ronald Reagan was elected in 1980 on a platform that called for deep cuts in government spending. The only problem was, Republicans in Congress refused to vote for the cuts Reagan proposed, rendering his budgets dead on arrival even before Democrats could so declare them. Still, Republicans said Reagan could not fight a Democratic Congress that cooked up all the new spending—but the Republicans solemnly vowed that if they controlled Congress things would be different.

As a matter of fact, this was just the message Republicans used in 1993 when they attacked Clinton's plan to reduce the deficit through increased taxes and nominal cuts in federal spending. First, Republicans refused en masse to support the president, depriving him of a single one of their votes in the House and Senate and forcing Democrats to stand alone with their president.

Let us take you back to 1993, when Clinton's budget plan was before the Congress and receiving nothing but condemnation from Republicans, who said it failed to cut spending enough. Listen carefully to these quotes from Republicans who saw themselves as the guardians of fiscal sanity and restraint:

"Mr. Clinton's economic plan proposes the largest tax increase in American history, contains few real spending cuts, proposes $60 billion in new spending and adds $1 trillion to the debt during the next four years," Republican Senator Pete V. Domenici complained in a column published in the June 13, 1993 edition of the *Washington Times*.

"If Americans believe that 'change' means higher taxes on everyone, bigger government, excessive defense cuts that harm both national security and the economy, and excuses instead of specifics, they will find plenty in the Democrat plan to support," said Congressmen John Kasich and Christopher Shays in a column published in the March 18, 1993 edition of the *Washington Times*.

"This is not deficit reduction, this is a grand old scheme that we have heard here for decades, and that is to tax more and spend more and to expect that out of that we will get more," said Senator Larry E. Craig of Idaho during debate over the Clinton budget.

"We ought to grow down the size of government to provide more freedom to grow up the private sector," said Congressman Dick Armey of Texas, during House debate over the Clinton budget.

Before we go any further, let us pause to let the air out of a lie Republicans repeated ad nauseam throughout the debate. They alleged, with considerable gusto, that Clinton's tax increase was the "largest in American history."

Wrong.

In inflation-adjusted dollars, the 1982 tax increases passed by a Republican-controlled Senate and Democratically controlled House and signed by President Reagan were larger than the Clinton tax increases. The Reagan increase was also larger as a percentage of the overall economy.

In the end, Clinton's budget, which included $267 billion in higher taxes, passed by one vote in the House and the Senate. From the day Clinton signed the bill into law, Republicans attacked every single vulnerable Democrat up for reelection in 1994 as having cast "the deciding vote" for Clinton's higher taxes.

Partially on the strength of animosity stirred up against Clinton's budget plan, Republicans won control of Congress in 1994 and promised to bring their principles of smaller government to the federal budget.

The Republicans' first budget tried to reduce federal spending, and some of the cuts survived a titanic struggle with Clinton that led to two government shutdowns. Clinton vilified Republicans for their supposed "cuts" in Medicare spending, but he also frightened them away from trying to abolish government agencies such as the departments of Education, Energy, Commerce, and Housing and Urban Development. Republicans had hoped to maintain the vital functions of these agencies and transfer them to other government agencies while shedding layers and layers of bureaucracy and saving taxpayers billions. After the political backlash over the government shutdowns, however, Republicans dropped these ideas like a hot rock.

That was the first year of the Republican Congress. And it was the only one that remotely kept faith with the party's limited-government philosophy. Since then, Republicans in Congress have gone back on their word: they have taken part in a feeding frenzy at the federal trough.

In their first three budgets, Republicans increased federal spending by $183 billion, compared to a three-year increase of $155 billion racked up by a *Democratically controlled Congress*. That's right. Republicans in charge of the nation's purse strings have devoted more to domestic spending than Democrats did while working with Clinton—a president Republicans once described tirelessly as a "tax-and-spend liberal."

In this budget year alone (1998), Republicans increased nondefense domestic spending by $22.6 billion. That translates into a 10-percent increase in nondefense domestic spending over 1997.

Hold on a minute. Republicans in control of the nation's budget are responsible for *increasing* the size and cost of government? Yes. In fact, the Republican party, supposedly the party dedicated to smaller government, decided to cut a five-year deal with Clinton that will *increase* federal spending in both 1998 and 1999. But wait, it gets worse. Republicans had the opportunity to balance the budget in 1998 but chose instead to increase spending for the next two years because that, allegedly, was the price of getting Clinton to accept tax cuts. Why didn't Republicans simply stick to their principles and eneact spending cuts without a tax cut? Wouldn't that have balanced the budget faster and made the government smaller?

While we are on the topic of budget deals, let's review the record of the Republican leadership on the three previous five-year budget deals negotiated since 1990. Bush and a Democratically controlled Congress negotiated a deal that included tax increases, nominal reductions in Medicare spending, and, for the first time ever, obligatory caps on domestic spending. It also included language that required Congress to offset the cost of tax cuts with equal reductions in the growth of entitlement spending and, conversely, required Congress to pay for new entitlement spending with higher taxes. These requirements began to reduce domestic spending gradually and blocked attempts from conservatives to cut taxes, and from liberals to add new entitlement programs. Though it was maligned at the time, many budget experts now view the 1990 agreement as the most-successful tool to control federal spending and as a legislative breakthrough that heralded the end of runaway deficits.

Every senior member of the current Republican leadership in the House and Senate voted against the 1990 budget deal. This list includes House Speaker Newt Gingrich, Senate Majority Leader Trent Lott, House Majority Leader Dick Armey, Senate Majority Whip Don Nickles, and House Majority Whip Tom Delay.

As we mentioned before, every Republican in the House and Senate voted against Clinton's 1993 budget deal.

In both cases, these Republican leaders said the 1990 and 1993 budget deals raised taxes too much and failed to cut spending. They predicted both would result in higher deficits and slower economic growth. In fact, both led to stronger economic growth, in part because Federal Reserve Chairman Alan Greenspan and financial titans on Wall Street saw them as credible attempts to reduce federal deficits—a judgment that led to lower interest rates. Over time those rates declined even further because the lower deficits reduced government borrowing, which left money available for private investors. It's worth pointing out that neither Greenspan nor the titans of Wall Street greeted 1997's so-called balanced-budget deal with the same enthusiasm they showed for the 1990 and 1993 budget plans.

As we've already conveyed, the balanced-budget deal of 1997 will not lead to a balanced budget in 2002 and stands as a monument to political cowardice because it does next to nothing to solve the looming financial crisis faced by Social Security and Medicare.

Instead of dealing with these very problems, Republicans papered them over and began gorging themselves on federal spending. And what kind of spending are we talking about? Well, some of it comes from the Democrats' old stomping-grounds: the pork farm.

According to Citizens Against Government Waste, a watchdog group that monitors congressional spending, the Republicans authorized $14.5 billion in pork-barrel spending in 1996, a 16-percent increase over the previous year and the highest amount since it began monitoring spending in 1990.

This is the Republican party led in the House by Speaker Newt Gingrich, who said in 1993 that he resented the Democrats' spendthrift habits because all they were about was "growing government to give politicians more pork-barrel handouts and bigger bureaucracies."

Together with President Clinton, the Republican Congress did enact cost-saving welfare reforms. But their zealous assault on welfare for the needy has not been matched by an equally aggressive assault on corporate welfare. Budget Committee Chairman John Kasich challenged his Republican colleagues to kill twelve specific industry subsidies, which he dubbed "the Dirty Dozen." According to *Congressional Quarterly,* a highly respected political journal, Kasich's activity during the 1997 budget cycle yielded minuscule savings. Congress took no action on several of the items. In other instances, budget cutting amendments were defeated, in most cases quite handily. Of the twelve projects, only two were subjected to any spending reductions, and those reductions were modest. The complete list follows:

Clean Coal Technology: Five-year cost, $500 million
The program assists private industry in devaluing environmentally sound ways to use coal as a fuel. Congress approved a $101 million rescission.

Fossil Energy Research and Development: Five-year cost, $1.37 billion
The House of Representatives defeated an amendment to cut $21 million from the program that develops alternative energy sources.

Animas-La Plata Project: Five-year cost, $432 million
Efforts to cut spending for this public works project in southern Colorado were defeated in the House and Senate. The project is intended to divert water from the Animas River and pump it to farm land at higher elevations.

Appalachian Regional Commission: Five-year cost, $500 million
The House rejected an amendment to cut $90 million from the road construction aspects of this program which duplicate other programs.

Market Access Program: Five-year cost, $347 million
The House voted to prohibit funds for administrative costs of the program that assists exporters of fresh food. The Senate tabled an amendment to the agriculture appropriations bill to cut funding for the program from $90 million to $70 million. No final action.

Timber Roads: Five-year cost, $100 million
Congress cut $5.6 million from the budget for timber road con-

struction in national forests that help private logging companies get access to tracts of forest.

Overseas Private Investment Corporation: Five-year cost, $3.5 billion
The House and Senate defeated amendments to cut the budget of OPIC, which provides loans and political risk insurance for U.S. business investments in developing countries.

Enhanced Structural Adjustment Facility: Five-year cost, $150 million
An International Monetary Fund (IMF) low-interest loan plan for developing nations. No action.

General Agreements to Borrow. No cost estimate.
International Monetary Fund loan reserve fund, intended to be used to prevent monetary crisis caused by loan defaults in developing countries. No action

Highway Demonstration Projects: Five-year cost, $4 billion
Road construction projects requested by individual members of Congress for their states and districts. No action.

Pyroprocessing Program: Five-year cost, $100 million
Energy Department research on ways to process spent nuclear fuel to separate plutonium and uranium from nuclear waste. No action.

Rural Utilities Services: Five-year cost, $190 million
Subsidizes loans to rural cooperatives for energy and telecommunications projects. No action.

In all, Kasich set out to eliminate twelve programs achieving five-year savings in excess of $11 billion. He succeeded in trimming only $106 million, or approximately 1 percent of the total. Kasich has vowed to repeat his effort to trim wasteful corporate subsidies in the future, though few political pundits believe his odds for success will improve.

When Republicans routinely beat back floor amendments to strike timber, export, peanut, and mining subsidies, is it any wonder that voters have concluded that neither party is really serious about controlling federal spending? Evidence of Republican profligacy keeps mounting like evidence in the case against the "unabomber," Theodore

Kaczinsky. Every year since regaining control of Congress, the Republicans have attempted to add the B-2 bomber to the defense budget, this despite objections from the Joint Chiefs of Staff. In 1991, the Bush administration agreed to limit production of the B-2 to 21 planes. At a cost of nearly $2 billion per plane, the Pentagon has decided that a tight defense budget can no longer accommodate such an expensive Cold War relic. Undeterred, the Republicans continue their annual campaign to build more B-2 bombers.

Worse, after making the line-item veto a centerpiece of their Contract with America, the Republican Congress voted to override President Clinton's veto of several dozen military construction projects that had not gone through the appropriate approval process.

And finally, with enthusiastic Republican support, the recently passed highway bill included over 1,500 pork-barrel projects (totalling $9 billion). That's more pork than in all the highway bills approved since the FHA was created in the 1950s.

REPUBLICANS are not demonstrating the resolve it takes to shrink the federal government. Like the Democrats before them, they, too, have overpromised and underdelivered. In short order, they have become addicted to the habit of spending other people's money. In the fiscal year 1998 budget, they achieved a dubious distinction by doling out more pork than any Congress in the nation's history. For those who believed the Republicans were serious about cutting government and reducing the federal role in our lives, the Republican Congress has been a major disappointment.

Republicans have abandoned their smaller-government philosophy entirely, veering instead toward policies of reckless profligacy that would make Democrats blush. In three short years Republicans have destroyed any claim they once had to being the part of smaller government. When they had the presidency but not Congress, Republicans said they could not cut spending without controlling Congress. Now that they have Congress, Republicans have not only failed to reduce government spending, they have actually outbid Clinton and previous Democratic congresses in terms of both domestic spending and pork-barrel legislation.

The Republican Party is about a lot of things in 1998. But reducing the size of government isn't one of them.

THE FIFTEENTH LIE

◆

DEMOCRATS ARE COMPASSIONATE

D EMOCRATS ARE SUFFERING from a serious nostalgia hangover.

Social Security. The GI bill. Medicare. Medicaid. Civil Rights. Head Start. The Peace Corps: all of these programs speak to the Democrats' century-old heritage as the party of compassion, the party of those who look to government for aid and comfort in times of hardship. Each of these programs sought to address an immediate social need in America, one that Democrats believed could never be adequately addressed through a laissez-faire economic structure. Each was a reaction to real human needs. Each in its own way offered the hand of government assistance as a bridge to future prosperity (the GI bill, civil-rights laws, and Head Start) or as a means of protecting the frail and weak from the privation this wealthy society could no longer tolerate (Social Security, Medicare, and Medicaid). Only one, the Peace Corps, sought to extend the unique definition of Democratic compassion overseas, and while the program has had mixed results, few can question its noble intentions and humanitarian goals.

It is this legacy that persuades most voters that Democrats are more compassionate than Republicans, more willing to use the government to assist the weak and politically powerless, more committed to seeking social justice in a nation of immense wealth.

That was true once, but it is no longer.

We're not arguing that Democrats have suddenly traded places with Republicans in the compassion department. Not at all. Just because Republicans have agreed to massive increases in federal spending doesn't make them compassionate. To our way of thinking, it only means they have bought into the "promise-everything" mentality that has hypnotized Democrats since the days of Lyndon Johnson.

Democrats are so drunk with nostalgia for their previous accomplishments that they're unwilling to make the programs of yesteryear workable now and in the future. Democrats who still claim credit as the protectors of Social Security, Medicare, and Medicaid are neglecting any responsibility for ensuring the long-term viability of these programs. Worse still, most Democrats in Washington seem more interested in adding government benefits to a list taxpayers are already having a difficult time financing. As our review of Social Security and Medicare suggested, the payroll taxes that partially finance both of these programs are only hampering our economy further.

Jonathan Rausch, in his book *Demoslerosis,* writes of the proliferation of interest groups since the inception of the Great Society. Every program now has a bureaucratic constituency inside and a special interest constituency (made up of beneficiaries, social workers, and nonprofit agencies) outside the government. Democrats in Congress cater to these constituencies. After all, Democrats are the traditional ally of civil service workers and Democrats, having initially created these programs, are loath to eliminate any of them. After thirty years of inexorable growth in the federal bureaucracy, rare is the domestic program that has been canceled. Even during the Reagan years, when on the strength of a veto the President could have made a determined effort to trim wasteful government, only a few small items were pared from the federal budget. Reagan succeeded in eliminating the General Revenue Sharing program and Urban Development Action Grants, but little else.

Like Reagan before him, President Clinton has found great difficulty in persuading Congress to restructure the federal bureaucracy. Case in point: For four years, the Clinton administration, to its credit, has attempted to advance legislation to consolidate over one hundred jobs programs into several block grants. The newly designed job-assistance initiative would allow states and localities enormous flexibility in tailoring job training and assistance programs to the unemployed. Currently, the phalanx of programs for the unemployed stretches across several Cabinet departments. Some programs are handled by the Department of Education. Others are managed by the Department of Labor. Still more are the domain of the Department of Housing and Urban Development. A few are housed with the Department of Health and Human Services. Is it any wonder that the citizenry decry government bureaucracy?

Why has this reform legislation been held up for so long? Simply put, interest groups prefer the status quo and are quite vocal about it. Average voters and taxpayers, who would benefit from the change, are silent. Their voices are not represented in the debate.

This dynamic is especially important in understanding how it is that the Democrats, who pride themselves on being advocates for the poor and disadvantaged, have in many ways become the nemesis of these groups. To too great a degree, Democrats have focused on increasing the size of government and the number of government programs, rather than in ensuring that the best programs are well funded and effectively implemented.

The Clinton administration has enjoyed modest success in restructuring the federal government. The Department of Agriculture has undergone a makeover. Various HUD programs have been consolidated and streamlined. Yet, despite these worthy accomplishments, the overall size of the government has not been reduced and few programs have actually been eliminated. Consequently, these activities have only chipped away at the tip of the iceberg, leaving a deadly threat lurking in the budgetary waters.

★

LIKE the Titanic, the ship of state is at risk of going under and the truly needy will be left with no lifeboats. Democrats, through the years, have been content to layer new programs on top of old, creating a patchwork of government agencies and services that leave beneficiaries confused and taxpayers outraged.

Let's examine a current example of this phenomenon. Democrat Clinton came to Washington promising full funding of the Head Start program. Head Start is a Great Society program aimed at providing preschool children a day-care setting offering certain educational opportunities. The purpose? To allow low-income families access to a preschool program to better help their children enter elementary school on an even par with other students. In other words, to give them a Head Start on learning the basics. Five years into his tenure, Clinton has yet to sign into law a budget that provides full funding for Head Start.

Nonetheless, he is now proposing a new program offering federal dollars to school districts so that additional teachers can be hired. The goal? To lower class size at the elementary level. In all, the Clinton plan would fund approximately 100,000 new teachers. You can make an arguments for the merit of the idea. Many scholars have touted the importance of reduced class size in advancing educational achievement. However, it might legitimately be questioned whether such a program is really the business of the federal government. Throughout our nation's history, elementary and secondary education has been the realm for state and local policymakers. Setting aside arguments about merit and federalism, this latest initiative does bear out our central point. One priority, Head Start for all disadvantaged preschoolers, is left underfunded, while a new education program is placed in competition for scarce federal resources.

This scenario has played out dozens of times over the years, leaving us with a federal government that promises too much and delivers too little.

★

DEMOCRATS would be deserving of the label—*compassionate*—if they were better focused on delivering full funding for their top priorities. Regrettably, they refuse to set priorities, which in a very real sense means nothing is given priority treatment. Instead they spread too few dollars over too many programs. Consequently, Democrats deliver mostly disappointment.

In late 1997 Democrats were talking about using any available government surplus (which there won't be in the first place) to pay for more social spending. On top of that, Clinton and other senior Democrats were seriously discussing extending Medicare coverage to the "near-elderly," those Americans between fifty and sixty-four who may have trouble maintaining health-care coverage.

What's more, we are not convinced that the so-called near-elderly need a blanket federal entitlement to health care. But we know that such care would cost billions and only make the job of saving Medicare and Medicaid all the more difficult—because, of course, new beneficiaries would claim additional benefits, adding to the government's costs, and putting still more pressure on taxpayers.

It seems to us that Democrats believe that once they establish a "compassionate" program they have no responsibility to properly manage it. In fact, the behavior of most contemporary Democrats suggests to us a butterfly approach to social policy as lawmakers flit from one social program to another, spreading promises of government benefits hither and yon. While this may look compassionate, it's precisely the opposite: it's cruel.

The expensive promises contained in the Democrats' Compassionate Three—Social Security, Medicare, and Medicaid—are gradually cannibalizing the entire federal budget. Since 1989 Medicare has grown by $69 billion, or 66 percent. Medicaid has grown by $47 billion, or 112 percent. Social Security, while on a pay-as-you-go financing schedule now, still cost the government $347 billion in 1996, nearly $100 billion more than we spent on national defense. As the costs of these programs increase, as they inevitably will, there will be less and less money available for other government programs such as medical research, space exploration, border patrol, national defense, and road and bridge construction.

If Democrats object to this trend, they have one or two choices: advocate higher taxes to pay for the entitlement programs *and the other government programs they are cannibalizing,* or reduce the cost of the entitlements so they can coexist with other government priorities without the need for higher taxes.

Now, Democrats so far have made it fairly clear that they will not propose higher taxes as long as Republicans are controlling Congress. Republicans, for their part, have made it even clearer that they intend to propose tax cuts each year of their tenure in power. With this political reality, it appears clear to us that the Democrats, to make good on their legacy of compassion, must be the first ones to propose means by which these programs can be saved.

Think about it. Republicans did not suggest or support any of these programs. Over time, as they became more popular, Republicans offered grudging political support. But these programs have never defined the Republican Party—far from it. If anything, in the minds of many voters, the Republican Party was defined by its hostility to Social Security, Medicare, and Medicaid.

So, we ask Democrats proud of their party's compassionate heritage: What political advantage is there for Republicans to fix problems with Social Security, Medicare, and Medicaid when they opposed them in the first place.

The answer? Not much at all.

That's especially true when most Democrats have exploited, for short-term political gain, even the best-intentioned Republican attempts to address the systemic financial problems of Social Security,

Medicare, and Medicaid. Democrats attacked Reagan in 1982 when it was suggested that he and his advisers were studying a possible reduction in Social Security benefits. This issue galvanized seniors in the 1982 campaign, because many of them believed Reagan had actually proposed a cut in benefits when, in fact, he had done nothing of the kind.

Democrats attacked again in 1985 when then–Senate Majority Leader Bob Dole single-handedly persuaded fellow Republicans to pass a budget that contained a tiny one-year reduction in Social Security benefits as part of a larger plan that promised to reduce the federal deficit dramatically. Reagan rejected the Dole plan, and the cuts never took effect. Nevertheless, Democrats pounded on the Dole plan in the 1986 campaign, and, thanks to the animosity stirred up among elderly voters, Democrats won several close Senate elections and regained control of the chamber.

Democrats attacked again in 1995 when, as we described earlier, Republicans proposed "cuts" in Medicare spending that were denounced in a cloud of absurd exaggerations by Clinton and a chorus of House and Senate Democrats—a protest that evaporated into thin air when in 1997 Clinton and these same Democrats signed onto a package of Medicare "cuts" of almost exactly the same size.

These attacks were all meant to prove to voters how devoted Democrats are to protecting and preserving compassionate government. But isn't their act wearing just a little bit thin?

Democrats can no longer credibly advertise themselves as the party of compassion when they refuse to deal seriously with the financial instability of programs millions of Americans are counting on.

When Democrats constructed Social Security they felt certain, on the basis of all the information before them, that the program would remain solvent in perpetuity. They had carefully balanced the size of the benefits against the magnitude of the payroll taxes required to finance them. The same was true of Medicare and Medicaid. The architects of these programs believed they had created self-financing health-care plans for the elderly and the poor, and all information at their disposal reinforced these conclusions. Those who built Social Security, Medicare, and Medicaid weren't basing their projections on flimsy accounting. They weren't pie-in-the-sky schemers willing to run up deficits simply to address profound human needs. They were circumspect and cautious. It's the circumstances that have changed, in ways they couldn't have foreseen.

We attribute no such conscientious prudence to the current crop of Democrats, who take so much pride in programs they had no part in building. Contemporary Democrats seem content to use questionable accounting and hang their vision of the future on baroque fibs about the soundness of Social Security, Medicare, and Medicaid. Their financial universe is a fantasyland where new benefits may be conferred upon the "near-elderly" without any budgetary consequences whatever.

This is not compassion. This is cowardice.

Democrats who defend the current entitlement structure, with its wage-busting payroll taxes and nebulous promises of retirement and medical benefits, are fooling themselves and—worst of all—fooling the American people. On top of that, they are protecting, not a personal-benefits system, but a scheme that takes the payroll-tax contributions of the young and reallocates them to the old. The entitlement structure as it exists today guarantees a gradual shift of wealth from young to old, a zero-sum game between generations that will do nothing to enhance our economic strength, could easily provoke bitter and utterly needless generational strife, and keeps each new generation from realizing its economic potential.

Is that the kind of America we want in the twenty-first century? We don't think so.

Democrats can do something about it. The party's legacy of compassion can be revived if Democrats decide to make good on the promises Social Security, Medicare, and Medicaid inherently make to today's baby boomers. To turn those promises into reality will require Democrats to rise above the politics of fear and exploitation and move back to the politics of compassion—politics that solve problems for people truly in need.

Until that happens, the Democrats have no claim to the mantle of compassion.

And, America, hampered by pork-barrel Republicans and neglectful Democrats, will have little claim to a secure and solvent future.